SUFI WARRIOR SAINTS

SUFI WARRIOR SAINTS

Stories of Sufi Jihad from Muslim Hagiography

Harry S. Neale

I.B. TAURIS
LONDON • NEW YORK • OXFORD • NEW DELHI • SYDNEY

I.B. TAURIS
Bloomsbury Publishing Plc
50 Bedford Square, London, WC1B 3DP, UK
1385 Broadway, New York, NY 10018, USA
29 Earlsfort Terrace, Dublin 2, Ireland

BLOOMSBURY, I.B. TAURIS and the I.B. Tauris logo are
trademarks of Bloomsbury Publishing Plc

First published in Great Britain 2022
This paperback edition published 2023

Copyright © Harry S. Neale, 2022

Harry S. Neale has asserted his right under the Copyright, Designs
and Patents Act, 1988, to be identified as Author of this work.

Series design: Adriana Brioso
Cover image: Najm al-Din al-Kubra, opaque watercolour, by Madhu, 1605.
Nafahat al-uns by Jami. Copied for Akbar at Agra AH1012-AD1605. Or. 1362 f.263.
(© Album/British Library/Alamy Stock Photo)

All rights reserved. No part of this publication may be reproduced or transmitted
in any form or by any means, electronic or mechanical, including photocopying,
recording, or any information storage or retrieval system, without prior
permission in writing from the publishers.

Bloomsbury Publishing Plc does not have any control over, or responsibility for, any
third-party websites referred to or in this book. All internet addresses given in this
book were correct at the time of going to press. The author and publisher regret
any inconvenience caused if addresses have changed or sites have ceased
to exist, but can accept no responsibility for any such changes.

A catalogue record for this book is available from the British Library.

A catalog record for this book is available from the Library of Congress.

ISBN:	HB:	978-0-7556-4337-0
	PB:	978-0-7556-4341-7
	ePDF:	978-0-7556-4338-7
	eBook:	978-0-7556-4339-4

Typeset by Integra Software Services Pvt. Ltd.

To find out more about our authors and books visit www.bloomsbury.com
and sign up for our newsletters.

In memory of my heroes
Don Montgomery
John Greider
Sheldon Rogers

CONTENTS

Preface	x
Notes on Transliteration, Dates, and Names	xii
Map	xiv

INTRODUCTION 1
   Sufi Hagiography and *Mujahid* Friends of God 1
   The Greater Jihad 2
   Sufism and *Tasawwuf* 3
   Sufi *Mujahids* and *Ghazis* in History 7
   Warrior Renunciants and Sufism 9
   Sufi Hagiography 11
   Recurrent Motifs in the Lives of God's Friends 13
   On the Sources, Structure, and Aim of This Book 19
   Ταῦτα δὲ ἐγένετο μὲν οὐδέποτε, ἔστι δὲ ἀεί 20
   Conclusion 21

Chapter 1
ASCETIC WARRIORS AND PROTO-SUFIS: THE EIGHTH AND
NINTH CENTURIES 23
   Ibrahim ibn Adham 24
      The Repentance of Ibrahim ibn Adham 24
      Ibrahim ibn Adham's Dicta, Exempla, and *Mujahada* 27
      Ibrahim ibn Adham and the Military Jihad 28
   Muhammad ibn Wasi' 29
      Dicta and Exempla of Muhammad ibn Wasi' 29
      Muhammad ibn Wasi' and the Military Jihad 30
   'Abdullah ibn al-Mubarak 31
      The Repentance of Ibn al-Mubarak 31
      Dicta, Exempla, and Miracles of Ibn al-Mubarak 32
      Ibn al-Mubarak and the Military Jihad 34
   Shaqiq al-Balkhi 36
      The Repentance of Shaqiq al-Balkhi 36
      Dicta and Exempla of Shaqiq al-Balkhi 37
      Shaqiq-i Balkhi and the Military Jihad 38

Chapter 2
MUJAHID FRIENDS OF GOD IN SUFISM'S FORMATIVE PERIOD: THE NINTH
THROUGH ELEVENTH CENTURIES 41

Bayazid al-Bistami 42
   Bayazid's Origins and Awakening 43
   Dicta, Exempla, and *Mujahada* of Bayazid 44
   Bayazid and the Military Jihad 46
   The Death of Bayazid 47
Junayd al-Baghdadi 47
   Junayd's Childhood 48
   Junayd's Dicta, Exempla, and *Mujahada* 49
   Junayd and the Complementary Nature of Jihad 50
   Junayd and the Military Jihad 51
   The Death of Junayd 52
Abu Ishaq al-Kazaruni 52
   Abu Ishaq's Childhood and Introduction to the Sufi Path 53
   Dicta, Exempla, and *Mujahada* of Abu Ishaq 54
   Abu Ishaq al-Kazaruni and the Military Jihad 56

Chapter 3
SUFI *MUJAHID*S OF THE CRUSADES AND THE MONGOL INVASION: THE TWELFTH AND THIRTEENTH CENTURIES 61

Najm al-Din Kubra 63
   The Spiritual Awakening of Najm al-Din 63
   Anecdotes and Exempla of Najm al-Din 64
   The Military Jihad and Martyrdom of Najm al-Din 65
'Abdullah al-Yunini—The Lion of Syria 66
   Exempla and Wondrous Deeds of 'Abdullah al-Yunini 66
   'Abdullah al-Yunini and the Military Jihad 67
   The Death of 'Abdullah al-Yunini 68
Abu'l-Qasim 'Abd al-Rahman al-Nuwayri—The Eloquent Martyr 68
   The Military Jihad and Martyrdom of al-Nuwayri 69
   Concerning the Sufism of 'Abd al-Rahman al-Nuwayri 70
Rumi 70
   Rumi's Childhood and Introduction to Sufism 71
   Dicta, Exempla, and Wonders of Rumi 73
   Rumi and the Military Jihad 74
   The Death of Rumi 75

Chapter 4
SUFI *MUJAHID*S OF AL-ANDALUS AND AL-MAGHRIB: THE TWELFTH THROUGH SEVENTEENTH CENTURIES 77

Abu 'Abdullah Muhammad al-Arkushi 79
   Abu 'Abdullah Muhammad al-Arkushi in *al-Sirr al-masun* 80
Abu'l-Hajjaj al-Mughawir 81
   al-Mughawir in Ibn Zafir's *Risala* 81
   The Jihad of Speaking a Just Word to a Tyrant 85
   Ibn 'Arabi's Description of al-Mughawir 86

Shaykh ʿUmar al-Tanji   86
    The Military Jihad of Shaykh ʿUmar al-Tanji in *al-Maqsad al-sharif*   86
ʿAli ibn ʿUthman al-Shawi   86
    ʿAli ibn ʿUthman al-Shawi in *Dawhat al-nashir* and *Tabaqat al-Hudaygi*   87
Muhammad ibn Yahya al-Bahluli   87
    al-Bahluli in *Dawhat al-nashir*   87
Muhammad al-ʿAyyashi   89
    Muhammad al-ʿAyyashi's Introduction to the Sufi Path and Jihad   89
    Muhammad al-ʿAyyashi and the Military Jihad   90
    The Death of Muhammad al-ʿAyyashi   91

Chapter 5
Sufi *Mujahids* of the Indian Subcontinent: The Eleventh Through Seventeenth Centuries   93
    Abu Muhammad Chishti   97
        Abu Muhammad Chishti in *Khwajagan-i Chisht*   97
    Shah Jalal al-Din al-Mujarrad   101
        Shah Jalal in *Gulzar-i abrar* and *Thamarat al-quds*   101
        Ibn Battuta's Description of Shah Jalal   103
    Sayyid Muluk Shah   104
        Sayyid Muluk Shah in *Tuhfat al-tahirin*   105
    Baba Palang Pūsh   105
        Baba Palang Pūsh Embarks on the Sufi Path   106
        The Wayfaring of Baba Palang Pūsh and His Meeting with Khizr   107
        Baba Palang Pūsh and the Defeat of the Qalmaqs   107
        The Military Jihad of Baba Palang Pūsh   108
        Baba Palang Pūsh Admonishes Sharif Khan   109
        Baba Palang Pūsh's Wondrous Journey to Rūm   110
        The Death of Baba Palang Pūsh   111

Conclusion   113

Glossary   118
Appendix: The Primary Hagiographical Sources and Their Authors   122
Notes   127
Bibliography   161
    Primary Sources   161
    Secondary Sources   165
Index   172

PREFACE

Sufi Warrior Saints tells the hagiographical stories of God's friends, concentrating on their depiction as the ideal practitioners of the Sufi understanding of the Islamic doctrine of jihad. Sufis conceived of jihad as complementary outward and inward struggles, and the many hagiographical anecdotes of God's friends reflect this conception. Jihad in Sufism begins with the inner struggle against the lower self and its passions. Since the earliest period of Sufism's unfolding, Sufis have held that the lower self must be overcome through self-mortification and spiritual exercises before engaging in the outer struggle. This outer form of jihad is generally understood to be the communal military jihad against the enemies of the faith; however, the less known but nevertheless important jihad of speaking a just word to a tyrant is also a significant component of the outer jihad in Sufism. The many stories herein explore this threefold jihad as it developed in Sufism.

Although translations of hagiographical lives of God's friends are readily available, most of these are single-source translations, relying on only one hagiography for each life. Furthermore, much of the Sufi literature translated into European languages reflects the interests of a Western readership, which tend toward the esoteric, mystical aspects of Sufism. This is not in itself objectionable, but the stories of God's friends transcend such narrow boundaries and contain a wealth of information that sheds light on nonmystical aspects of Sufism, as well as the complexities of premodern Islamic society and history. The multifaceted Sufi understanding of jihad that these stories present is rarely noted in translations of Sufi hagiography. It is therefore hoped that *Sufi Warrior Saints* will offer Western readers a more nuanced picture of the role of Sufis in Islamic culture.

In composing *Sufi Warrior Saints*, I have drawn from many kinds of sources in both Arabic and Persian. These sources include Sufi hagiography, poetry, manuals, and treatises. They also include premodern Muslim histories and travel narratives, as these, too, contain many anecdotes of God's friends. All translations from these sources in *Sufi Warrior Saints* are my own, and I take full responsibility for any errors in this regard.

* * *

My sincere thanks are due to Paul Psoinos, who has patiently edited the entire manuscript of *Sufi Warrior Saints*. His meticulous and indefatigable efforts in this regard have saved me from manifold errors and omissions. Without his expert help and unerring eye for discrepancies (especially those concerning bibliography and citation), this book would be much the poorer. I also wish to thank my wife, Katherine, for her encouragement and support during the five years I spent researching and writing this book; my friend and erstwhile colleague Raymond Farrin, who graciously helped me translate several poems and anecdotes from Arabic when I had all but given up hope of rendering them into readable English; Olga Louchakova-Schwartz for helping me obtain a much-needed source; and the cartographer Bill Nelson for the splendid map.

H.S.N.
Boise
August 2021

NOTES ON TRANSLITERATION, DATES, AND NAMES

With regard to the transliteration of Arabic and Persian names and terms, I have generally dispensed with the sundry diacritics that scholars customarily employ for this purpose. I have used the apostrophe to represent both the Arabic *'ayn* and the Arabic *hamza*. The macron indicating long *a* (i.e., *ā*) is used only to distinguish Arabic verbs and verbal nouns, and several other words for the sake of clarity (e.g., Rūm, rather than "Rum"), and is not used in any other transliterations.

It should also be noted that the spelling of Persian names and words does not reflect standard modern Iranian pronunciation, since the stories in this book generally predate the sound shifts that have occurred in Iranian Persian over roughly the last 500 years.

All dates herein are Common Era, with the exception of the year of death that follows, in parentheses, the first mention of an individual; the format of which is: Islamic calendar year/Common Era year. Likewise, all century dates are Common Era.

The form of the names of God's friends sometimes varies, depending on whether an anecdote is a translation from Arabic or Persian. Thus, the reader may encounter both Ibrahim ibn Adham (the Arabic form) and Ibrahim-i Adham (the Persian form); 'Abdullah ibn al-Mubarak and 'Abdullah-i Mubarak; Abu Yazid al-Bistami and Bayazid-i Bistami; and so forth.

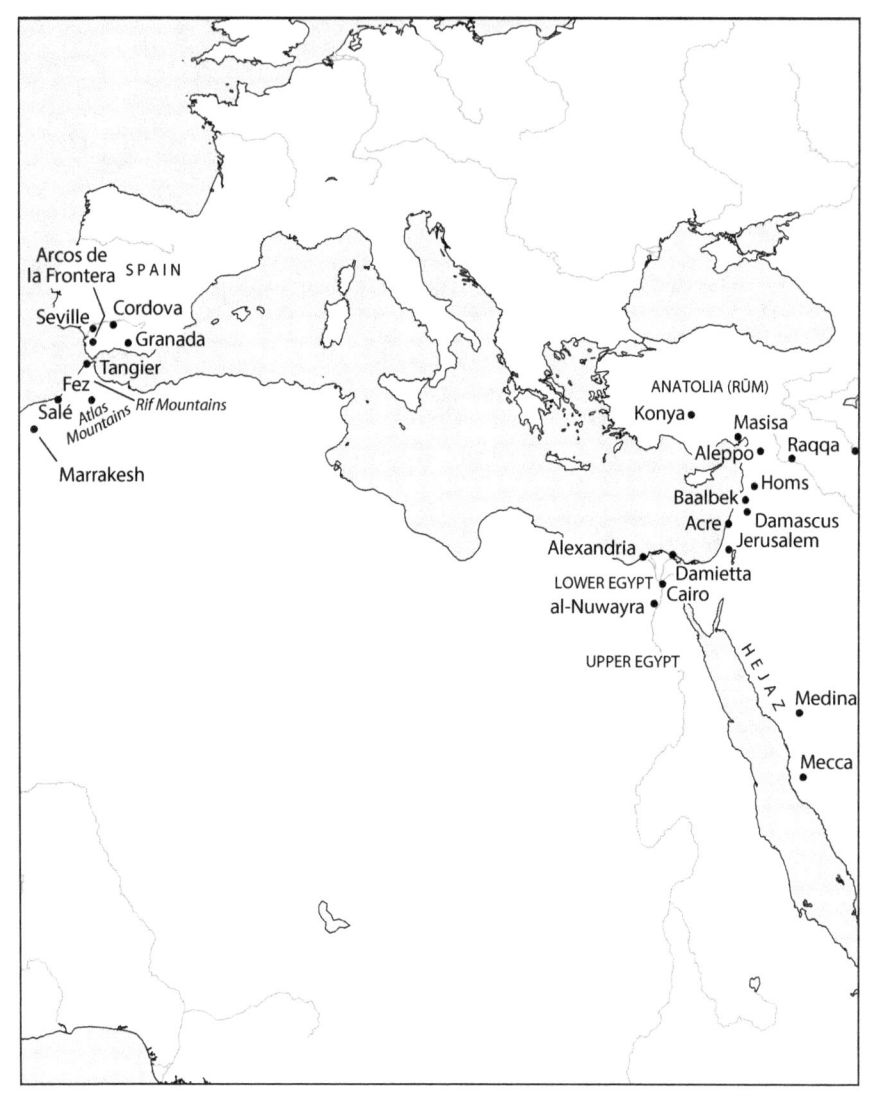

Map: Cities, towns, and historical regions in the stories of *Sufi Warrior Saints*. (Cartography: Bill Nelson.)

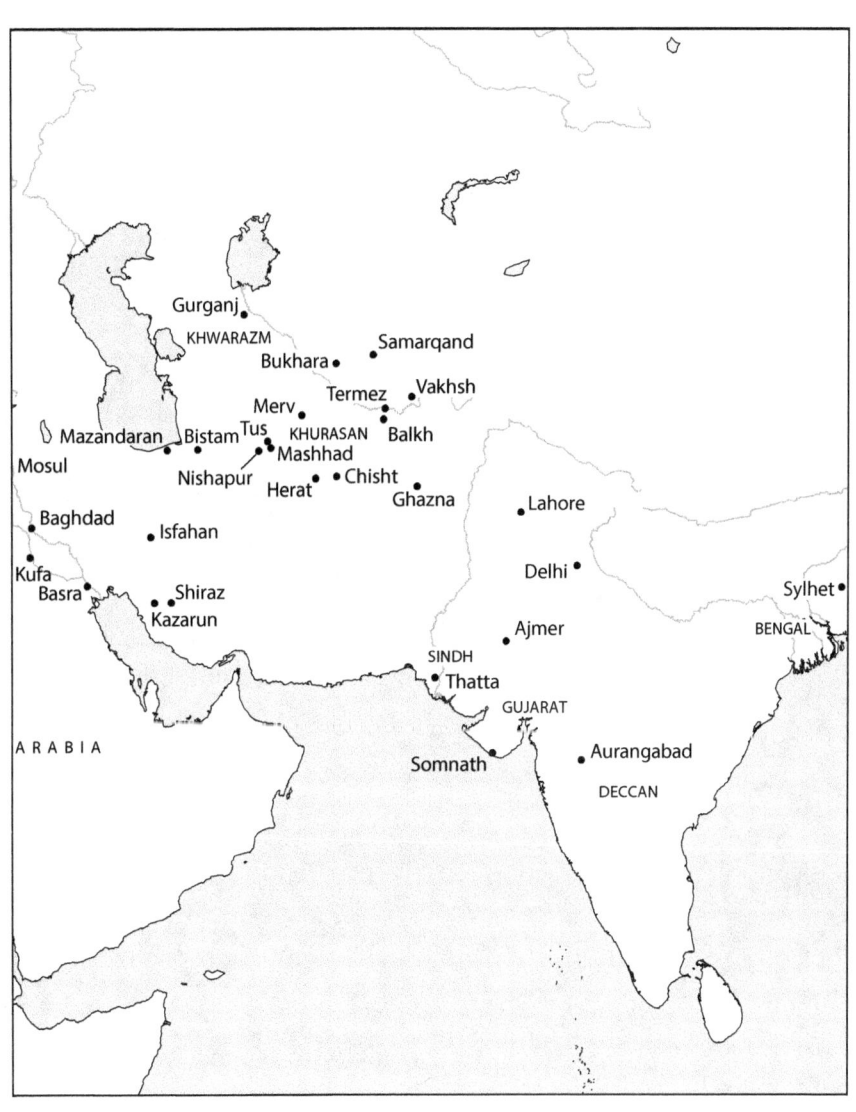

INTRODUCTION

*The stories of God's friends are one of His armies,
with which He strengthens the hearts of the Sufi initiates.*

—Junayd al-Baghdadi

Sufi Hagiography and Mujahid *Friends of God*

In the introduction to the twelfth-century Sufi hagiography *Tadhkirat al-awliya'* (*Memorial of God's Friends*),[1] Farid al-Din 'Attar of Nishapur set forth his reasons for composing his *tadhkira* ("memorial," "memoir") in Persian.[2] Perhaps the most significant reason he gave was his belief that after the Qur'an and *hadith*, the best words are those of God's friends, for their words are, in fact, an explication of Islamic scripture.[3] 'Attar further explained that whereas the majority of Persian-speaking Muslims of his time did not have sufficient knowledge of Arabic to read Islamic scripture, a collection of stories and sayings of God's friends in Persian would serve to instruct them in fundamental Islamic doctrine and piety.[4]

'Attar's words succinctly convey the essential role that God's friends have played in Sunni Muslim culture—from North Africa to the Indonesian Archipelago—as paradigms of godliness, devotion, and Islamic practice. And although this role has diminished in recent times, the stories of God's friends continue to be an invaluable source regarding premodern Muslim culture. Moreover, many Sufi hagiographies are classics of Islamic literature and deserve to be read for their literary merit.

Following the appearance in the eleventh century of the first, rather terse, Sufi hagiography in Arabic (i.e., al-Sulami's *Tabaqat al-sufiyya*, which we will discuss in more detail below), the Sufi hagiographical tradition would gradually develop into a genre that included wondrous tales of God's friends, their didactic sayings and pious exempla, allusions to historical events, and explanations of Qur'anic verses and *hadith*, as well as poetry. It is, thus, fortunate that several excellent anthologies of Sufi hagiographical anecdotes are available in translation.[5]

Among the many motifs encountered in stories of God's friends is that of the Sufi as warrior for the faith (*mujahid/ghazi*).[6] Anecdotes of Sufis fighting the enemies of Islam or rendering miraculous assistance to Muslim armies are common throughout the Sufi hagiographical tradition, and these anecdotes confirm the centrality of the doctrine of jihad in Islamic history.[7] Nevertheless, few examples of Sufi warrior stories are available in European languages, even though a collection of such stories would benefit a readership interested in Sufism, Islamic literature, and the challenging topic of jihad.

Sufi Warrior Saints endeavors, therefore, to provide such a collection of stories from the lives of God's friends translated from the original Arabic and Persian hagiographical sources. As is the case with much premodern Islamic literature, the majority of these sources are not available in translation, and as a result many of the anecdotes that make up the stories herein appear in English for the first time.

Before we turn to the subjects of Sufism and Sufi hagiography, however, it may be helpful to address some of the enduring misconceptions about Sufism. This is essential if we are to understand, for example, why the current Western conception of Sufis as peaceful mystics does not easily permit consideration of Sufis as agents of military jihad.

Much of the popular Sufi-related literature available in European languages presents Sufism as a tradition of poetry, music, and dance concerned with mystical closeness with God. Sufi poetry, in particular, enjoys a modest degree of popularity in the West, to which the many available versions of Rumi's poetry attest. Moreover, Western Sufi scholarship has tended to concentrate on the mystical and theoretical aspects of Sufism, and this concentration has contributed to the popular notion that Sufism is primarily an esoteric mystical tradition. These two factors have led to the widespread belief in Western countries that Sufis practice an alternative, more tolerant form of Islam that downplays doctrinal differences while emphasizing the spiritual and ethical basis that all religions are commonly believed to share. The influence of this popular image of Sufism is especially apparent in the equation of Sufi jihad with the "greater jihad," which has become the dominant Western interpretation of jihad in the Sufi context.

The Greater Jihad

You must carry out the greater jihad, which is the jihad against your passions, ... for if you accomplish this jihad against your lower self, your other jihad— the jihad against enemies—will be sincere.

—Ibn 'Arabi

The greater jihad[8] (i.e., the inner spiritual struggle) plays a significant role in contemporary Western discourse regarding Islam, in which it is not confined only to discussions about Sufism, as those wishing to counter the notion that Islam is fundamentally a militant faith often tout the greater jihad as the true or primary form of jihad in traditional Islamic practice. Such attempts at historical and doctrinal revisionism concerning jihad have steadily increased over the last two decades, largely in response to the various forms of militant Islamism that have manifested in the twenty-first century. The greater jihad has received considerable publicity in Western media and scholarship in recent years, as we have mentioned, and it is increasingly promoted as the primary and, occasionally, the only meaning of the Islamic doctrine of jihad.[9] Although the greater or inner jihad is a fundamental component of Sufism, the complementary inner and outer aspects of Sufi practice, which we will discuss further below, are also reflected in the Sufi understanding of jihad: the inner jihad is the struggle against the passions, and the outer jihad is the military struggle against unbelievers and the foes of the faith. In discussing the inner jihad, however, Sufis have generally not employed the verbal noun *jihad,* instead, they have used the alternative verbal noun *mujahada* (and the attendant and often-synonymous term *riyada*) to describe struggling with the lower self (*nafs*).[10] Thus, in most Sufi writings, *mujahada* refers almost exclusively to the individual spiritual struggle, whereas the use of the term *jihad* generally denotes the outer, communal, military struggle with the unbelievers.[11] The terms *mujahada* and *riyada* will therefore denote the inner jihad in the stories of God's friends that we will read in the following chapters—rather than the term "greater jihad."

It bears mentioning that the doctrine of jihad has a long and complex history, as elaborated in the theoretical realm of Islamic law and as exemplified in the deeds of historical *mujahid*s. And throughout Islamic history the definition and practice of jihad have *always* included religiously sanctioned warfare. The Sufi practice of jihad likewise has neither been single-faceted nor has it excluded the traditional legal definitions of jihad. It is therefore hoped that the stories related herein will help clarify the complementary nature of Sufi jihad by providing a nuanced depiction of its various forms as exemplified by God's friends.[12]

Sufism and Tasawwuf

It is assumed that "Sufism" is a term familiar to readers of this book, given its consistent use in most scholarly and popular writing on Islamic mysticism. For this reason, throughout *Sufi Warrior Saints* "Sufism" will refer to what in Arabic is called *tasawwuf,* even though the English term is problematic for several reasons, not the least of which is that it seems to suggest a sect of Islam or even a separate religious tradition.[13]

The word *tasawwuf* is derived from the Arabic word for wool—*suf*—and literally means "to adopt or follow the way of the Sufis; to become a Sufi."[14] To describe the friends of God, early Muslim writers chose the adjective *sufi,* alluding to the wool frocks they were said to wear. Much like the donning of hair shirts by early Christian anchorites, the wearing of wool was an ascetic practice that symbolized the renunciation of comfort, the elimination of worldly desires, and, above all, unwavering devotion to God.[15]

Here we ought to clarify the position of Sufism within Islam before proceeding with our discussion of *tasawwuf.* Despite popular assumptions to the contrary, Sufism is *not* a sect, unlike the Sunni and Shi'ite traditions, which do constitute separate sects of Islam. Moreover, throughout its history Sufism has developed primarily within the Sunni Islamic tradition. In this regard, Sufi writings relate that many of the early Sufis were recognized authorities in the Islamic religious sciences (e.g., interpretation of scripture, jurisprudence, etc.) that comprise the Sunni scholarly tradition.

With respect to the traditional religious sciences, it is said that Sufis particularly excelled in the science of *hadith*,[16] which consisted of collecting and recording oral narratives concerning the deeds and words of the Prophet Muhammad as related by his Companions (*Sahaba*) and then evaluating the veracity of each *hadith* on the basis of its chain of oral transmission (*isnad*).[17] For this reason, Sufi archetypes and early Sufi scholars, and the eponyms of Sufi orders as well (e.g., Junayd al-Baghdadi, al-Qushayri, Najm al-Din Kubra, et al.) were often reckoned worthy *hadith* scholars (*muhaddithun*).[18] Bearing this in mind, it is hardly surprising that *hadith* and the methodology of *hadith* scholarship would play a significant role in the unfolding and elaboration of the Sufi hagiographical tradition, a topic that we will examine in further detail when we discuss the genesis of Sufi hagiography.

In addition to associating the earliest friends of God with *hadith*, the traditional sources depict them as exemplars of pious scrupulosity (*wara'*) and exclusive reliance on God (*tawakkul*) for their daily bread.[19] These sources further describe the ascetic Sufi archetypes as devoting themselves to God by following the inner spiritual path and by assiduously fulfilling their outward religious duties, which included communal responsibilities. For an example of how God's friends themselves defined Sufism, it is worth considering the definition attributed to the early Sufi shaykh Junayd al-Baghdadi (d. 297/910), which describes *tasawwuf* as embodying the following eight qualities: generosity, contentment, patience, intimation, exile, wearing wool, travel, and poverty.[20] This description further associates each of these qualities with a prophet from Islamic sacred history and, in doing so, connects the Sufis with the paradigms of piety and exemplary conduct in Islam. Likewise, early Sufi writers would portray the friends of God as the spiritual heirs of the Prophet Muhammad, his Companions, and the early Muslim renunciants/ascetics (*zuhhad*).[21] Indeed, some Sufi writers even went so far as to say that associating with God's friends was equivalent to associating with God.[22] It is especially worth noting that this manner of depicting God's friends is common not only to Sufi writings but to many other genres of premodern Islamic literature as well. The ubiquity of these depictions in Islamic literature strongly indicates that God's friends, as they are portrayed in stories and anecdotes, have served as spiritual intermediaries and models of godliness for Muslims since at least the formative period of Sufism.[23]

Early Sufi literature sought to secure the status of God's friends as paradigms of Muslim piety and correct practice, and in this respect the first Sufi hagiographers, 'Abd al-Rahman al-Sulami (d. 412/1021) and Abu Nu'aym al-Isfahani (d. 430/1038), and Sufi scholars such as Abu'l-Qasim al-Qushayri (d. 465/1072), seem to have had in mind the opinion of traditional religious scholars—many of whom were initially skeptical of Sufism's validity. One of the ways these early hagiographers and treatise writers bolstered their claims that Sufism was a legitimate development within Sunni Islam was to emphasize the religious learning of God's friends and their adherence to the fundamental tenets of the faith. As an example of such adherence, al-Sulami, in his seminal hagiography *Tabaqat al-sufiyya* (*Generations of the Sufis*), relates the following words of his teacher, Abu'l-Qasim Nasrabadi (d. 367/978): "The foundation of Sufism is cleaving to the Qur'an and the *Sunna*."[24] This dictum underscores the scriptural and doctrinal basis for Sufism and forfends against claims that it is an aberrant innovation—an accusation that Sufis faced in the eleventh century and, unfortunately, face again today (primarily from followers of Salafist and Wahhabist interpretations of Islam).[25]

As we have mentioned, most literature in European languages that deals with Sufis defines them as the mystics of Islam. Such a definition, however, does not do justice to the complex and multifaceted Sufi tradition. Islamic mysticism certainly exists and is primarily expressed through Sufism; moreover, most Sufi practices and doctrines that complement outward Sunni practice are of a mystical character. Nevertheless, "Sufi" cannot be simply glossed as "Muslim mystic," as this would exclude significant nonmystical facets of the Sufi tradition.[26] In this regard, the significant difference between scholarship on Sufism in Islamic languages and in European languages is worth noting; for example, scholarship in the Muslim world prefers to downplay the mysticism of Sufis, which is so appealing to a Western audience, in favor of Sufi bravery and leadership in times of crisis, which appeals to the historical Islamic *mujahid* ethos. Conversely, scholarship in European languages has often overlooked the militant component of Sufism, preferring instead the study of Sufism's mystical and aesthetic aspects. Both perspectives are valid, and—like drunken and sober Sufism, which we will discuss below—they are not mutually exclusive.[27] One of the aims of *Sufi Warrior Saints* is to show how these two perspectives, the Sufi warrior and the Sufi mystic, are united in the stories of God's friends.

With respect to the essence of Sufism, William Chittick has succinctly defined it as "the interiorization and intensification of Islamic practice."[28] This definition underscores the fact that Sufism in essence generically designates a multiplicity of spiritual and ascetic practices and modes of conduct that have developed since the late ninth century.[29] To illustrate this multiplicity, we need only consider the unfolding of distinct Sufi orders since the appearance in the late tenth century of the first of them (i.e., the Kazaruni order of Fars) while also bearing in mind that historically not all Sufis have been associated with particular orders, especially during the formative period of Sufism (i.e., the tenth through twelfth centuries), and that many Muslims have engaged in certain Sufi practices or been affiliated with a Sufi order without themselves being Sufi initiates. Moreover, although most Sufis have historically been Sunni Muslims, there have been notable exceptions (e.g., the Ne'matollahi Sufi order, which is Twelver Shi'ite, and the heterodox Bektashi order, which was known for its antinomian practices).[30]

In considering the various Sufi devotional practices, it is worth noting that the Sufi orders have differed considerably in doctrine and practice.[31] We may contrast, for example, the Naqshbandi order's preference for silent *dhikr* (recollection of God through repeating His name or reciting the *shahada*) and rejection of *sama'* (musical audition)[32] with the Qadiri and Shadhili orders' practice of vocal *dhikr*, and the Chishti and Mevlevi orders' use of *sama'* to induce emotional and spiritual states that can lead to spiritual unveilings.[33] Even more striking, perhaps, is the fact that the first Sufi order—the aforementioned Kazaruni order—does not seem to have been based on any kind of mysticism and did not develop any particular regime of spiritual exercises for initiates (*murids*).[34] All such differences and exceptions suggest that it is unduly restrictive, not to mention misleading, to treat Sufism as a uniform Islamic mystical phenomenon, even if we may reasonably describe much of what constitutes Sufi practice—insofar as it differs from outward Sunni practice—as mysticism.[35]

Notwithstanding the different manifestations of Sufi devotion, some practices and doctrines of recognizably Sufi origin are essential to most forms of Sufism. One example is the fundamental Sufi belief that Islamic scripture contains both an inner, spiritual aspect and an outer, doctrinal aspect (e.g., Rumi described the Qur'an as "a two-sided brocade").[36] This complementary view of Islamic doctrine is especially important for understanding Sufi jihad as epitomized by God's friends.[37]

The complementary nature of Sufism is further illustrated by the concepts of spiritual intoxication (*sukr*) and sobriety (*sahw*). Intoxication is said to occur when the Sufi wayfarer is overwhelmed by God's nearness, whereas sobriety is the discernment and insight that allows him to perceive the difference between the eternal God and His finite creation. Both intoxication and sobriety are necessary to experience oneness with God and yet distinguish Him from what He has created.

Though many of God's friends were reckoned either "drunken" or "sober" Sufis, none of them was wholly one or the other. For example, Bayazid (d. 261/875), whom we will read more of in Chapter 2, is often described as a drunken Sufi because of his ecstatic utterances and eccentric actions; however, a careful reading of the many anecdotes and dicta from hagiographical accounts of Bayazid's life shows his concern for strict adherence to the *shari'a* (Divine Law) and following the Prophet's *Sunna*.

One can even descry the complementary Sufi concepts of intoxication and sobriety in the various genres of Sufi writings; poetry is "drunken" writing, in that it expresses the experience of God's nearness—or distance—in allegorical and mystical language, whereas prose is generally "sober," as it deals with complex matters of belief and practice that often require thorough knowledge of Islamic scripture and the traditional Islamic sciences.[38]

For a Western readership, perhaps the best example of a historical Sufi figure who embodied drunkenness and sobriety (i.e., the mystical aspects of Sufism as well as its intellectual tradition and the dictates of outward Sunni Islamic practice) is Jalal al-Din Balkhi (d. 672/1273)—better known in European languages as Rumi. Rumi is reckoned one of the greatest Sufi poets of his—or any—era. His poetry, composed primarily in Persian, has been translated into many languages, and it is no exaggeration to say that these translations of Rumi's poetry are responsible for much of the current interest in Sufism in the West.

Rumi is popularly imagined as a mystic poet who transcended religious orthodoxy and promoted a spiritual rapprochement between the various faiths. This image of Rumi is inaccurate, however, for although Rumi may be ranked among the most renowned Sufi poets, he was also a Sunni Muslim religious scholar of the Hanafi legal school. Moreover, Rumi unequivocally held Islam to be superior to other faiths, and his *Mathnavi-yi ma'navi* can be properly understood only in its Qur'anic context.[39] It is especially necessary to emphasize these facts, as some of the literature in European languages concerning Rumi presents the mystical content of his poetry as panspiritualist, devoid of Islamic character.[40] As we shall see in Chapter 3, however, the hagiographical portrayal of Rumi combines an account of the wonders attributed to him with anecdotes that highlight his learning and adherence to the *Sunna*.

It is hoped that the foregoing consideration of the differing practices of the various Sufi orders and the complementary states of intoxication and sobriety, as well as the example of Rumi, has helped dispel the reductive notion that Sufis are nothing more than Muslim mystics—however attractive such a notion may be. Sufism deserves to be considered on its own terms, and this requires that we expand our understanding of Sufi doctrine and practice. A broader perspective that comprehends the many realms of Sufi activity will allow us to better discern the complementary character of Sufi words and deeds, as well as the aspects of Sufism that are not of a mystical nature.

As we mentioned earlier, God's friends have served as exemplars of piety, religious practice, and inner spiritual cultivation for Sunni Muslim communities since the formative period of Sufism. And the historical record affirms the complex social role of Sufis in premodern Sunni Muslim culture—a role that went far beyond composing mystical poetry and writing treatises on complex esoteric doctrine.

Sufi Mujahids *and* Ghazis *in History*

The stories of God's friends are hagiographical and literary narratives that at times accord with the historical record but are not themselves historical accounts. Nevertheless, hagiography can shed light on historical circumstances, especially when combined with careful analysis of other historical evidence that corroborates or suggests the historicity of an anecdote or story.

The twelfth-century hagiography *Asrar al-tawhid* relates the following anecdote. "During the life of our shaykh [Abu Sa'id], another shaykh went on a military campaign with a group of Sufis to Rūm. One day, while he was journeying in that Abode of War, he saw Iblis (the Qur'anic Lucifer) and said to him, 'O Accursed One! What are you doing *here*? You don't bother yourself with the folk of this land?' 'I'm not here by choice,' replied Iblis. 'How did you get here, then?' asked the shaykh. 'I was passing through Mayhana when Shaykh Abu Sa'id Abu'l-Khayr came out of the mosque there and began wending his way home. On the way, he suddenly sneezed, and that sneeze blew me all the way here.'"[41] In another collection of hagiographical anecdotes contemporary with *Asrar al-tawhid*, it is said that a certain Shaykh Abu'l-Hasan al-Tusi devoted his life to worship and jihad and led five of his *murids* on a military expedition to Tarsus to join in the jihad against the Byzantines.[42] Similar anecdotes are related in *Tadhkirat al-awliya'* and the Indo-Persian hagiography *Gulzar-i abrar,* among others.[43] The recurrence of anecdotes of Sufis carrying out the military jihad under the leadership of their shaykh suggests two possibilities, neither one of them excluding the other. They may represent historical Sufi involvement in the military jihad, which could indicate that Sufis undertook a military role more often than is generally imagined. Their recurrence may also reflect a trope of Sufi shaykhs leading their *murid*s into battle in order to show Sufis performing the outward Islamic duty of jihad. In any event, such anecdotes deserve serious consideration when examining the social role of Sufis in history.

Notwithstanding the fact that this book concerns hagiographical accounts of Sufi warriors rather than the history of Sufis *as* warriors, it is worth pausing here to address historical Sufi involvement in warfare to show that Sufi writings and Sufi military activities were, in fact, in accord.

Throughout much of Sufism's history, Sufis have at various times served as exemplary warriors for the faith.[44] Contemporary chronicles relate that Sufis fought to defend the Abode of Islam during the Crusades; for example, Shaykh Arslan al-Dimashqi (d. mid-twelfth century) is said to have defended Damascus when the Crusaders besieged the city in 1148.[45] During the Mongol invasion of Central Asia and Iran in the early thirteenth century, Sufis were undoubtedly among those who defended the cities of Khurasan and Transoxiana, where Sufism had flourished since the eleventh century. In this regard, Shaykh Najm al-Din Kubra, whom we will discuss further in Chapter 3, is said to have perished while leading a group of Sufis in battle against the Mongols when they attacked the city of Khwarazm in 1221.

Nonetheless, as recent scholarship has shown, hagiographical portrayals of Sufis as warriors sometimes reflected an idealization of the past or sought justification for a contemporary political ideology rather than presenting an account based on historical events. This is especially true of Sufi warrior narratives composed centuries after the death of their subject.[46]

An example of this idealization may be seen in symbolic accounts of friends of God such as those of 'Abdullah al-Arkushi and 'Umar al-Tanji (see Chapter 4) fighting the Christians in al-Andalus during the period of the Reconquista. The miraculous events told in relation to the military deeds of these two rather obscure Sufi figures are too vague to be placed in any historical context. Notwithstanding the legendary origin of these hagiographical anecdotes, such stories may still adumbrate historical Sufi involvement in defending Muslim territory in the Iberian Peninsula before the fall of Granada in 1492 and the subsequent end of Muslim rule in what is now Spain and Portugal.

Although the historicity of anecdotes regarding Sufi friends of God during the early period of the Reconquista can be difficult to substantiate, accounts of Sufis in the Maghrib taking part in the military jihad following the Reconquista are on firmer historical ground. The reason for this is that Maghribi Sufis began to play an increasingly important defensive role in response to the growing threat the Iberian Christian kingdoms posed to the Muslims of North Africa. And during the fifteenth and sixteenth centuries, several Sufi shaykhs were indispensable in the military effort to resist the predations and invasions of the Spanish and Portuguese. Among these shaykhs we may mention Muhammad al-Jazuli (d. 870/1465), who exemplified the role of the Sufi as *mujahid* in both the military and the political sense, as well as the nonmystical Sufi role of teacher and paradigm of Islamic practice in Muslim society.[47]

Sufis were especially important in the development of Indian Islam; the stories of God's friends in Chapter 5 offer many examples of their multifaceted role in the subcontinent. Sufism arrived in northern India during the late twelfth and early thirteenth centuries, and Sufis played a significant part in the Islamization of the Indian subcontinent.[48] Wherever Islam gained a foothold, Sufis often served as teachers, proselytizers, and reformers, and their status as such continued throughout the premodern period. In addition to these social roles, Sufis also took part in the military jihad to expand the Abode of Islam in India.[49] The tradition of *ghazi* friends of God has remained an important component of popular Sufi shrine worship in the subcontinent and gives some credence to the military role of Sufis in the history of Muslim India.[50]

Even though *Sufi Warrior Saints* does not include anecdotes from hagiographical sources in Turkic languages, it goes without saying that Sufism was an integral part of Muslim culture throughout the lands of the Ottoman Empire. Ottoman history furnishes many examples of Sufi *mujahid*s, and in this regard contemporary accounts record Sufis taking part in the Ottoman conquest of Constantinople in 1453.[51] Moreover, following the conquest of Constantinople, Sufis would also play a significant role in Islamizing Ottoman territory.[52]

The foregoing historical examples of Sufi *mujahid*s remind us that Sufis have often played an active military role in both defending Muslim communities and expanding the domain of Islam since the eleventh century and that this role accords with the explication of the military jihad found in Sufi treatises and other writings.[53] And although it can be difficult to distinguish sacred history from historical fact in premodern accounts of Sufi warriors, it is nevertheless possible to glean a general idea of Sufi involvement in warfare that has some historical basis.[54] This may be achieved by comparing a variety of sources and evidence, as several scholars have successfully demonstrated in research that concerns premodern Sufi figures and Sufi activities. Hagiography is essential to such research, for although it does not present a historically reliable picture of Sufi friends of God, it can tell us much about the era during which the hagiographer lived and the social and political circumstances that inspired his composition.[55]

Warrior Renunciants and Sufism

Sufism does not, in general, call for monasticism (rahbaniyya) *in the Christian sense of the word; rather, it is monasticism of a special kind that accords with Islam's shari'a ... the Prophet explained this monasticism as jihad in God's path.*
—Muhammad Jalal Sharaf

The stories in *Sufi Warrior Saints* present idealized accounts of Sufi *mujahid*s and *ghazi*s from the hagiographical tradition.[56] The origin of the *mujahid* ideal, however, precedes the historical advent of Sufism by several centuries and therefore merits consideration before we turn to the topic of Sufi hagiography. In the following paragraphs, we will explore the literary precursors of Sufi *mujahid*s as well as the origin of the Sufi term *ribat*, both germane to our overview of Sufi jihad.

Though historical Sufism appeared sometime in the late ninth or early tenth century, the Sufi tradition traces the Sufi path back to the Prophet of Islam in an unbroken initiatic chain through his closest companions and kin (i.e., 'Ali and Abu Bakr), the generation that came immediately after (*Tabi'un*), and the earliest renunciants. For this reason, Sufi hagiography reckons the renunciant *mujahid*s, as well as other godly Muslim figures from the centuries following the advent of Islam, among the first generation of Sufis.[57]

The ubiquity of stories of early Sufi archetypes such as Ibrahim ibn Adham (d. 161/778) and 'Abdullah ibn al-Mubarak (d. 181/797)—who could not have been Sufis from a historical perspective—suggests that anecdotes of these ascetic/renunciant warriors provided the principal models for depicting Sufis as bold *mujahid*s in Sufi hagiography. The stories of these ascetic warriors were in turn modeled on the *maghazi* of the Prophet and his Companions, which were the narrative accounts of the Muslim conquest of Arabia in the early seventh century. The compilers of these sacred battle narratives—Ibn Hisham (d. 213/828) and al-Waqidi (d. 207/823)—relied primarily on oral sources. Their accounts present an idealized depiction of the first Muslims as courageous warriors for the faith, who exemplified piety, bravery, and asceticism in their many battles with the enemies of the burgeoning Islamic polity.[58]

The Muslim scholar al-Tabari (d. 310/923) relied heavily on anecdotes of these early battles, as narrated in Ibn Hisham's *al-Sira al-nabawiyya*, in the composition of his monumental *Tarikh al-rusul wa'l-muluk* (*History of Prophets and Kings*).[59] It is likely that Tabari's highly influential history thus helped to further establish the ethos of the ascetic *mujahid* in Muslim sacred history. It is also conceivable that these stories of the Prophet's military campaigns as related in the *sira* literature and early histories, as well as anecdotes of ascetic *mujahid*s in early Sufi hagiography, served to inspire historical Sufi warriors, whose deeds would in turn be related in later hagiographical accounts of Sufi *mujahid*s.[60] In this way, Sufi hagiography and the military deeds of historical Sufis brought forth a kind of symbiosis between an idealized narrative tradition of *mujahid* friends of God and living Sufi *mujahid*s.

Not only did the early renunciants serve as archetypes of devotion and bravery in Islamic sacred history; their military endeavors were also the source of several important Sufi concepts and terms, notably the aforementioned *mujahada*, as well as *ribat*. As *ribat* is significant in the history of Sufism, let us now consider its historical and lexical origins.

Many of the Muslim warriors who fought the Byzantines during the Umayyad and early Abbasid periods (roughly the eighth through the tenth century) would dwell in the border region—known as the *thughur*[61]—in outposts referred to as *ribat*s. The verbal noun *ribāt* originally signified the action of two hostile groups tying their horses at their respective frontiers in preparation for battle, or holding a post at the enemy's frontier.[62] These Muslim warriors—often referred to as *ghazis*—would lead an ascetic life while fighting to defend and expand the Abode of Islam.[63] It was from this ascetic military tradition that Sufis developed the idea of the *ribat* as a hospice where they could engage in spiritual exercises.[64] Moreover, a secondary meaning of the verb *rābata* is to apply oneself constantly and assiduously to prayer,[65] which perfectly accords with the complementary interpretation of the inner and outer meanings of scripture to which we referred earlier. It is also likely that the Sufi adoption of the term *ribat* was, in part, inspired by the final verse of *Surat Ali 'Imran* in the Qur'an (3:200), which says: *O you who believe, be constant, and forbear, and keep your post* (rābitū), *and fear God that you may prosper.*

The terms *ribat* and *mujahada* are important to our discussion of Sufi *mujahid*s, in that they offer succinct examples of the complementary outer and inner significance of Sufi terminology. Although the original meaning of the two words was unequivocally military, and this military meaning remained current, *ribat* and *mujahada* acquired a second, spiritual, meaning in Sufism, which reflected both the military activity of the early ascetics as well as their godliness, spiritual purity, and martial zeal.[66]

Sufi Hagiography

As the majority of the material for this book is found in the premodern Sufi hagiographical tradition, which spans roughly the eleventh through the seventeenth century, we ought to consider the origins and development of Sufi hagiography in order to provide some context for the stories of Sufi *mujahids* and *ghazis*. With this in mind, we will begin by discussing the two earliest comprehensive Sufi hagiographies, which were composed in Arabic, and the methodology of their authors in relation to contemporary attitudes toward Sufism. We will then address the development of hagiography composed in Persian, noting in particular how it evolved as Sufism became a generally accepted and integral part of Sunni Muslim culture. Following this, we will touch on the hagiographical tradition in the Maghrib before turning to consideration of some of the recurrent motifs in the lives of God's friends.

The earliest extant work of Sufi hagiography is al-Sulami's *Tabaqat al-sufiyya*, which dates to the late tenth or early eleventh century.[67] The structure and method of *Tabaqat al-sufiyya* owe much to the science of *hadith* collection and narration, which, as we mentioned earlier, was the branch of traditional Islamic learning for which Sufis were said to manifest a strong affinity. *Tabaqat al-sufiyya* divides the lives of the Sufis into five generations, beginning with the Companions of the Prophet and ending with the generation of Sufis closest to the era of the book's composition. The narrative of each friend of God in al-Sulami's hagiography consists of an introduction, followed by a *hadith* transmitted by the Sufi subject, and a biography.[68] Generally preceding the biographical details of each life, a chain of transmission mirrors the structure of the canonical *hadith* compendia (e.g., those of al-Bukhari, Muslim, etc.) and reflects how they introduce each tradition of the Prophet. It is worth noting that the majority of the biographies in *Tabaqat al-sufiyya* consist primarily of statements rather than developed narratives that tell a story.[69]

The second Sufi hagiography, which was composed several decades after al-Sulami's seminal work, is that of Abu Nu'aym al-Isfahani, whose *Hilyat al-awliya'* is structured similarly to *Tabaqat al-sufiyya* while expanding the narrative of each biography.[70] *Tabaqat al-sufiyya* and *Hilyat al-awliya'* were composed in Arabic, which was still the language of learning for most Persian-speaking Muslims, and they both rely on chains of transmission for authentication of their content.

As Sufism continued to unfold, it gradually became an accepted part of Sunni Muslim culture, so that by the end of the twelfth century, Sufi writers no longer felt so compelled to defend Sufism. With this in mind, we may consider 'Attar's *Tadhkirat al-awliya'*, which is the finest literary example of a Sufi hagiography from this period and is the source for many anecdotes in the stories that make up the contents of *Sufi Warrior Saints*. 'Attar's hagiography continues the tradition that his predecessors established while at the same time departing from them in several important ways: *Tadhkirat al-awliya'* dispenses with chains of transmission, is composed in unadorned Persian rather than Arabic, and presents entertaining, accessible narratives composed by a poet who cherished the stories of God's friends.[71] (This is not to say, however, that all subsequent Sufi hagiographies followed the innovations of *Tadhkirat al-awliya'*.) Insofar as it does not include chains of transmission, it could be said that *Tadhkirat al-awliya'* followed the precedent set by earlier works of Persian prose.[72]

It is also worth mentioning that hagiographies such as *Tadhkirat al-awliya'* probably contain a valuable record of the kinds of stories that Sufi proselytizers and preachers would have told either to edify an audience of ordinary (possibly unlettered) believers or to persuade potential converts of the miraculous power of God's friends and thereby the truth of Islam.[73] Such a record thus gives us an insight into popular forms of worship and religious practice that would otherwise be unavailable.

A significant development in hagiography of the Muslim East that occurred after the composition of *Tadhkirat al-awliya'* was the appearance of Sufi hagiographies composed in relation to a specific Sufi order. This development roughly coincided with the crystallization of the Sufi orders following the devastating Mongol conquests of the thirteenth century.[74] Hagiographies composed to support the legitimacy of a given order are generally of two kinds: *tabaqat*, which present the generations of Sufis and godly figures according to a Sufi order's initiatic chain, and monographic hagiographies that concentrate on the life and deeds (*manaqib*) of an order's eponym or namesake.[75] An example of the former is the extensive hagiography in Persian *Nafahat al-uns*, which 'Abd al-Rahman Jami (d. 898/1492) of Herat composed in support of the Naqshbandi Sufi order, to which he belonged. Examples of monographic hagiographies include *Firdaws al-murshidiyya*, which concerns the life of Abu Ishaq al-Kazaruni; *Asrar al-tawhid*, which relates the life of Abu Sa'id Abu'l-Khayr of Mayhana (in present-day Turkmenistan); and

Manaqib al-'arifin, regarding the life and deeds of Mawlavi Jalal al-Din Rumi—the eponym of the Mevlevi Sufi order in Anatolia—whom we discussed earlier, and his successors. It is also important to note that none of these hagiographies contains chains of transmission and they were all composed in Persian.

As regards the Sufi hagiographical tradition of the Muslim West, examples of which we will read in Chapter 4, the *rijal* genre proved to be the most important in defining *walaya* in the Maghrib.[76] *Rijal* (Arabic plural of *rajul*, "man") collections relate concise narratives of God's friends as transmitters of Islamic practice and paradigms of *walaya* and do not generally follow the birth-till-death structure common to the monographic *manaqib* genre.[77] Among the most important early Maghrib *rijal* collections are *Kitab al-tashawwuf ila rijal al-tasawwuf* of Abu Ya'qub al-Tadili (d. 627/1230) and *Kitab al-mustafad fi dhikr al-salihin wa'l-'ubbad* of Muhammad 'Qasim al-Tamimi (d. 603/1207). Later *rijal* collections include *Dawhat al-nashir* of Ibn 'Askar (d. 986/1578) and *Tabaqat al-Hudaygi* of Muhammad b. Ahmad al-Hudaygi (d. 1189/1775).

It is hoped that this brief introduction to Sufi hagiography has provided the reader with a basic understanding of the sources for the stories in *Sufi Warrior Saints*. Before moving on, however, we ought to mention that Sufi hagiography is not the only important source of hagiographical material for the lives of God's friends. In fact, many premodern Arabic chronicles and histories, some of which were composed by Sufis, likewise furnish anecdotes of Sufi *mujahids*, as does the *rihla* (travel-narrative) genre also. Examples of these histories and travel narratives include Ibn 'Asakir's *Tarikh madinat Dimashq*, al-Khatib al-Baghdadi's *Tarikh Baghdad*, al-Yafi'i's *Mir'at al-janan*, Ibn al-'Imad's *Shadharat al-dhahab*, Ibn Kathir's *al-Bidaya wa'l-nihaya*, and Ibn Battuta's *Rihla*. These histories and travel narratives have contributed many fascinating and illuminating anecdotes to the stories of God's friends related herein, underscoring the fact that Sufi hagiographical anecdotes were a significant component of premodern Islamic literature in general.

Having discussed the hagiographical sources for the lives of God's friends, we will now turn to the topic of recurrent hagiographical motifs and their significance for our narratives. Following this, we will say a few words regarding the methodology for the composition of the stories and will then conclude our introduction to *Sufi Warrior Saints* with several points to keep in mind when reading these stories.

Recurrent Motifs in the Lives of God's Friends

If someone tells you stories of the wonders of God's friends,
and these stories seem to you far from the path of reason and impossible,
do not doubt them until you acquire knowledge of the reality of their truth,
for the heart does not perceive the mark of truth by means of reason or formal effort,
but rather through God's grace.

—Qabus Nama

As with hagiography in general, Sufi hagiographies contain a significant number of recurring motifs and tropes that communicate fundamental characteristics of God's friends.[78] Some of these motifs are common to multiple religious traditions or specific geographical regions and thus attest the universal nature of hagiographical narrative.[79]

Several common motifs in Sufi hagiography merit our consideration, as they help illuminate the essence of God's friends and shed some light on how a popular audience would have understood and identified this essence. The use of these motifs also represents a kind of hagiographical methodology, in that their recurrence serves to substantiate miracles as well as to present Sufi ideals and truths symbolically.[80] For a premodern audience, the relation of one instance of a miraculous deed would recall similar deeds in the lives of other friends of God and would thereby confirm the essential truth of such deeds.[81] For this reason, in the following paragraphs we will consider important recurring motifs from Sufi hagiography that are germane to our topic of Sufi *mujahid*s. These motifs include precocity, repentance (*tawba*) and discarding books, wandering in the wilderness, admonishing rulers (the jihad of the tongue), admonishments from non-Muslims, addressing the importunate lower self and prodigious *mujahada*, encounters with dogs and other animals, miraculous conversion of unbelievers, various battle tropes, and miracles and dreams following the death of a friend of God. Though some of these motifs involve miracles and wondrous deeds, others speak more to the social role of Sufis.[82]

The first recurrent motif we will consider is that of precocity. In many religious and mythological traditions, precocity is often a foretoken of a future prophet, saint, or hero. Sufi hagiography is no exception, and there are many examples of friends of God whose precocious deeds or words indicate their spiritual status, sometimes even before they are born. God's friends often speak precociously, which is also a common motif in the lives of prophets in the Islamic tradition.[83] Several examples of this motif occur in *Sufi Warrior Saints*: at the age of only seven, Junayd al-Baghdadi (see Chapter 2) defines thankfulness to God before four hundred shaykhs in a mosque in Mecca and receives their unanimous approbation; the young Najm al-Din Kubra receives his nickname *al-Tamma al-kubra* (the Great Calamity—see Chapter 3) while studying the religious sciences, as he wins every argument with his fellow students regarding learned topics. A rather extreme example may be found in the life of Abu Muhammad Chishti (see Chapter 5), who while still an infant speaks Arabic to his father and, at the age of four, begins leading the Friday prayer. Other friends of God exhibit spiritual and doctrinal precocity. For example, while still in the womb, Bayazid (see Chapter 2) lets his mother know that she is eating something that may be religiously unclean by kicking until she spits out the suspect morsel of food. The boy Rumi (see Chapter 3) exhorts his playmates not to jump from roof to roof like animals and is then carried up into the heavens by the angels before returning to his friends. All these anecdotes of miraculous precocity foretell the spiritual might these future friends of God will exemplify throughout their lives.

Anecdotes of repentance (*tawba*), whereby a future friend turns from his worldly life to closeness with God, are important in the lives of several early friends of God whose lives we will read in Chapter 1. One of the best-known examples is that of Ibrahim ibn Adham, whose repentance occurs after several wondrous events, which include an encounter with the enigmatic prophet Khizr,[84] an encounter with a wild ass that speaks to him and upbraids him for wasting his time in the frivolous pursuit of hunting,[85] and hearing an admonishing voice emanating from his saddle. Sometimes an encounter with an unbeliever is the catalyst for repentance, as when Shaqiq al-Balkhi (d. 194/810) repents after a Buddhist and then a Zoroastrian upbraid him for his failure to rely solely on God for his daily bread.[86] Romantic love is the catalyst for Ibn al-Mubarak's turning to God and forsaking worldly concerns: after spending the entire night standing before the house of his beloved, he hears the dawn call to prayer and chides himself for having spent so much time in the pursuit of a girl while not having the patience to listen to a Friday sermon in the mosque. In all these examples, God's friends reevaluate their priorities and internalize the fundamental aspects of the faith, which, among other things, include strict adherence to the dictates of the *shari'a*.[87]

There are many anecdotes in the Sufi hagiographical tradition of friends of God abandoning their books, which generally symbolizes their having passed beyond mere external learning and reached a higher station of spiritual knowledge. In one example, Ahmad-i Havari (d. 230/844/5) begins by devoting himself to the study of the Islamic religious sciences; however, when he attains the state of perfection (*kamal*), he takes his books and casts them into the sea, saying: "These were a good guide; however, having reached the goal, what would I need a guide for?"[88] In a similar manner, Abu Sa'id Abu'l-Khayr is said to have gathered all his books and buried them after having attained a spiritual state that resulted from *mujahada* and *riyada*.[89] The Chishti friend of God Mawlana Zia al-Din Hakim, having eaten the roasted leg of a crane that Mu'in al-Din Chishti (d. 633/1236) places before him, renounces philosophy and then casts his philosophy books into the water and becomes a follower of the Chishti shaykh.[90] Najm al-Din Kubra (see Chapter 3), having turned toward the inner spiritual path after an encounter with a dervish, does not finish reading the final pages of a book his teacher has assigned to him, despite the latter's plea that he complete his studies. The motif of abandoning one's books and outward learning may also symbolize a kind of *tawba* in the literal sense of turning toward God, in that friends of God who do so turn away from their previous life of prestigious outward knowledge toward a new, inner life of the spirit.

Many friends of God spend a period wandering alone in the wilderness as part of their repentance and spiritual reorientation. Following his repentance, Ibrahim ibn Adham (Chapter 1) wanders in the mountains and the wilderness, lamenting his sins before finally making his way to the city of Merv. Bayazid (Chapter 2) wanders for thirty years in the wilderness while undertaking *mujahada* and *riyada*. Baba Palang Pūsh wanders naked in the wilderness contemplating God until Khizr appears to him and tells him his time of wandering in repentance is complete. In these three examples, each friend of God seeks spiritual purification and rebirth in wandering and after this period of loneliness and deprivation is ready for the next stage of his spiritual career. Thus, these examples of wandering in the wilderness symbolize the final break with worldly concerns and the subject's former life.

The motif of a friend of God admonishing a ruler—often a caliph who is not living up to his role as Commander of the Faithful—is common in hagiographical literature. This motif is especially important in that it reflects a third aspect of Sufi jihad, which is based on the *hadith* "The best jihad is a word of justice to an unjust ruler."[91] In one example from al-Isfahani's *Hilyat al-awliya'*, Fudayl ibn 'Iyad (d. 187/803) upbraids the Abbasid caliph Harun al-Rashid (d. 193/809) for not attending to the welfare of the Muslim community.[92] Fudayl warns the caliph that his face will be blackened in the flames of hell should he not live up to his title and counsels him to seek guidance in the Qur'an.[93] Similar anecdotes are found in the lives of Shaqiq al-Balkhi (see Chapter 1) and Junayd (see Chapter 2), both of whom admonish the caliph for neglecting his duties to the Muslim polity. The motif of God's friends admonishing an unjust ruler emphasizes their role as protectors of their fellow Muslims, in that they do not fear confronting a tyrant—an act that could result in punishment or death for an ordinary man. It also shows the superiority of *wilaya* to temporal power while reminding Muslim rulers to heed the counsel of God's friends and seek the well-being of the Muslim community in all their actions.

Friends of God themselves may be admonished—often by a non-Muslim, which is a common motif in Sufi hagiography. We have mentioned Shaqiq al-Balkhi's repentance following his being chided by a Buddhist and then a Zoroastrian regarding his failure to rely on God. Ibn al-Mubarak (Chapter 1) likewise encounters a Christian monk known for *mujahada* and asks him what the path to God is. The monk upbraids him, saying "If you knew God, you would know the path to Him."[94]

God's friends struggle with the lower self (*nafs*) through spiritual warfare, which, as we mentioned earlier, Sufi texts generally refer to as *mujahada* and *riyada*. A common motif of this struggle involves a friend of God addressing his *nafs*, which is invariably tempting him to give in to his base desires. In many examples of this motif the *nafs* wishes to eat something toothsome; for example, the *nafs* of Bishr al-Hafi (d. 227/841) yearns to eat chicken stew, while the *nafs* of Abu'l-Husayn al-Nuri (d. 295/907) importunes him for a date. The motif of the *nafs* longing to eat dates is also found in anecdotes of Malik ibn Dinar, Rabi'a, and Ibrahim ibn Adham (see Chapter 1).[95] Indeed, dates often symbolize luxury and worldly desire in Persian hagiography; thus Abu Ishaq al-Kazaruni, whose life we will consider in detail in Chapter 2, forbade himself dates and sugar as well.[96] In an example from Sufi hagiography from the Maghrib, the *nafs* of the North African friend of God Muhammad ibn Ahmad al-Tamazuti (d. 1007/1599) would appear to him as a weak-willed and delicate slave girl who would complain of the self-mortification that he made her undergo. While engaging in *mujahada*, he would admonish her to cease complaining and accept whatever God had ordained.[97] In a rather unusual anecdote involving the military jihad, Ahmad Khizravayh of Balkh (d. 240/854) wishes to take part in a campaign against the unbelievers and is astonished to discover that his *nafs* also wishes to go. He then realizes that his *nafs*, which has grown weary of *mujahada* with its unrelenting regime of self-mortification, sleep deprivation, and solitude, sees the campaign as a chance for food, companionship, and sleep. Ahmad tells his *nafs* that he will continue to impose on it the same strict regime, but it cheerfully agrees to this. In the end, Ahmad prays to God and beseeches Him to deliver him from the wiles of his *nafs*. God answers his prayer by causing his *nafs* to reveal its plan to him. The *nafs* says to Ahmad: "Every day, you slay me one hundred times [through *mujahada* and *riyada*], and no one knows anything about this; whereas in battle I may die a martyr, for which the people will praise me." Upon hearing this confession, Ahmad, convinced that he cannot trust his *nafs* regardless of the circumstances, redoubles his efforts to oppose it.[98]

With regard to *mujahada*, it is not surprising that prodigious self-mortification is another common motif in the lives of God's friends. Abu'l-Hajjaj al-Mughawir, whose life we will read in Chapter 4, sits outside for forty days without stirring, wearing only a cloak, and does not seem to be affected by temperature fluctuations or lack of sustenance. Abu Muhammad Chishti (see Chapter 5) suspends himself upside down in a pit to pray, which recalls the anecdote concerning Abu Sa'id Abu'l-Khayr in *Asrar al-tawhid* in which his father relates that he saw him lay a beam with a rope tied thereto athwart the mouth of a pit; then he tied his foot to the rope, let himself down into the pit, hung upside down, and recited the entire Qur'an.[99] In an extreme example of self-mortification, Bayazid (see Chapter 2) refuses his *nafs* water for an entire year to punish it for an infraction.

Animals are common in Sufi hagiography, where they sometimes play a didactic role. This may be seen in anecdotes concerning dogs, which are considered ritually unclean in Islam. Contact with a dog requires completion of ablutions (*wudu'*) to return to a state of ritual purity. For this reason, dogs often symbolize humility, owing to their lowly status. In the life of Bayazid, for example, a dog becomes his walking companion and reminds him of the essence of *tawakkul*.[100] Dogs can also be a means of showing the spiritual power of one of God's friends, as when Najm al-Din Kubra bestows *walaya* on a dog by means of his glance after having read the thoughts of one of his *murid*s who doubts the shaykh's power.[101]

Animals can also symbolize a friend of God's *walaya*. An especially curious example of this is that of a (presumably venomous) snake attending to a sleeping friend of God. In the life of Ibrahim ibn Adham, one of his companions relates that he beheld a snake with a narcissus bouquet in its mouth shooing the flies from the friend of God while he slept. A similar anecdote regarding Ibn al-Mubarak tells of a snake with a sprig of basil in its mouth keeping the flies from disturbing him while he sleeps in a garden. In the life of Abu Ishaq al-Kazaruni, his *murid*s witness a black snake bearing a narcissus in its mouth approach their shaykh while he is taking a nap. The snake lays the narcissus on the shaykh's breast, leaves, and then returns with another narcissus, which it likewise places on his breast. The snake continues to leave and return in this manner until there is a bouquet of narcissus on the shaykh's breast. When Abu Ishaq awakes, he explains to his *murid*s that one who truly loves God receives the love of all creatures.

The power of God's friends to convert unbelievers is another common motif in Sufi hagiography. For example, Fudayl ibn 'Iyad, whom we mentioned above, converts a Jew to Islam through an alchemical miracle whereby he transforms a lump of earth under the Jew's pillow into gold.[102] In another anecdote, a Brahmin becomes a Muslim after having witnessed Shaykh Baha' al-Din al-Sindi rise aloft and revolve in the air.[103] 'Abdullah al-Yunini of Syria, whose life we will read in Chapter 3, brings about the conversion of a Christian wine merchant by turning the merchant's wine to vinegar. A single glance from Najm al-Din Kubra (Chapter 3) has the power to convert an unbeliever, as does the very presence of Abu Muhammad Chishti (Chapter 5).

God's friends often assist in waging war against the unbelievers, either sending aid from afar through their *wilaya* or by taking part in battle as a *mujahid* or *ghazi*. For example, *Hilyat al-awliya'* relates that Ibrahim ibn Adham took part in many battles on both land and sea. In another anecdote from *Hilyat al-awliya'*, Shaqiq al-Balkhi spends the entire day fighting the unbelievers, and then when night comes he lies down between the two armies and uses his Sufi cloak (*khirqa*) for a pillow, trusting in God to keep him safe.[104] In another example, Abu Ishaq al-Kazaruni (see Chapter 2) sends an army of *ghazi*s to do battle with the Byzantines. The Byzantines overwhelm the Muslims, so they call to Abu Ishaq for help. Abu Ishaq appears among them as a great warrior on horseback, and by means of his *wilaya* they rout the unbelievers—all while Abu Ishaq has remained in Kazarun, where his companions witness him vigorously flailing his staff about on the roof of the mosque. In a similar manner, Abu Muhammad Chishti, who is fighting the unbelievers at Somnath, in Gujarat, calls out to one of his *murid*s, who is in Chisht, in Khurasan, to help him turn the tide of the battle. The *murid* appears at once and helps defeat the unbelievers; at the same time, however, the *murid*'s companions in Chisht are astonished to see him furiously striking walls and doors with a stave, and only later do they learn the significance of his actions.[105] Though not a war motif, but involving a similar motif of journeying a great distance in the blink of an eye to aid someone, Baba Palang Pūsh (Chapter 5) in India hears his friend's cry of distress in Anatolia and immediately journeys there miraculously to help him.

Miraculous events and dreams often follow the death of God's friends, which serve to further confirm their status as such. In some cases, a friend of God appears to a *murid* or contemporary in a dream after his death, and the latter asks him about his recompense in the hereafter for his earthly deeds (e.g., Ibn al-Mubarak in Chapter 1 and Junayd in Chapter 2). Following the death of Muhammad ibn Wasi' (Chapter 1), a Sufi has a dream in which Ibn Wasi' enters heaven before Malik ibn Dinar on account of his owning only one shirt during his life, whereas Malik owned two, thus exemplifying the former's superior renunciation (*zuhd*). Sometime after the death of Abu Ishaq al-Kazaruni (Chapter 2), his successor calls upon him to aid the Muslims of Kazarun in their campaign against a Christian city, which they have besieged. Abu Ishaq's spirit tells his successor what the Muslims must do to defeat the Christians, which leads to the fall of the Christian city and victory for the Muslim host. In what is perhaps the most colorful post-mortem deed related in *Sufi Warrior Saints*, 'Abd al-Rahman al-Nuwayri (Chapter 3) is beheaded by a Crusader, who mocks his corpse with a quotation from the Qur'an. The severed head of al-Nuwayri immediately responds by repeating the final phrase of the Qur'anic quotation. Upon witnessing this, the Crusader becomes a Muslim.

Throughout *Sufi Warrior Saints* we shall encounter these (and other) recurrent motifs, especially those dealing with the various forms of jihad. The primary forms of jihad in Sufi hagiography (which we mentioned earlier) are the jihad of confronting tyrants and rulers who do not uphold their duty as leaders of the Muslim polity, the jihad of struggling with and subduing the *nafs* (i.e., *mujahada*), and the communal military jihad waged either to defend the Abode of Islam or to spread Islam in the lands of unbelief.

On the Sources, Structure, and Aim of This Book

The anecdotes of Sufi *mujahid*s and *ghazi*s from which the stories herein are composed are primarily from Sufi hagiographies, although, as mentioned above, Sufi treatises and poetry, as well as a variety of premodern sources that include histories, chronicles, and travel narratives have also provided many anecdotes. Though the authors of most of these texts were themselves Sufis, some of them (e.g., Ibn Kathir and Ibn ʿAsakir) were Sunni Muslim historians and did not necessarily have any formal Sufi affiliation but included anecdotes about Sufis and renunciants in their histories. In this regard, it is worth noting that many of the same early renunciants and Sufis appear in virtually every kind of premodern Islamic narrative—even in the frame-tale story cycle *Alf layla wa-layla* (*The Arabian Nights*)—and this bespeaks the significance of the stories of God's friends in premodern Sunni Muslim culture.[106]

As regards the structure of the stories, each chapter will concentrate on several friends of God from a particular era or region significant in Islamic history and will begin with a brief introduction that surveys the major historical events and social circumstances that pertained. The structure of each life will depend on the available sources. For some of the lives (e.g., the life of Muhammad ibn Wasiʿ in Chapter 1), there is no single source that presents a birth-till-death narrative, but only brief anecdotes dispersed among various sources; where this is the case, I have assembled the anecdotes into a coherent narrative, while denoting each anecdote's provenance in the footnotes. Where there are multiple hagiographical sources that relate a complete narrative of a given friend of God's life (e.g., the life of Ibrahim ibn Adham in Chapter 1), I generally present the source that is either the most detailed or has the most literary merit for the main narrative of the subject's life, while including translations of anecdotes from other sources where applicable. In the case of Abu Ishaq al-Kazaruni (Chapter 2), Bayazid al-Bistami (Chapter 2), Rumi (Chapter 3), and Baba Palang Pūsh (Chapter 5), entire monographic hagiographies are dedicated to them, and I have not, of course, endeavored to translate the entire hagiography for each of these friends of God; rather, I have selected anecdotes that represent the aspects of their lives and deeds that are relevant to the focus of this book. In the above cases, the selections will highlight anecdotes that portray the subject as an exemplar of Sufi jihad in its three primary outward manifestations: fighting in battle as a *mujahid/ghazi,* leading Muslim warriors to victory by means of *wilaya,* and admonishing kings and others who wield temporal power (e.g., emirs, governors, and generals) in the Muslim community. Anecdotes that relate the preliminary inner struggles of God's friends to overcome their lower selves will precede those dealing with outward forms of jihad, in accordance with the general Sufi belief that the Sufi wayfarer must first complete the inner jihad before he can selflessly undertake the outer. For several lives (e.g., the life of Abu 'Abdullah Muhammad al-Arkushi in Chapter 4 and that of Sayyid Muluk Shah in Chapter 5), there is—to my knowledge—only one brief extant source; in these cases, I have translated the entire hagiography of the friend of God without rearranging or omitting any of the anecdotes.

The primary aim of this book is to offer readable narratives about Sufi *mujahid*s to a readership that does not have access to the many sources in Arabic and Persian from which these stories are composed. Although, as mentioned above, I have generally followed one or two main sources for the majority of each subject's life, I have also supplemented the narrative using other sources where possible. I have chosen this method not only to present as complete a story as possible but also to include anecdotes from every available source, as I believe these will be of interest to the reader while also providing examples of the diverse literary tradition of Sufi hagiography. In this way, *Sufi Warrior Saints* takes inspiration from the Sufi hagiographical tradition—namely 'Attar's *Tadhkirat al-awliya'*—by weaving a seamless narrative from sundry sources, so as to present the reader with a compelling and coherent story that distills the essence of what each friend of God's life embodies. The purist may object, but I contend that this methodology is true to the cultural tradition, which goes beyond the confines of one particular hagiographical text and reflects the living oral tradition regarding God's friends.

With regard to the format of the stories, all the anecdotes presented in each life are careful translations from the original Arabic and Persian sources. I have inserted words and phrases that are implied but not actually present in the original text in brackets in order to render the anecdotes into coherent English. I have also indicated original Arabic or Persian terms in parentheses where necessary and have preceded some anecdotes or selections of quotations with my own explanatory statements in italics. All quotations from the Qur'an are also in italics.

Ταῦτα δὲ ἐγένετο μὲν οὐδέποτε, ἔστι δὲ ἀεί

In reading these stories,[107] the reader ought to bear in mind that the lives of God's friends are not factual accounts of historical deeds and events, as we noted earlier; rather, they are part of Muslim sacred history: that is, they embody the essential truths of the faith through stories that premodern believers—even the most humble or unlettered—could understand. Sacred history is not unique to Islam; indeed, it is a part of every religious tradition (e.g., the Gospels of Christianity, the *Jataka*s of Buddhism, the Hindu *Purana*s).

Sacred history is the narrative that provides a religious tradition with a structure as it unfolds and to which believers may return in order to give spiritual meaning to contemporary events. With regard to the nature of sacred history, Ananda Coomaraswamy reminds us: "What is... far more important than the record of fact is the expression of all that the facts, as understood, implied to those to whom they were a living inspiration."[108] The actors in sacred history serve as archetypes of piety, heroism, and wisdom—and, occasionally, villainy. In the context of Islamic sacred history, an illustrative example of this may be found in the martyrdom of the Prophet's grandson Husayn at Karbala, in Iraq, on the tenth day of Muharram (known as 'Ashura) in the year 680. Husayn and his seventy-two supporters, made up of his followers, friends, and kin, embody suffering for the sake of truth and the struggle against worldly evil and injustice—which the Umayyad caliph Yazid I (d. 64/683) epitomizes. Husayn and his supporters knew beforehand that in upholding the truth they would perish at the hands of Yazid's soldiers. Throughout Islamic history, Husayn has represented virtue, patience, and bravery, not only for Shi'ite Muslims—for whom he is the third imam—but also for many Sunni Muslims. Yazid, conversely, has represented cruelty, perfidy, and oppressive, unjust rule.

During the Iranian Revolution, Ayatollah Khomeini and his followers often invoked these archetypes in support of their aims, identifying the shah as the Yazid of his day and those struggling against him as taking part in a contemporary Karbala resistance.[109] An important slogan of the Islamic Revolution was "Every day is 'Ashura,"[110] a powerful and persuasive statement that Khomeini's faction in the revolution used in order to define opposition to the shah as a spiritually significant struggle connected in sacred time to Husayn's martyrdom at Karbala.

Like Husayn and his followers at Karbala, the realm that God's friends in Sufi hagiography inhabit is sacred history, governed by sacred time. Sacred time is recurrent, and thus it follows that the deeds of God's friends are always exemplary and always meaningful. Indeed, these stories of God's friends provide believers access to the essence of Islamic godliness while also allowing them to return in sacred time to the era of the faith's unfolding in sacred history.

Conclusion

It is hoped that *Sufi Warrior Saints* will help clarify the multifaceted role Sufis have played in Islamic culture and history and dispel some of the misconceptions concerning Sufis, especially the limited view that they are nothing more than the mystics of Islam. It is further hoped that the stories related herein will elucidate some of the nuances of jihad, as this fundamental Islamic doctrine is still poorly understood in the West.

Current Western definitions of jihad range from the polemical (e.g., a brutal "holy war" that condones terrorism) to the apologetic (e.g., a nonviolent struggle for spiritual purity and justice). Both definitions show strong ideological bias, and neither takes into account the legal complexities of the doctrine of jihad. As mentioned previously, the doctrine of jihad is the struggle to expand the Abode of Islam or to defend it. With regard to expanding the Abode of Islam, jihad may involve proselytization or, if necessary, war. The rules for carrying out the military jihad are regulated by a well-established legal tradition, which requires that the *mujahid* be utterly selfless and seek no personal gain.[111] The stories of Sufi *mujahids* often reflect these strict legal stipulations and thereby refute the above-mentioned simplistic, ideologically motivated definitions of jihad.

Despite its original (primarily military) meaning in Islamic jurisprudence, jihad did not remain static and would eventually come to embrace other forms of religious and spiritual struggling. By the twelfth century, extramilitary interpretations of jihad had gained some currency, as may be seen in the fourfold definition of Ibn Rushd (d. 595/1198), which comprised "The jihad of the heart, the jihad of the tongue, the jihad of the hand, and the jihad of the sword."[112] Likewise, al-Raghib al-Isfahani had previously defined jihad as "Fighting the outer foes, fighting Satan, and fighting the *nafs*."[113] Ibn Rushd's fourfold complementary understanding of jihad, as well as the threefold definition of al-Raghib al-Isfahani, undoubtedly influenced the formulation of the greater jihad in Sufism. God's friends exemplify this complementary spiritual aspect of jihad in the many anecdotes depicting their *mujahada* and *riyada* in Sufi hagiography.

Notwithstanding the development of a threefold understanding of jihad and the current—and, we may add, timely—emphasis on the greater jihad, we must neither ignore nor downplay the military jihad in Islam. For if we are to fully understand the history of this dynamic faith, it is imperative that we recognize the militant ethos that assured the initial survival and subsequent spread of Islam. This militant ethos also pervades the history and literature of Sufism, and the attempt on the part of some—in both Western and Muslim countries—to seek in Sufism a solution to militant Islamism not only is patronizing but also shows how poorly they understand the complexity of the Sufi tradition.[114] In this regard, *Sufi Warrior Saints* seeks to reveal the symbolic—and to some degree historical—part that Sufis have played in the military jihad through relating anecdotes of Sufi warriors.

As regards the cultural and artistic value of these stories of God's friends, it is hoped that *Sufi Warrior Saints* will provide nonspecialist readers with an introduction to some of the essential components of Muslim piety while also allowing them to appreciate Sufi hagiography as literature.

Through storytelling we define what it means to be human, connect the present to the past, and make sense of our place in the world. The appeal of stories is universal, and a good story—regardless of the time or place of its composition—draws us into its timeless realm of essential truth and wisdom. It is for this reason that the fundamental truths of every religious tradition are often best conveyed through stories. The stories in *Sufi Warrior Saints* will, it is hoped, introduce readers to the spiritual and ethical lessons that the lives of God's friends impart in a way not unlike the experience of many premodern Muslims for whom these stories were originally told.

Chapter 1

ASCETIC WARRIORS AND PROTO-SUFIS: THE EIGHTH AND NINTH CENTURIES

In many ways, the eighth and ninth centuries (second and third centuries of the Islamic calendar) were the defining period of early Islam. In the seventh century, following the death of the Prophet in 632 and the establishment of the caliphate, the Muslims defeated the Byzantines and Sassanids in several decisive battles and thereby gained considerable territory in Western Asia and North Africa.[1] During the eighth century, the Muslim armies under the Umayyad dynasty completed the conquest of the Near East, North Africa, and Central Asia begun in the previous century. The Muslims also succeeded in gaining a foothold in Europe in 711, when a Muslim army led by Tariq ibn Ziyad (d. early second/eighth century) began the invasion of the Iberian Peninsula, which brought much of what is now Spain and Portugal into the Abode of Islam.

The eighth and ninth centuries not only were significant for the territorial expansion of Islam, for they also witnessed the first efforts of early Muslim scholars to undertake the systematic study of Islamic scripture and elaborate the principles of Islamic law. These efforts included the collection of *hadith* and working out a method for evaluating their veracity on the basis of chains of transmission, as well as the composition of the first examples of Qur'anic exegesis (*tafsir*). The science of *hadith* was fundamental in the development of the Islamic scriptural tradition and would influence the way both historical and hagiographical narratives would be composed in the following centuries. It is also worth noting that what Sunni Muslims would come to consider the six canonical *hadith* compendia, including those of al-Bukhari (d. 256/870) and Muslim ibn al-Hajjaj (d. 261/875), were all composed during the ninth century.[2]

A state of almost perpetual war and raiding obtained during this period between the Abbasid Caliphate (established in 750 after the fall of the Umayyads), with its capital at Baghdad, and the Byzantines in the *thughur* region of northern Syria and southern Anatolia.[3] As a result, an ascetic Muslim warrior culture arose in the *thughur* garrisons. And this, in turn, inspired the important oral tradition regarding the wondrous and courageous deeds of the semilegendary *ghazis* who would become influential figures in Muslim sacred history. The anecdotes about these warrior ascetics eventually found their way into most genres of the burgeoning Islamic literary tradition, including the first Sufi hagiographies.

Hagiographers such as al-Sulami and al-Isfahani would include these frontier ascetics in the first generation of Sufi friends of God and would thereby establish Ibrahim ibn Adham, Muhammad ibn Wasi', 'Abdullah ibn al-Mubarak, and Shaqiq al-Balkhi, among others, as Sufi *mujahid* archetypes.

These warrior ascetics were known in particular for their *tawakkul* and *wara'*, accordant with the austere life that they led in military outposts, which differed greatly from life in Baghdad and Damascus with their abundant luxuries and worldly pleasures. Most important, these early friends of God embodied the essential qualities of the *mujahid*—piety, selflessness, and courage—and their stories would serve to inspire these same qualities in Muslims throughout the premodern period, to which the retelling of their wondrous and godly deeds in Sufi hagiography and poetry over the centuries bears witness.

Ibrahim ibn Adham

Ibrahim ibn Adham of Balkh (in present-day Afghanistan) is one of the earliest Sufi archetypes, and the Sufi hagiographical tradition relates many anecdotes about his life and deeds. Ibrahim was known especially for his *wara'* and *tawakkul*; he exemplified the complementary aspects of jihad—both military and spiritual[4]—in overcoming his *nafs* through *mujahada* and *riyada* so that he became a fearless *mujahid* and *ghazi*.[5] Ibrahim is described as a brave horseman[6] who fought the Byzantines on the frontier between the Abode of Islam and the realm of Eastern Christendom in what is now Syria, Iraq, and Turkey[7]; he is also said to have fought several battles at sea.[8]

Regarding the primary sources for the life of Ibrahim ibn Adham as presented hereunder: the narrative of Ibrahim's repentance is primarily from *Tadhkirat al-awliya'*, with some additional anecdotes from *Pand-i piran* and the *Risala* of al-Qushayri. The anecdotes of his miracles, dicta, and exempla are from *Hilyat al-awliya'*, *Fazayil-i Balkh*, *Tarikh madinat Dimashq*, and *al-Tabaqat al-kubra*. The military jihad anecdotes are from *Hilyat al-awliya'*, *Tarikh madinat Dimashq*, *Fazayil-i Balkh*, and *al-Bidaya wa'l-nihaya*.

The Repentance of Ibrahim ibn Adham

He was the king of Balkh. The beginning of his [inner] transformation was during his kingship when a world was under his command, and forty golden shields were borne before him and forty golden maces behind him. One night, he was sleeping on his throne. At midnight, the roof began to quake as though someone was on the roof, and so he called out, "Who goes there?" [A voice] answered, "I am an acquaintance and have lost my camel." Ibrahim replied, "You foolish man, you seek a camel on the roof? How could a camel be on the roof?" [The voice] answered, "You careless man, you seek God on a golden throne, clad in silk? Is seeking a lost camel on the roof truly stranger than *that*?" On account of these words, awe filled Ibrahim's heart and a fire blazed therein; he became thoughtful and was amazed and melancholy.

It is related that one day, while Ibrahim was holding court with his nobles, each one standing in his place, and his servants were arrayed before him, a man of awe-inspiring demeanor suddenly entered through the door, such that no one among the servants or attendants dared ask him who he was or why he had come. The man then drew nearer until he stood before Ibrahim's throne. "What do you want?" said Ibrahim. "I've alighted at this guesthouse," he said. "This is my *palace*, not a guesthouse!" replied Ibrahim. "To whom did this palace belong before this?" asked [the man]. "It belonged to my father." "And to whom did it belong before that?" "To someone else." "And before him?" "To his father." "And where did they all go?" he asked. "They have all died and passed on," said Ibrahim. "And this is *not* a guesthouse where one man arrives, and another departs?" As soon as he had spoken these words, he left the palace forthwith. Ibrahim hastened after him, swearing an oath and crying, "Stop! I must speak with you." [The man] halted. "Who are you, and whence have you come that you should kindle a fire in my breast?" [The man] answered, "I am a land and a sea, a shore and a heaven, and the name by which I am best known is Khizr." Ibrahim replied, "Wait, so that I may return home and then come back!" "The matter is more urgent than that," replied [Khizr], and he vanished.

Ibrahim's ardor grew and his pain increased, and he said, "What is this that I have seen by night and heard by day? Have them saddle my horse in order that I may go hunting and find out how this affair will turn out." He mounted and turned his face toward the wilderness. He traversed the wilderness in a state of madness so that he did not know what he was doing. In that state he became separated from his retinue and wandered far off. He heard a voice saying, "Awake!" He was unwilling to listen to it. He heard the same voice a second time. The third time, he moved away thence and ignored the voice. The fourth time, he heard, "Awake! before you are made awake!" When he heard this speech, he lost all possession of his senses. Suddenly a wild ass appeared, and he directed his attention toward it. The wild ass began speaking and said, "I have been sent to hunt *you*, not you to hunt *me*. You cannot hunt me. Were you created to pursue and shoot helpless creatures? Don't you have something else to do?" Ibrahim said, "What is all this about?" and turned away from the wild ass. Then he heard the same words coming from his saddlebow that he had heard from the wild ass. He was overcome with sorrow and fear, and his unveiling unfolded.

When God decided to complete [the unveiling of Ibrahim's heart], he heard [the same words] again, this time from the buttonhole of his collar. Thereupon the unveiling was complete; the kingdom of heaven was made manifest to him, and he witnessed the hidden realities vouchsafed God's men and attained certain knowledge. It is said that he wept so much that his horse and clothing became soaked with tears, and he sincerely repented. He turned away from the road and saw a shepherd boy herding his sheep before him, wearing coarse clothing and a hat of coarse cloth. [Ibrahim] perceived that the youth was one of his servants, took off his golden cloak, gave it to him, and made him a gift of the sheep. He then donned the shepherd boy's coarse cloak and hat, and after this he began wandering on foot in the mountains and the wilderness, bewailing his sins, until he reached the city of Merv, where he saw a bridge and a blind man falling from the bridge. Ibrahim said, "God keep him!" to stop him from falling. The blind man became suspended in midair, and the people took hold of him and brought him down. They were in awe of Ibrahim and said, "What a great man!"

Ibrahim then continued on his way till he reached the city of Nishapur. He was seeking an empty place to devote himself to the worship of God. There is a well-known cave there, in which he dwelled for nine years, three years in each chamber. Who knows what kind of *mujahada* he performed day and night in that cave? Every Thursday he would emerge from the cave and collect a fagot of firewood, bear it to Nishapur the following morning, and sell it. He would perform the Friday prayer; with the money he received, he would buy a loaf of bread. He would give half the bread to a beggar and would [eat of] the other half and was satisfied until the next week. And this is how the affairs of his life passed.[9]

It is said that when the people learned a little of what Ibrahim was doing, he fled the cave and set out for Mecca. And when Shaykh Abu Sa'id—may God hallow his secret[10]—went to that cave to make a pilgrimage, he said, "Praise be to God! If this cave were full of musk it would not give off such a scent; it has become all rest and repose because a brave and generous man spent several days here in sincerity."[11]

It is said that it took him fourteen years to cross the wilderness. The entire way he prayed and supplicated God until he arrived in Mecca. The elders of the sacred precinct received tidings [of his arrival] and came out to welcome him. He moved himself to the front of the caravan so that nobody would recognize him. The servants came out before the elders [and] saw a man coming before the caravan. They asked him, "Has Ibrahim-i Adham almost arrived? For the elders of the sacred precinct have come to welcome him." Ibrahim said, "What do they want with that old heretic?" [So] they raised their hands to him and slapped him about the neck without letting up, saying, "You would call such a man a heretic? You're the heretic!" "That's just what I'm saying," replied [Ibrahim]. When they ceased, [Ibrahim] said to his *nafs*, "Are you satisfied now? You wanted the elders of the hallowed precinct to come meet you, praise be to God that I perceived your intention." In the end, they recognized him and asked his pardon; so he began residing in Mecca, and they ended up becoming his friends and companions. But he always ate of what he himself earned: sometimes he was a bearer of firewood, and sometimes he looked after people's gardens.[12]

It is related that Ibrahim-i Adham said: "I was once in Jerusalem. When evening came, everyone said the night prayer and then the people dispersed, but I remained alone in the mosque. When a portion of the night had passed, two angels entered. One of the angels said to the other, 'I sense a man and believe someone is here.' [The other angel] replied, 'Indeed, Ibrahim-i Adham is here.' [The first angel then remarked,] 'The wretched fellow—he struggled so diligently and engaged in self-mortification until he attained such a lofty station, and suddenly made one mistake and fell from that station.' 'What did he do?' [the other angel] asked. 'He was once in Basra and he bought some dates. He saw a single date that had fallen and imagined that it must belong to him, so he picked it up and ate it. As soon as that date reached his stomach God caused him to fall from his lofty station.'

"When I heard this," Ibrahim said, "I gave a loud cry and began weeping and striking myself about the head. I left the mosque, [still] weeping, and journeyed to Basra. I approached the date seller and gave him a dirham to buy some dates. I gave him one of the dates and said to him, 'O Generous man! I once bought dates from you, and [saw that] one date had fallen on the ground; I believed it was one of mine, so I picked it up and ate it. Now take this one in exchange and pardon me!' When the date seller heard this, he wept and said, 'I pardon you.'" Ibrahim then returned to Jerusalem and sat down beside a large stone. When it was night and [the city was] empty, the same two angels descended, and the one said to the other, "I sense a man." The other angel replied, "It is Ibrahim-i Adham who is here." "The same Ibrahim who fell from that [lofty] station on account of one date?" "Yes, God has raised him once again to his [former] station."[13]

Ibrahim ibn Adham's Dicta, Exempla, and Mujahada

Ibrahim was once invited to a party, which he attended. The others in attendance began to talk about a man who had not come, saying, "He's boring." Ibrahim said, "My *nafs* has done this to me, and I have come to a place where people are talking badly about someone behind his back." Ibrahim left forthwith and did not eat for three days.[14]

It is said that once, the cost of meat had become quite high, and [the people] went before [Ibrahim] to inform him of this. He told them that it would be easy to make meat cheap again, and so they asked how. He said that if they ceased eating meat it would become cheap again.[15]

Many wondrous anecdotes are told about Ibrahim ibn Adham: The histories have related that, Ibrahim, Shaqiq [al-Balkhi], and Fudayl ibn 'Iyad were recalling the words of God's friends and the *awtad*[16] while standing on Abu Qubays Mountain.[17] Ibrahim said, "There are servants of God who—if one of them should bid a mountain burst asunder, straightaway it bursts asunder and it comes crashing down." Immediately, Abu Qubays Mountain began to move and rumble as if it would burst asunder, quaking beneath their feet. When Ibrahim witnessed this, he stamped his foot on the ground and said, "Be still, mountain!" At once the mountain ceased moving.[18]

It is also related that one of Ibrahim's companions said, "I beheld Ibrahim ibn Adham lying down in a garden in Syria, and a snake with a narcissus bouquet in its mouth kept shooing the flies from Ibrahim until he awoke."[19]

Regarding Ibrahim as an exemplar of tawakkul: One of his companions said, "We went out journeying with Ibrahim ibn Adham along the seashore when we came to a thicket in which there was much wood, and it was near a fortified position. We said to Ibrahim ibn Adham, 'How about we spend the night here and kindle a fire with this wood?' Ibrahim said, 'Do so!' So we sought fire from the fortification and kindled a blaze. We brought forth the bread and food we had, and then one of us said, 'How splendid these coals are! If we only had some meat to roast on them.' Ibrahim ibn Adham said, 'Indeed, God is able to provide you with [meat].' And while we were [speaking] in this way, a lion came hunting a camel. When [the camel] neared us, it fell to the ground and broke its neck. Ibrahim rose and said, 'Slaughter it, for God has indeed provided you with sustenance.' So we slaughtered it and roasted the meat, and the lion remained at a distance watching us."[20]

Ibrahim was known for his rigorous mujahada. When he could find no food that was religiously licit, he would eat dirt—he once ate only mud for an entire month.[21] Someone asked Ibrahim, "When did you settle in Syria?" Ibrahim replied, "Twenty-four years ago. I did *not* come to [Syria] to carry out the military jihad and dwell on the frontier." "For what reason then did you settle in [Syria]?" "To eat licit bread."[22] Someone asked Ibrahim what he thought about marriage, Ibrahim said, "If I could divorce my *nafs*, I would."[23] Regarding the struggle against the *nafs*, it is related that Ibrahim said, "The most difficult jihad is the jihad against the passions. Whoever forbids his *nafs* its passions is delivered from the world and its afflictions and is preserved from its pains."[24]

Ibrahim ibn Adham and the Military Jihad

It is related that Ibrahim said, "Whoever wishes—even slightly—to permit deviation from jihad and to delay [carrying out this duty]—it is as if he is a partner with the unbelievers in destroying Islam."[25]

Ibrahim exemplified wara' *and* zuhd—*even when fighting the unbelievers. When he would go forth on one of his many military campaigns against the Byzantines, he would cleave to his stringent asceticism, countenancing nothing save what was absolutely necessary for the completion of the military endeavor.*

One of Ibrahim's companions related, "I went on a military expedition with Ibrahim. I had two horses, and Ibrahim was on foot. I wanted him to mount [the other horse], but Ibrahim would not consent. I swore an oath [entreating him to mount the horse]. So he mounted until he was seated on the saddle, and said, 'I have fulfilled your oath.' He then dismounted. We journeyed thirty-six miles with that raiding party, and he was on foot."[26] Another companion related, "Ibrahim went raiding with us on two military expeditions…, and he would not take a share of the spoils, nor would he eat any of the Byzantines' goods. We brought him delicacies, and honey, and chicken, but he would not eat of them, saying, 'It is religiously licit, but I am abstaining therefrom.' Ibrahim would eat only what he had carried with him and would fast. He would go to war on a worn-out old horse worth one dirham. He also had a donkey that he would compare to that old horse, and if I were to have given him a horse of gold or silver, he would not have received it. And he would not accept a sip of water."[27]

The following anecdotes regarding Ibrahim's wilaya *are related by* ghazis *who are said to have gone to sea with him:* "We were at sea with Ibn Ma'yuf[28] when the wind began to blow, and the waves crashed, and the ships were in disarray. The people began to weep. They said to Ibn Ma'yuf, 'This is Ibrahim ibn Adham—could you ask him to supplicate God?' [Ibrahim] was sleeping in a corner of the ship with his head swathed. [The commander] approached him and said, 'O [Ibrahim]! Do you not see the state the people are in?' [Ibrahim] raised his head and said, 'My God! Thou hast shown us Thy might—now show us Thy mercy!' Then the ships became calm." *Another ghazi related* that he was with Ibrahim ibn Adham on a ship during a sea raid, when the wind began blowing violently, and they faced drowning. Then they heard an invisible voice loudly say, "You are afraid when Ibrahim is among you?"[29]

A ghazi *companion related*, "We were with Ibrahim ibn Adham aboard a ship on the sea, when the enemy attacked us. Ibrahim and another man hurled themselves into the sea—that is, toward the enemy—and the enemy was soundly defeated."[30]

Once, the call went out to prepare for war against the unbelievers: Ibrahim had nothing with which to prepare for the military expedition, and so he sat down and thought about what to do, "I have neither friend nor brother from whom I could borrow what I need." This concern occupied him for some time. In the end, he prostrated himself in prayer and addressed God, saying, "Alas, I sought help from other than Thee, and now I beseech Thee and know I must ask [Thy] forgiveness!" He then made his ablutions and performed two *rak'ats* of prayer. And [God] bestowed on him the very amount [needed] to equip himself with a horse and weapons.[31]

It is said that Ibrahim died on an island in the Mediterranean Sea while fighting the Byzantines. On the night his death occurred, he went to relieve himself nearly twenty times and he performed his ritual ablutions anew after [each time], for he had a stomach ailment. When at last the swoon of death was upon him, he said, "String my bow!" So they strung it. He grasped it and died clutching it while striving to shoot at the enemy.[32]

Muhammad ibn Wasi'

Muhammad ibn Wasi' al-Azdi (d. mid second/eighth century)[33] of Basra was reckoned among the early renunciant *mujahid*s of Iraq and fought under the Umayyad general Qutayba ibn Muslim (d. 96/715) during the conquest of Khurasan and Transoxiana.[34] Though the anecdotes regarding his life are not abundant, the fact that Muhammad ibn Wasi' is mentioned in many important Sufi treatises and hagiographies indicates his significance as an early Sufi archetype. Sufi hagiography emphasizes his asceticism and renunciation (*zuhd*), as well as his knowledge of the Qur'an, *shari'a*, and Sufism.[35] Like many of the early *mujahid* friends of God, Muhammad ibn Wasi' was also known for his *wara'*.[36]

Regarding the primary sources for the life of Muhammad ibn Wasi' as presented hereunder: the anecdotes of his dicta and exempla are from *Hilyat al-awliya'*, the *Risala* of al-Qushayri, *Tadhkirat al-awliya'*, *Mir'at al-janan*, *Kimiya-yi sa'adat*, *al-Ta'arruf li-madhhab ahl al-tasawwuf*, *Siyar a'lam al-nubala'*, and *Tahdhib al-asrar*. The military jihad anecdotes are from *Hilyat al-awliya'* and *Rawd al-rayahin*.

Dicta and Exempla of Muhammad ibn Wasi'

Muhammad ibn Wasi' epitomized austerity and self-mortification: He would dip dry bread in water and eat it, saying, "Whoever is satisfied with this has no need of mankind."[37] *As regards the scrupulosity this friend of God exemplified in carrying out his devotions, one of the Sufis said,* "Whenever I find myself becoming lax in matters of worship, I look upon Muhammad ibn Wasi' in his diligence, and the desire to worship abides with me for a week."[38]

The Sufi tradition attributes the following statement concerning God's oneness to Ibn Wasi': "I see nothing without that I see God therein."[39]

Several important sayings and dicta are ascribed to Ibn Wasi', including the following: "If the servant brings his heart nigh unto God, God brings unto him the hearts of those who believe."[40] "It is harder for people to guard their tongue than it is for them to guard a dirham or a dinar."[41] "If sins had a smell no one would sit next to me."[42]

A man once asked Ibn Wasi' for a precept, and he said, "I will give you a precept so that you can be a king in both this world and the next." "How's that?" asked the man. "Lead an ascetic life in this world so that you desire nothing from anyone and regard all mankind as needy—without a doubt, you will be wealthy and a king! Everyone who does so will be a king in this life and also in the hereafter."[43]

Muhammad ibn Wasi' was asked, "Do you know your Lord—may He be exalted?" He remained silent for an hour, and then he replied, "Whoever knows Him, his speech wanes and his wonder waxes."[44]

The emir of Basra once asked Ibn Wasi', "What do you have to say regarding the question of predestination and free will?" Ibn Wasi' answered, "O emir! On the Day of Reckoning, God—may He be exalted—will not ask His servants about predestination and free will; rather, He will ask them about their deeds."[45]

They asked Ibn Wasi', "How are you?" He replied, "How do you think someone is whose life is diminishing while his sins are increasing?"[46]

One day he came before Qutayba ibn Muslim, clad in wool. [The general] asked him, "Why do you wear wool?" [Ibn Wasi'] was silent. "Why don't you answer?" "I wish to say, on account of renunciation, but then I would be praising myself, and if I should say [that it is] owing to poverty, then I would be reproaching God—may He be exalted."[47]

Muhammad ibn Wasi' and the Military Jihad

When Ibn Wasi' was with Yazid b. al-Mulahhab[48] fighting in Khurasan, he asked leave to perform the Hajj. The governor gave him permission and said, "We enjoin you to do so." "Enjoin the entire army to do so," said [Muhammad ibn Wasi']. "No," said [the governor]. "I have no need [of the army, replied Muhammad ibn Wasi']."[49]

Muhammad ibn Wasi' related, "I desired for forty years to eat roasted liver, and I said one day, 'I will go forth on jihad, and perhaps a sheep will fall to me as my portion of the spoils, and I will eat my fill thereof.' So I went forth with the people on jihad, and we fought the unbelievers and acquired spoils. And I took a sheep as my portion and asked one of my companions to roast its liver for me. Then slumber overcame me, and I fell asleep. [I dreamed that] I saw angels descend from heaven and they wrote down: 'So-and-so went forth on jihad to be called brave, and this one went forth to acquire booty, and this one went forth to boast.' Then they came to me and said, 'This greedy wretch desired roasted liver!' So I said, 'Don't do this! I turn to God—may He be exalted—in repentance.' Then I said, 'I will not do [this] again—I [say this] thrice; indeed I turn to Thee and repent of all my desires!'"[50]

After the death of Muhammad ibn Wasi', one of the Sufis related the following dream: "It was as if the Day of Reckoning was at hand, and it was said, 'Let Malik ibn Dinar and Muhammad ibn Wasi' enter Paradise!' And I looked to see which of the two would enter first, and Muhammad ibn Wasi' entered. I asked the reason for his entrance, and it was said to me, '[Muhammad ibn Wasi'] owned only one shirt, whereas Malik [ibn Dinar] owned two.'"[51]

'Abdullah ibn al-Mubarak

'Abdullah ibn al-Mubarak lived during the first decades of the Abbasid Caliphate and is traditionally regarded as one of the earliest renunciant warriors. Like Ibrahim ibn Adham, Ibn al-Mubarak spent most of his adult life fighting the Byzantines on the *thughur*, where he was known especially for his bravery and *wara'*.[52] Sufi hagiographers included Ibn al-Mubarak in the first generation of Sufis, and there are many anecdotes in Sufi literature regarding his pious and courageous deeds. Hujviri referred to him as "chief of the renunciants" and "learned in all matters and states regarding the Sufi path and *shari'a*"[53]; 'Attar named him "exemplar of the two jihads"[54]; al-Isfahani described him as closely acquainted with the Qur'an, the Hajj, and jihad[55]; similarly, al-Munawi referred to him as "Glory of the *mujahids*."[56] A number of poems as well as sundry writings are traditionally ascribed to him,[57] notably the *Book of Renunciation (Kitab al-zuhd)* and the *Book of Jihad (Kitab al-jihad)*—a treatise based on *hadith* and concerned primarily with the military aspects of jihad.[58]

Regarding the primary sources for the life of Ibn al-Mubarak as presented hereunder: the story of his conversion is from *Kashf al-mahjub*. Anecdotes of his dicta, exempla, and miracles are from *Hilyat al-awliya'*, *Kashf al-mahjub*, *Tarikh Baghdad*, the *Risala* of al-Qushayri, *Hazar hikayat-i sufiyan*, and *Tadhkirat al-awliya'*. The military jihad anecdotes are from *Tarikh Baghdad* and *Hazar hikayat-i sufiyan*.

As regards 'Abdullah ibn al-Mubarak's origins, it is said that he was born to a Turkish father and a Khwarazmian mother in Merv and that he was a client of the Arab Bani Hanzala tribe.[59]

The Repentance of Ibn al-Mubarak

The event that caused Ibn al-Mubarak to repent of his worldly ways and begin following the Sufi path was his infatuation with a girl. One night[60] he arose from among [a party] of drunken [revelers] and took one of them with him and went and stood beneath the wall of [the home of] his beloved. The girl ascended to the roof, and they remained till dawn gazing at each other. When 'Abdullah heard the dawn call to prayer, he supposed that it was the prayer before sleep, but when the day began to break, he realized that he had spent the entire night captivated by the beauty of his beloved. And this led to his spiritual awakening. He said to himself, "Shame on you, son of Mubarak! That you should remain standing the entire evening because of your passion and feel no weariness, and yet, when the prayer leader recites an especially long *sura,* you are driven mad." Thereupon he repented and devoted himself to knowledge and its acquisition until his spiritual station was such that his mother once went into the garden and saw him sleeping, and a great snake was keeping the flies off him with a sprig of basil in its mouth.[61]

Dicta, Exempla, and Miracles of Ibn al-Mubarak

Thereafter, Ibn al-Mubarak traveled from Merv and spent time in Baghdad, where he associated with the Sufi shaykhs. Thence he went to Mecca, where he dwelled for a time, and then he returned to Merv. The people of Merv befriended him and had him give lessons in lecture sessions. At that time, half the people of Merv followed *hadith,* and the other half followed opinion, just as [they do] today.[62] They called him "agreeable to both parties" because he agreed with each of them. And both sides claimed him for their own. Ibn al-Mubarak established two *ribat*s, one for the followers of *hadith,* and the other for the followers of opinion—and to this day the two remain as they were originally founded. Thence, he returned to the Hejaz and settled in Mecca.[63]

It is said that during his lifetime Ibn al-Mubarak's knowledge of hadith *was unparalleled. In this respect a religious scholar said,* "Among the *hadith* scholars Ibn al-Mubarak was like the Commander of the Faithful among the people."[64]

He was asked, "What wonders have you witnessed?" He replied, "I saw a Christian monk who had grown thin through *mujahada* and was bent over from fear of God. I asked him, 'What is the path to God?' 'If you knew God, you would know the path to Him.' [The monk] then said, 'I worship Him Whom I know not, whereas you sin against Him Whom you know.' In other words, knowledge of God (*ma'rifa*) entails fear, but I see you secure, whereas security entails unbelief and ignorance, and I find myself always fearful. This was counsel for me and kept me from doing much one ought not to do."[65]

As for the exemplary manner in which Ibn al-Mubarak lived his life, it is said that he would divide his time among three pious endeavors: One year he would perform the Hajj; the following year he would go to war against the unbelievers; and he would then engage in mercantile affairs for one year and distribute the profits among his companions. He would give the poor dates and would count the date seeds—to whomever had eaten the most dates he would give a dirham for each seed.[66]

Ibn al-Mubarak said, "I beheld a pious woman and while she prayed, a scorpion stung her forty times, and yet no change could be seen in her demeanor. When she completed her prayers, I asked her, 'Mother, why didn't you defend yourself from that scorpion?' She replied, 'My son, you are a child. How would it be permissible to engage in my own affairs while carrying out my duty to God?'"[67]

Harun al-Rashid came to the city of Raqqa, but the people [of the city] hastened after 'Abdullah ibn al-Mubarak, their sandals tattered and raising clouds of dust.

The mother of one of Harun's sons looked down from a palace tower, and when she saw the people, she asked, "What is this?" They replied, "A learned man from Khurasan named 'Abdullah ibn al-Mubarak has come to Raqqa." "By God," she said, "This realm does *not* belong to Harun [al-Rashid], for he can gather the people only by means of his armed attendants and guards."[68]

Ibn al-Mubarak related, "One year there was a drought in Mecca, and the people of Mecca prayed for water many times, but the rains did not come. I said to myself, 'I will arise and withdraw from the people and go to the mountains where I will pray two *rak'at*s in seclusion (*khalvat*) and beseech God, and perhaps God—may He be exalted—will answer.' I journeyed in the mountains, and there I found a cave. I entered therein and began earnestly remembering God and invoking His name (*dhikr*). I saw a black man enter; he was stupefied and overcome by love of God. He prayed silently for a long while. When he had finished his prayers, he said, 'My God! I know what it is Thy servants seek from Thee.' No sooner had he spoken these words than a cloud appeared and began to pour forth rain in abundance. This slave then went out of the cave and headed toward the city. I followed after him. He went to Mecca and went down an alley. There was a tall mansion, and he went into it. I asked to whom this mansion belonged. 'It belongs to a slaver,' they said. I approached [the slaver] and told him I needed a slave. He presented every slave he had to me, but I did not see him among them. 'Do you have another?' I asked. 'I do have another, but he is lazy and always goes to a corner and utters something like one bewildered. If you would like, I will bring him to you and sell him to you for whatever price you wish.' 'That is reasonable,' I replied. He left and brought that slave. When I saw him, my heart bore witness and I gave the slaver what he asked and I bought him. The slave said, 'O Ibn al-Mubarak! What will you do with me, for I am weak and cannot serve you.' 'O slave! I bought you so that I might serve *you*.' Then I said to him, 'How did you know my name?' 'The friend knows the friend,'[69] he responded. I took him home and undertook to serve him. After a while, he rose, performed his ablutions, and prayed two *rak'at*s of prayer while he moved his lips. I went near him and listened to what he was saying. He said:

> O Lord of the secret! The secret has indeed become manifest, And I do not desire life after it has become known.

He uttered this and was silent. I shook him, but he had surrendered his soul to God. I prepared his body and buried him. When evening came, I beheld him in a dream: he was coming with the Friend [of God][70] on his left and the Beloved [of God][71] on his right, and both of them said to me, 'May God repay you for having treated our beloved (*habib*) well.'"[72]

It is related that one day [Ibn al-Mubarak] was passing through [a place where a blind man lived]. They told the blind man, "Abdullah ibn al-Mubarak is coming—ask for anything you wish." The blind man said, "Halt, O 'Abdullah!" 'Abdullah halted. "Supplicate God—may He be exalted—that He restore my sight." 'Abdullah bowed his head and prayed, and immediately [the blind man] regained his sight.[73]

Many pithy sayings are attributed to Ibn al-Mubarak, among them: "Asceticism is faith in God with love of poverty."[74] And "The people of this world leave this life before aspiring after the best thing in it." "And what is that?" they said. "Knowing God—may He be exalted."[75] It is also related that Ibn al-Mubarak said, "When a man knows the measure of his *nafs*, he becomes—in his own estimation—more despicable than a dog."[76]

It is said that a youth once came before Ibn al-Mubarak, threw himself at his feet, and began to weep, saying, "I have sinned, and out of shame I cannot say what I have done!" "Tell me what it is you've done," said 'Abdullah. "I have fornicated!" said [the youth]. [Ibn al-Mubarak] said, "[Oh,] I feared that you had spoken ill of someone behind his back."[77]

A man once asked Ibn al-Mubarak for guidance. "Behold God" [said Ibn al-Mubarak]. The man replied, "What does this mean?" "Always comport yourself as if you were beholding God—mighty and exalted."[78]

Once they asked [Ibn al-Mubarak], "Which trait is most beneficial in a man?" "Abundant intelligence," said he. "And if that is not present?" they asked. "Good comportment." "And if that is not present?" "A compassionate brother to advise him." "And if that is not present?" "To be ever silent." "And if that is not present?" "Instant death."[79]

One of Ibn al-Mubarak's companions related, "I was going with 'Abdullah-i Mubarak to wage war against the Byzantines. He said to me, 'The corruption of the common folk happens only after [the corruption of] the elite.' 'And how is that so, 'Abdullah?' said I. 'There are five classes of the elite: the religious scholars (*'ulama*), the renunciants (*zuhhad*), the *ghazi*s, the merchants, and the rulers. The religious scholars are the heirs of the prophets[80]; the renunciants are the pillars (*awtad*) of the earth; the *ghazi*s are God's army; the merchants are the guarantors of God; and the rulers are shepherds of the people. When the religious scholar disparages the religion and exalts wealth, whom will the ignorant imitate? And when the renunciant desires earthly pleasures, who will tread the path of God? And when the *ghazi* is covetous, how will he gain victory over the enemies of the religion? And when the merchant is deceitful, whom will the people trust? And when the ruler shepherds the wolf, who will protect the sheep?"[81]

Among the many poems attributed to Ibn al-Mubarak are the following lines concerning renunciants and the military jihad[82]:

O wool-clad reciter[83] of the Qur'an!	You are reckoned among God's servants.
Abide ever on the border serving God;	Baghdad is not the place for renunciants!
Indeed, Baghdad is a residence of kings,	and but a way station for the reciter pursuing [unbeliever] quarry.

Ibn al-Mubarak and the Military Jihad

There are many anecdotes regarding Ibn al-Mubarak's military campaigns; among them is the following well-known story: 'Abdullah ibn al-Mubarak—may God hallow his spirit—had gone to war. An unbeliever (*kafir*) approached the ranks and slew many Muslims. A fervor overcame 'Abdullah, and he took up his shield and sword and went to that unbeliever. They strove much with one another—neither of them gaining the upper hand. When the time for prayer came, 'Abdullah—may God have mercy upon him—said to the unbeliever, "The time has come for me to worship my God; you stay here." The unbeliever ceased [fighting]. 'Abdullah performed his prayer, and they returned to battle and strove in the same manner—neither having gained the upper hand. When the sun was near setting, the unbeliever said to 'Abdullah, "The time has come for me to bow down before my deity—give me your leave and swear that you will not be treacherous with me." "So be it," said 'Abdullah. The unbeliever set aside his shield and sword and fell down before the sun in prostration. 'Abdullah said to himself: "This is an unbeliever, and God—mighty and exalted—has said, *Verily there are no oaths that bind them*,[84] there are no covenants made with unbelievers. Now that he is prostrating himself before the sun, I shall slay him." He took up his sword, intending [to slay] that unbeliever. When he neared the unbeliever, a voice came into his inner heart: *Fulfill God's covenant when you make a promise.*[85] He let fall his sword. When the unbeliever completed his prostration, he said, "O 'Abdullah! What restrained you from what you intended to do to me while I was bowing down before the sun, which is my deity? Were you to have cut me to pieces, I would not have raised my head from worshipping my deity. Why did you let fall your sword when your victory was at hand?" 'Abdullah said, "When I was intending to strike you with my sword, a voice came to me saying, *Fulfill God's covenant when you make a promise*. When the unbeliever heard this, he said, 'A religion in which fidelity and fulfillment of promises are thus cannot be any other than that of God—I bear witness that God is one and Muhammad—on whom be prayers and peace—is his messenger in truth.'"[86]

One of the Sufis related, "Ibn al-Mubarak left Baghdad for Masisa,[87] and the Sufis accompanied him. [Ibn al-Mubarak] said to them, 'You have pride and would be ashamed to be provided for [without contributing]—bring a tray hither, boy!' Then he placed a cloth on the tray and said, 'Let each man among you deposit whatever he has with him under the cloth.' So one man placed ten [silver] dirhams beneath the cloth; another placed twenty; and [this money] sustained them till Masisa. When they reached Masisa, [Ibn al-Mubarak] said, 'This is a land of warfare, and so let us divide up whatever remains.' And he gave one of the men twenty gold dinars. The man was astounded and said, 'O [Ibn al-Mubarak]! But I gave only twenty silver dirhams!' 'Doubt not that God blesses the *ghazi* by providing for him,' replied [Ibn al-Mubarak]."[88]

A ghazi related, "One year I went with the army of Islam on a military campaign. When we reached the land of the unbelievers, their army came forth and formed ranks before the Muslims. A warrior stepped forward from among them, wishing to fight. That unbeliever warrior defeated every Muslim who came forth and fought with him. The Muslims became discouraged. Then a man came forth from the Muslim host, his face concealed behind a veil, and he cast the unbeliever warrior from his horse and cut off his head. The folk of Islam rejoiced and cried, *Allahu akbar!* No one knew who [the champion] was. I approached him and endeavored [to have him remove his veil] and swore an oath; he removed his veil—it was 'Abdullah ibn [al-]Mubarak! I said, 'O 'Abdullah! Why did you conceal your identity at such a time and in such a place when by *your* hand is this victory?' [Ibn al-Mubarak] replied, 'I have pledged my life to Him Who knows me and created my body and soul in the eternity without beginning (*azal*). He knows His creation well, and whoever has made a covenant with Him is among those He has selected, and [such a one] has no business making himself known among the people. Go back, and do not reveal my secret, for He to Whom I have given my life knows me and what is in my heart.'[89]

It is related that Ibn al-Mubarak died in the city of Hīt, in Iraq.[90] It is said that he opened his eyes at the time of his death, laughed, and uttered, *For the like of this, let those who labor, labor.*[91] After Ibn al-Mubarak's death, Fudayl ibn 'Iyad said, "I saw 'Abdullah ibn al-Mubarak in a dream and asked, 'Which deeds did you find most preferable?' 'That for which I was noted [during my life].' 'Jihad and fighting on the frontier (*al-ribat wa'l-jihad*)?' 'Yes!' [Ibn al-Mubarak] replied. 'And what have they done with you?' 'I have been pardoned twice, and a woman from the folk of Paradise has spoken to me, as has a woman from among the houris.'"[92]

Shaqiq al-Balkhi

Shaqiq al-Balkhi was another well-known *mujahid* friend of God from Balkh who lived during the early Abbasid period. The traditional sources relate that Ibrahim ibn Adham, also of Balkh, introduced Shaqiq to the Sufi way and that he, in turn, became the teacher of Hatim al-Asamm (d. 237/852). Like many of the early friends of God, Shaqiq was known for his renunciation and his *tawakkul*.[93] One of the earliest treatises regarding the stages of the Sufi path is attributed to Shaqiq, *Adab al-'ibadat*.[94] The sources also depict Shaqiq as an exemplar of the complementary nature of Sufism who was learned in all matters of *shari'a* and *haqiqa*: that is, the outer and inner aspects of Islam. During his life, Shaqiq associated with the leading Sufi shaykhs[95] and had many *murids*.[96] The hagiographical sources relate that Shaqiq was a pious warrior for the faith[97] and that he died a martyr during a military campaign in the region of Khuttalan, in present-day Tajikistan.[98]

Regarding the primary sources for the life of Shaqiq al-Balkhi as presented hereunder: the story of Shaqiq's conversion is from *Tadhkirat al-awliya'*. Anecdotes of his dicta, exempla, and miracles are from *Hilyat al-awliya'*, *Kashf al-mahjub*, *Hazar hikayat-i sufiyan*, *Kimiya-yi sa'adat*, and *Tadhkirat al-awliya'*. The military jihad anecdotes are from *Tadhkirat al-awliya'*, *Siyar a'lam al-nubala'*, and *Shadharat al-dhahab*.

The Repentance of Shaqiq al-Balkhi

The reason for [Shaqiq's] turning to God in repentance (*tawba*) was that he had gone to Turkestan as a merchant and he went to have a look at a temple [wherein] he beheld an idol worshiper praying to an image and weeping.[99] Shaqiq said to him,

"You have a living Creator who is all-knowing and all-powerful. Worship Him and have shame, and worship not an idol, from which you will gain nothing." [The idol worshiper] replied, "If this is as you say, is He not then able to give you your daily bread in your own land so that you don't have to come [seeking it] here?" Shaqiq awoke on account of these words, and he set out for Balkh. A Zoroastrian became his traveling companion. The Zoroastrian asked Shaqiq, "What is your occupation?" "I am a merchant." "If you seek after daily bread that is not ordained for you, you will never attain it—even were you to seek until the Day of Reckoning. And if you are seeking daily bread that has been ordained for you, cease, for it will come to you itself." When Shaqiq heard this, his heart truly awakened, and this world became dead to him.[100]

Dicta and Exempla of Shaqiq al-Balkhi

Shaqiq's wife once demanded that he find a job. She said, "Shaqiq! The children are hungry, and we are poor. If you were to work for a while as a laborer today, perhaps we could have what we need." Since Shaqiq considered his wife to be of little faith, he left the house. There was a mosque in Balkh, which he entered and then sat down relying entirely on God (*tawakkul*) [for his livelihood]. He worshiped God and returned home at [the time of] the evening prayer. His wife said, "What did you do?" Shaqiq—God's mercy be upon him—replied, "I didn't do any labor today, I did the Lord's work, and my work was good, He said, 'Work for Me for a week, and I will give you your pay all at once.'" "So be it," said his wife. Shaqiq worshipped God for seven days and placed himself utterly in His hands. On the eighth day, he said to himself, "If today there is nothing [for us], my wife will be very angry." [So] he went to work with the laborers. [On that same day], God—may He be exalted—sent an angel in the form of a man bearing a purse in which there were seventy gold dinars to Shaqiq's house. The angel knocked on the door. "Who is it?" [said Shaqiq's wife.] [The angel replied], "The Lord has sent me—this is Shaqiq's wages for seven days, give them to him and say, 'For seven days you worked for Us, and what reproach did you receive from Us, that today you should go [to work] for someone else?'" His wife put [the wages] aside until Shaqiq came home [at the time of] the evening prayer. His wife placed the purse before Shaqiq, and he opened it and beheld the seventy gold dinars, upon each of which were written: *And whosoever relies on God, then He is All-sufficient for him.*[101]

Many sayings are attributed to Shaqiq, among them: "The path to God consists of four things. The first is trust in [receiving one's] daily bread; the second is purity in [one's] deeds; the third is enmity toward Satan; the fourth is preparing for death."[102] One day, they asked Shaqiq about the daily bread *hadith*. Shaqiq said, "Seeking one's daily bread is ignorance, and working for one's daily bread is to find fault with God."[103] *Shaqiq also said,* "God makes those who are obedient to Him alive in their moment of death, and those who are sinful He makes dead while they are living."[104] Hatim al-Asamm related that Shaqiq once said to him, "Deal with people the way you deal with fire—take what benefits you, and avoid what burns you."[105] *Regarding the inner jihad, Shaqiq said,* "As for knowing the enemy of

God, you must learn that you have an enemy [regarding which] God will accept naught save [that you] wage warfare, warfare in the heart, and that you be a tireless *mujahid* fighting against the enemy."[106]

As for the jihad of speaking just words to a ruler, it is related that Shaqiq once went to see the caliph Harun al-Rashid. "So you're Shaqiq the renunciant (*zahid*)?" said Harun. "I'm Shaqiq, but I'm no renunciant." [The caliph] said, "Give me counsel!" "God—may He be exalted—has made you the successor of [Abu Bakr] al-Siddiq (the truthful)—and He demands truthfulness of you, as He did of him; and He has made you the successor of ['Umar] al-Faruq (the discerner]—and He demands discernment from you between what is true and what is false, as He did of him; and He has made you the successor of ['Uthman] Dhu al-Nurayn[107]—and He demands humility of you, as He did of him; and He has made you the successor of 'Ali ibn Abi Talib—and He demands knowledge and justice of you, as He did of him."[108] [The caliph] said, "Give me further counsel!" [Shaqiq] said, "Indeed God—mighty and exalted—has an abode called Hell and has made you [Hell's] doorkeeper, and He has given you three things: the treasury, a sword, and a whip, and He has said: 'With these three things, you are to keep the people from [going to] Hell.' Do not withhold money from anyone who comes before you in need; apply the whip to those who disobey God's commandments, so that they might learn how to behave; and kill with the sword anyone who wrongfully kills another. Should you not do this, you yourself will be the first to enter Hell, and the people will follow after you." "Give me more counsel!" [said the caliph.] "You are a spring and the others—those who are your governors—a stream. If the spring is clear, the turbidity of the streams will be harmless; but if [the spring] be turbid, there is no hope that the streams will be clear."[109]

Shaqiq-i Balkhi and the Military Jihad

Regarding the military jihad, it is said that Shaqiq was among the leaders of military campaigns owing to his devotion and renunciation.[110]

It is related that Hatim-i Asamm said, "I went to war [against the unbelievers] with Shaqiq. One day, it was hard, and [the two sides] formed ranks. It was such that all one could see was spearheads, and arrows were whizzing through the air. Shaqiq said, 'O Hatim! How do you find yourself? Do you imagine that it's last night when you were sleeping in the bedclothes with your wife?' 'No,' said I. 'By God,' said [Shaqiq], 'I find my body now as you were last night in the bedclothes!' Night fell, and [Shaqiq] lay down between the two armies, made a pillow out of his patched Sufi cloak, and went to sleep. And this he did among such foes, owing to the trust he had in God."[111]

It is related that one day, [Shaqiq] was holding an assembly, when suddenly a cry was heard in the town that the unbelievers had come. Shaqiq rushed out, put the unbelievers to flight, and returned. A *murid* laid several flowers before the shaykh's prayer rug, and Shaqiq inhaled their fragrance. An ignorant man saw this and said, "An army is at the gates of the city and the leader of the Muslims is sniffing flowers!" "Hypocrites see everything as sniffing flowers—they do not see the defeat of an army," replied [Shaqiq].[112]

Regarding his death, it is related that, in [the year 194], Abu 'Ali Shaqiq al-Balkhi the renunciant and shaykh of Khurasan was martyred during a military campaign. He traveled once and with him were eighty *murid*s. And he was the shaykh of Hatim al-Asamm.[113]

Chapter 2

MUJAHID FRIENDS OF GOD IN SUFISM'S FORMATIVE PERIOD: THE NINTH THROUGH ELEVENTH CENTURIES

The formative period of historical Sufism began in the late ninth century, when Abbasid power had begun to wane, and continued well into the eleventh century, when much of the eastern Islamic world came under the rule of various Turkic dynasties—beginning with the Ghaznavids and Ghurids and culminating in the rise of the Seljuks. Before the advent of the Turkic dynasties, the Persian-speaking Tahirids ruled most of Khurasan from 821 through 873 as the local governors of the Abbasids; Tahirid rule signaled the beginning of the end of Arab rule in the region. The political and cultural situation really began to change, however, with the founding of the Samanid Empire in 892 in Transoxiana and the accession of the Buyid dynasty to dominion over much of what is now western Iran and eastern Iraq by 935. With the establishment of these two dynasties, the eastern Islamic lands became in effect independent of central Abbasid rule. Arabic remained the language of religious scholarship; nevertheless, under the patronage of the Samanids, New Persian began to develop as the second great cultural language of the eastern Islamic world.

This era also witnessed the emergence of the Sufi schools of Baghdad and Khurasan with their "sober" and "drunken" approaches, respectively.[1] It was during this era, as well, that Sufis began composing treatises and manuals to set forth and explain fundamental Sufi concepts. In the late ninth/early tenth century, Hakim al-Tirmidhi composed some of the first mystical treatises dealing with the spiritual struggle (*mujahada*) and the conduct of God's friends.[2] Tirmidhi's writings, with their focus on God's friends and *mujahada*, adumbrated the hagiographical tradition that would unfold in the following centuries as one of the most influential developments of Sufism. In the latter part of the tenth century, Abu Nasr al-Sarraj (d. 378/988) of Tus composed *Kitab al-luma'*, and Abu Bakr Muhammad al-Kalabadhi (d. 380/990) wrote *al-Ta'arruf li-madhhab ahl al-tasawwuf*. These two treatises set forth a sacred historical narrative of Sufism and established Sufi doctrine while also defending Sufism as an orthodox Sunni Islamic practice. Sufism truly began to flourish in the eleventh century with the genesis of Sufi hagiography, which related the lives, words, and deeds of

God's friends, as well as the burgeoning culture of the first Sufi orders and lodges. It was also during the eleventh century that Sufis began seriously to cultivate poetry as a vehicle for expressing mystical concepts.[3]

This chapter will treat the lives of three friends of God from this period, two of whom—Bayazid and Junayd—are among the best-known figures in the history of Sufism, while the third, Abu Ishaq al-Kazaruni, is distinguished for having organized the first historical Sufi order. Though we must carefully sift through the traditional accounts regarding Bayazid, Junayd, and Abu Ishaq for verifiable historical events, we may contrast the lives of these three seminal Sufi figures with those of God's friends in Chapter 1, in that they were, indeed, historical Sufis.

With respect to the historical role of these three friends of God in the military jihad, only Abu Ishaq al-Kazaruni is likely to have been directly involved in the raids and campaigns that the Sunni Muslims of western Iran carried out against the local Zoroastrians and the Byzantine Christians; whereas the anecdotes concerning the participation of Bayazid and Junayd in military endeavors probably tell us more about the ongoing state of war that obtained between the Byzantines and the Abbasids rather than indicating their particular role as *mujahid*s on the frontier. Notwithstanding such historical concerns, the lives of these three early Sufis epitomize the complementary character of Sufi jihad, which includes the original Islamic ethos of jihad as a military endeavor, the spiritual struggle (*mujahada*) against the *nafs*, and the admonishment of tyrants and rulers who neglect their duty as guardians of the Muslims.

Bayazid al-Bistami

Abu Yazid Tayfur al-Bistami, known in Persian as Bayazid, was an early Sufi from the town of Bistam, in Greater Khurasan (present-day northeastern Iran). Bayazid was known for his "drunken Sufism," characterized by unguarded and seemingly blasphemous utterances and deeds for which some religious scholars pronounced him an unbeliever,[4] as well as for his austerity and self-mortification. Notwithstanding his rather extreme qualities, there are several anecdotes in which Bayazid expresses either directly or implicitly his adherence to the Qur'an and *Sunna*,[5] and in this way, he exemplifies the complementary nature of Sufism, as discussed earlier. Bayazid is a significant figure in early Sufi literature: for example, 'Attar devotes more pages to Bayazid's life in *Tadhkirat al-awliya*' than he does to any other friend of God; indeed, *Tadhkirat al-awliya*' relates the *mi'raj* of Bayazid, in which he embarks on a mystical journey to the Heavenly Throne. *Kitab al-nur*—the earliest extant hagiography concerning Bayazid—refers to him as "Sultan of the Knowers"; *Tadhkirat al-awliya*' names him "shaykh of his era" and "greatest of the shaykhs and friends of God."[6] *Mir'at al-zaman* states that Bayazid had no predecessor in regard to his knowledge of annihilation in God and abiding in God (*fana*' and *baqa*').[7] Though controversy attended Bayazid both within the Sufi tradition and without, such controversy did not diminish Bayazid's importance to Sufi sacred history, for he would continue to occupy a prominent place among God's friends in Sufi literature throughout the Muslim world.

Regarding the primary sources for the life of Bayazid al-Bistami as presented hereunder: the narrative of Bayazid's origins and awakening is from *Tadhkirat al-awliya', Tabaqat al-sufiyya, Kitab al-nur,* and *Dastur al-jumhur.* The anecdotes of his dicta, exempla, and *mujahada* are from al-Qushayri's *Risala, Asrar al-tawhid, Tadhkirat al-awliya',* and *al-Tabaqat al-kubra.* The military jihad anecdotes are from *Hazar hikayat-i sufiyan* and *Tadhkirat al-awliya'.* Anecdotes of Bayazid's death are from *Tadhkirat al-awliya'* and *Kitab al-nur.*

Bayazid's Origins and Awakening

Regarding Bayazid's origins, one of the Shaykhs said, "His grandfather Sharushan was a Zoroastrian and he converted to Islam, and his submission (*islam*) was correct, and he surrendered, and his surrender (*istislam*) was correct... the reason for the conversion of Sharushan, the grandfather of Abu Yazid—may God hallow his spirit—was that the son of Ibrahim, who had come to Bistam at the beginning of Islam, associated with him and befriended him. [Ibrahim] asked him about this and reproached him for it, saying, 'If only you had associated with anyone else and befriended one of the Arabs instead of him, it would be better for you—you befriend a Zoroastrian man and continue your friendship with him!' So his son responded, 'O father! He is a man of admirable character, who does not refute questions, and is generous and loyal, and that's why I am his friend.' [Ibrahim] said, 'Tell him your father is coming to him as a guest.' [The son] told [Sharushan], who replied, 'Indeed! If he comes, my actions will be [to show him] honor and generosity.' When they came, Sharushan placed food before them. [Ibrahim] said, 'I will not eat of it until you fulfill my wish and satisfy my need.' 'And what is that?' [asked Sharushan]. 'That you become a Muslim.' 'I shall do so most gladly!' And [Sharushan] said, 'I bear witness that there is no god save God and that Muhammad is a prophet.' And he became a Muslim. This is the reason for his conversion to Islam. May God—exalted—bless him and his family."[8]

They were three brothers: Adam, Tayfur, and 'Ali. And they were all renunciants and worshipers and endowed with [mystical] states.[9]

Bayazid exemplified wara' *when he was still in his mother's womb:* It is related that his mother said, "Whenever I would place a morsel of food in my mouth, if there was any doubt about its being religiously licit, he would begin kicking in my belly until I spat out that morsel."[10]

It is related that when Bayazid's mother sent him to school [to learn the Qur'an], and they reached *Surat Luqman*, [they read] the verse *Give thanks unto Me and unto thy mother and father*, and Bayazid asked his teacher the meaning of this verse. When the teacher explained it, it affected his heart so greatly that he put down his slate and asked permission to return home. His mother asked, "O Tayfur! Why have you come back? Have you attained success, or have they given you a gift?" "No. We reached this verse wherein God—exalted—commands [that we] serve Him and you. How can I manage two households? This verse has entered my soul. Either ask God to let me be all yours or give me to God so that I may be all His." His mother said, "I have released you to God's work and relinquished my own claim to you."[11]

So Bayazid left Bistam and wandered in the wilderness of Syria for thirty years engaging in self-mortification, continually depriving himself of sleep and food while he served one hundred and thirteen Sufi shaykhs, and he benefited from all of them—one of whom was Ja'far al-Sadiq.[12]

As for how Bayazid found the Sufi path, it is related that God willed that he should first spend considerable time among the various classes of Muslims.[13] Bayazid said, "At the beginning of this, I associated with the religious scholars, teachers, and seekers of knowledge for a long time. When I had attained learning in regard to divine matters, I said to myself, "This is a great degree of learning I have achieved. God—may He be exalted—has made me understand so that I might see the dignity of the religious scholars and the knowers in His court and witness their station there. [Nevertheless,] I saw no place for myself [among them] and sundered myself from them. For a time, I joined those who devote themselves to worship, spending their nights standing and their days fasting. So it was that I would utter the first *Allahu akbar!* with the imam. When I understood their station, I saw no place for myself in their company and again despaired. After that, I joined the pilgrims who journey to the *Ka'ba;* when I did not see them in the presence [of God], I also saw no grace for myself among them. After that I joined the *mujahid*s for a time and drew my sword and killed unbelievers. I also saw no place for myself among them .... Then I said, "My Lord! Have mercy on me and grant me the station of Thy generosity, in which I may not be disturbed by others the way that I am among [all] these companions! God—may He be exalted—called to me, 'O Bayazid! render something unto Us that We do not possess so that it may be to your benefit!' 'Whence may I render unto Thee what Thou havest not?' 'I do not have need, poverty, lowliness, or weeping.' [Bayazid] answered, 'O Lord! As Thou didst show me the station of that multitude, show me the folk who possess these things!' When I looked, I beheld a very small group of people who did not vie with one another and eschewed idle talk and distractions. I swore to choose nothing save need, poverty, lowliness, and humility."[14]

Dicta, Exempla, and Mujahada *of Bayazid*

It is related that it took Bayazid twelve years to reach the *Ka'ba*. Every few steps he would unroll his prayer rug and perform two *rak'at*s of prayer. He would say, "This is not the hallway of some earthly king, such that one can hasten down it all at once." So Bayazid reached the *Ka'ba* but did not go to Medina that year, saying, "It would not be courteous to the Prophet—upon whom be prayers and peace—to visit following this. I will undertake [that pilgrimage] separately." He returned [home] and then undertook the pilgrimage [to Medina] another year. As he made his way to the city, a great host of people began flocking to him, and when he went out [of Medina], people followed him. Bayazid looked and said, "Who are [all these people]?" "They will keep you company." [Bayazid called out,] "O Lord God! conceal Thyself not from Thy servant with Thy people!" He then wished to rid himself of the people's love for him and remove his troublesomeness from their path. He performed the dawn prayer, looked at the people, and said, "*I* am God;

there is no god but *me*, so worship *me!*" The people said, "This man must be mad." They left him and went on their way. The shaykh was speaking to them there with the speech of God—may He be exalted—which is called "Speaking by means of his lord."[15]

The shaykh Abu 'Ali al-Juzjani was asked regarding the utterances of Bayazid, and he said—may God have mercy on him, "Abu Yazid—let us concede his state to him—perhaps in [that state] had uttered idle words or [was] in a state of [spiritual] drunkenness, but anyone who wishes to reach Abu Yazid's station must struggle with his *nafs* as Abu Yazid struggled—only then would he understand Abu Yazid's speech, and God—exalted—knows best."[16]

As regards Bayazid's extraordinary piety, it is related that whenever he would reach the door of the mosque, he would stand there for an hour weeping. "What is it?" they asked. He replied, "I find myself like a menstruating woman, who fears entering the mosque lest she defile it."[17]

It is said that Abu Yazid al-Bistami beheld a group of houris in his sleep. He looked upon them and was robbed of his time for several days. Then he saw a group of [houris] in his sleep [a second time], but he did not turn toward them and said [only], "You are a distraction."[18] It is also related that Abu Yazid al-Bistami said, "I beheld my Lord—mighty and exalted—in a dream, and I asked, 'What is the path to Thee?' [God] replied, 'Abandon your *nafs* and come.'"[19]

Abu Yazid al-Bistami went to find someone who was described as a friend of God. When he reached [the man's] mosque, he sat down and waited for him to come out. The man came out, and [as he did so,] he spat in the mosque. Abu Yazid departed and did not greet him, saying, "This man can't be trusted [to follow] the conduct prescribed by the *shari'a*; how, then, could he be trusted with the mysteries of God?"[20]

Many wondrous deeds are ascribed to Bayazid. It is said that when he was journeying on the Hajj, he had a camel laden with his provisions. Someone saw the burden and said, "The poor camel—its load is so heavy; this is truly wrong!" Bayazid replied, "O young man! The bearer of the burden isn't the camel—look and see whether any burden is on the camel's back." When he looked, there was the space of a hand's span above the camel's back. The young man exclaimed, "Praise be to God; what a wonder this is!" Bayazid said, "If I conceal my state from you, you wag your tongue in blame, and if I unveil it, you are unable [to handle it]. What is to be done with you?"[21]

The early Sufi shaykh and friend of God Abu Sa'id Abu'l-Khayr once described Bayazid in the following manner: "He would ride upon a lion, and he used a venomous snake as a whip; and yet, when he would pray, he would say, 'My Lord, we swoon at Thy veil, and yet, wert Thou to remove Thy covering from us, our faults would be exposed [and we would thereby be disgraced].'"[22]

It is related that Bayazid was walking one day when a dog joined him. [Bayazid] pulled his robe away [so that the dog would not defile him]. The dog said, "If I am dry then there is no problem between us, and if I am wet seven washings will put things to right between us. Nevertheless, if you pull your robe away from me, you'll not become clean even if you should wash in seven seas." Bayazid said,

"You have outer uncleanliness, and I have inner uncleanliness—come, let us join together, and it may be that on account of our union cleanliness will result between us." The dog replied, "You are not worthy of my companionship, for I am spurned by the people, whereas you are accepted. Everyone who comes upon me throws a stone at me, but everyone who comes upon you says, 'Peace be upon you, O Sultan of the Knowers!' While I have never put aside a bone for the morrow, you have a bushel of wheat." Bayazid said, "If I'm not worthy of a dog's company, how could I be worthy of the company of Him Who is Everlasting?"[23]

Many sayings concerning Sufism are attributed to Bayazid. Someone once asked him, "How did you attain this mystical knowledge?" "By means of a hungry belly and a naked body," said [Bayazid].[24] *Regarding the difference between Sufis and renunciants*, he said, "The Sufis fly while the renunciants travel on land."[25] It is related that one of the great [shaykhs] said, "I saw [Bayazid] in a dream and said, 'Give me counsel!' [Bayazid] replied, 'Mankind is in a sea without end; far from mankind is a ship; strive till you board the ship and save your wretched body from the sea.'"[26]

It is said that [God's friend] Dhu al-Nun al-Misri sent one of his companions to Bistam to bring him a description of Abu Yazid al-Bistami. When the man arrived in the town of Bistam, he asked for the home of Abu Yazid and went in. Abu Yazid said, "What do you want?" "I want Abu Yazid." "Who is Abu Yazid?" said [Bayazid]. "Where is Abu Yazid? I *too* am seeking Abu Yazid." So the man left and said, "This man has gone mad." He returned to Dhu al-Nun and told him what he had witnessed. Dhu al-Nun wept and said, "My brother Bayazid is in the company of those who are vanishing in God—may He be exalted."[27]

Concerning Bayazid's struggle with his nafs, it is related that he said, "I engaged in *mujahada* for thirty years, but I found nothing so difficult as following [the law of God]. If it were not for the difference of opinion of the religious scholars, I would have been left behind. And difference of opinion of the religious scholars is a mercy, save with regard to grasping [God's] oneness."[28] Once, some people asked Bayazid, "Tell us something about your *mujahadat*." "If I were to tell you the greatest [of my self-mortifications] you would not be able to bear it, but I will tell you about the least of them: One day, I bade my *nafs* do something, and it stubbornly refused, so I did not give it water for a year and told it, 'Either make your body obey or die of thirst.'"[29]

Bayazid and the Military Jihad

Regarding the military jihad in the life of Bayazid, a *murid* once asked Bayazid-i Bistami—may God's mercy be upon him, "Who in the world [has attained] a rank greater than anyone else's?" [Bayazid] answered, "Abu 'Abdullah al-Nibaji—may God's mercy be upon him."[30] [The *murid* then] asked, "By what means of worship and devotion did he attain this rank?" "By means of *tawakkul* and jihad," said [Bayazid].[31]

It is related that once, the army of Islam was in Rūm and had faltered, and they were near to being defeated by the unbelievers. They heard a voice: "Bayazid, help them!" Straightaway, a fire appeared from the direction of Khurasan so that the [unbeliever] host was filled with dread, and the army of Islam achieved victory.[32]

The Death of Bayazid

It is related that in the beginning, the shaykh would continually say, "Allah, Allah"; when he was on the point of death he was still saying, "Allah." Then he said, "O Lord, ever have I remembered Thee heedlessly, and now that my soul is leaving [my body], I am heedless still in worshipping Thee, and I know not when my soul will be wholly present!" Bayazid gave up the ghost repeating God's name, and [his soul] was present.[33]

It is said that [Bayazid's nephew] Abu Musa was away the night Bayazid died. Abu Musa said, "I dreamed that I had placed the Heavenly Throne on my head and was bearing it and I wondered at this. The following morning, I hastened to tell the shaykh. The shaykh had died and countless people had gathered from everywhere. When they raised the bier, I strove to be given a corner of the bier, but it did not happen. I could not abide this. I went under the bier and raised it with my head and continued walking. I had forgotten the dream. I saw the shaykh, and he said, 'O Abu Musa, this is the explanation of the dream you had last night: that Heavenly Throne that you placed on your head in the dream was Bayazid's bier.'"[34]

After the death of Bayazid, one of the Sufis said, I visited the grave of shaykh Abu Yazid, Sultan of the Knowers—may God hallow his dear spirit—and lo, a sparrow was pursuing an ant. [The sparrow] was hastening to catch [the ant] until it neared the grave, but when it had almost reached the grave, it went away, leaving [the ant in peace]. I realized that [the sparrow] had desisted [from catching the ant] out of respect for the shaykh. I wondered at [this]—and God knows best what is right.[35]

Junayd al-Baghdadi

Abu'l-Qasim al-Junayd al-Baghdadi is considered one of the foremost Sufis of the early historical period of Sufism. In contrast to Bayazid, Junayd embodied the "sober" school of Sufism, which eschewed unguarded and ecstatic utterances and outwardly controversial behavior.[36] Junayd was born and raised in Baghdad, the capital of the Abbasid Caliphate; however, his father, who was a glass seller, was originally from Nihavand, in Persia.[37] In his youth, Junayd's uncle Sari al-Saqati (d. 253/867) encouraged him to study the traditional Islamic religious sciences, including *fiqh* (jurisprudence) and *hadith*.[38] It was also Sari al-Saqati, himself a friend of God, who initially guided Junayd along the Sufi path.[39] Junayd would eventually become the greatest Sufi shaykh of his era, and many later Sufis would trace their spiritual lineage to him as the paradigm of sober Sufism.[40] The early Sufi Ibn al-'Ata of Baghdad (d. 309/922) said of him, "Junayd is our leader in this knowledge [*tasawwuf*] and our source of imitation in the practice thereof."[41] Junayd was known as the Sultan of the Sufi Path, and it is said that his inner and outer states were in perfect harmony with the Prophet's *Sunna*.⁴² A body of writings, primarily in the form of letters, is also attributed to Junayd.⁴³

Regarding the primary sources for the life of Junayd as presented hereunder: the narrative of Junayd's childhood is from *Tadhkirat al-awliya'*. The anecdotes of his dicta, exempla, and *mujahada* are from *Kitab al-luma'*, *al-Ta'arruf li-madhhab ahl al-tasawwuf*, *Kashf al-mahjub*, al-Qushayri's *Risala*, *Tabaqat al-sufiyya*, *Hilyat al-awliya'*, *Tadhkirat al-awliya'*, *Pand-i piran*, *al-Tabaqat al-shafi'iyya al-kubra*, and *al-Fawa'id*. The military jihad anecdotes are from *Tadhkirat al-awliya'* and *Rawd al-rayahin*. Anecdotes of Junayd's death are from *Hilyat al-awliya'*, *Tadhkirat al-awliya'*, *Pand-i piran*, and *Kimiya-yi sa'adat*.

Junayd's Childhood

*The hagiographical anecdotes about Junayd's childhood portray him as a precocious boy with a sharp mind, whose manners, understanding, and spiritual insight were indeed wondrous.*⁴⁴ One day, he came home from school and found his father weeping. "What has happened?" he asked. [His father] said, "Today I took a portion of the *zakat* (prescribed alms)⁴⁵ to the house of your maternal uncle—to wit, Sari [al-Saqati], but he did not accept [the money]. I weep because I have spent my life earning these five dirhams, and yet it is not worthy of any of God's friends." "Give me [the money] and I will take [it to him] so that he will accept it," said Junayd. Junayd took the money and went [to his uncle Sari's house] and knocked on the door. "Who is it?" said [Sari], "It is I," said [Junayd]. [Sari] did not open the door. "Take this small sum," said Junayd. "I won't take it," said Sari. Junayd said, "By the God Who bestowed grace upon you and a religious obligation on my father, take [the money]!" Sari replied, "O Junayd! "What grace has He [bestowed on] me and what religious obligation on your father?" Junayd said, "He has bestowed grace on you by giving you a life of poverty and has placed a religious obligation on my father by occupying him with the affairs of this world. You [can either] accept [the money] or refuse it, but my father *must* pay the *zakat* money to someone who merits it whether or not he wishes to." These words pleased Sari, and he opened the door, saying, "[My] boy, before I accept this *zakat,* I accept you!" Sari took the money and [thenceforward] Junayd held a special place in his heart.⁴⁶

Junayd was seven years old when Sari took him on the Hajj. In the Sacred Mosque in Mecca the meaning of thankfulness (*shukr*) was being discussed among four hundred elders, and each of the four hundred gave his own definition and explanation of thankfulness. Sari said to Junayd, "You also say something!" Junayd said, "Thankfulness means not being sinful by means of whatever beneficence God—mighty and exalted—has bestowed on you and not making His beneficence a source of sin." When Junayd said this, the four hundred elders said, "Well done, O beloved of those who are truthful!" And they all agreed that no one could say better. Sari said, "Young man, God's gift to you will soon prove to be your speech." Junayd said, "I was pondering this when [Sari] said, 'Whence did you come by this [wisdom]?' 'From your gatherings,' [answered Junayd]."⁴⁷

Junayd's Dicta, Exempla, and Mujahada

Junayd returned to Baghdad and took up [his father's trade of] selling glass. Every day he would go to the shop, pull down the curtain, and perform four hundred *rak'ats* of prayer. He did this for a time, and then he abandoned the shop. There was a room near the entranceway of Sari's house; he dwelled therein and occupied himself with guarding his heart, and he unrolled his prayer rug and concentrated on prayer so that nothing save God would occupy his thoughts. He dwelled in this manner for forty years and spent thirty years performing the night prayer and would stand until morning repeating God's name and would also perform the ablutions for the morning prayer. He said, "When forty years passed, the thought occurred to me that I had achieved my aim. Thereupon an unseen voice said, 'Junayd! The time has come for Us to manifest to you the belt of seclusion.' 'What sin has Junayd committed that this is so?' Then I heard a voice say, 'Do you require a greater sin than the fact that you exist?'" [Junayd] sighed, bowed his head, and said, "Whoever is not fit for union with God, all his good deeds are sins." So Junayd remained in that room, where he would repeat God's name all the night long. People began to talk about this, and they told the story to the caliph. The caliph said, "We cannot forbid him without some kind of proof." They said, "His words are sowing discord among the people." Now the caliph had a slave girl, whom he had purchased for three thousand dinars, and no one could rival her in loveliness. The caliph was in love with the girl. He bade them dress her in fine clothing and array her in costly jewels. Then they told [the girl], "Go before Junayd and show him your face and your clothes and jewels, and say, 'I have much money and my heart is weary of this world. I have come so that you will want me and that in your company I may devote [myself to God], for my heart will not be at rest with anyone else.' Show yourself to him and remove your veil and exert yourself in this matter." A servant accompanied her, and the slave girl came before [Junayd] with the servant. Everything she had agreed to do, they accomplished twofold. Without wishing to do so, Junayd's eyes fell upon her, but he was silent and gave no response. The slave girl repeated her story, and Junayd looked down. Suddenly he raised his head, uttered a sigh, and breathed on the slave girl, and she immediately fell dead. The servant left and told the caliph what had happened. The caliph burned with remorse and said, "Whoever does to men what ought not to be done will see what ought not to be seen." He rose and went to Junayd, saying, "One must go unto such a man." Then he said to Junayd, "O Shaykh! How could your heart allow you to burn such an image [of comeliness]?" Junayd responded, "Is this how you show kindness to the Muslims, O Commander of the Faithful—by trying to bring to naught my forty years of austerities, sleeplessness, and physical agony? Who am I amid [all this]? Do not [wrong], lest they should do [wrong]."[48]

Regarding Junayd—may God's mercy be upon him—it is related that he saw a Christian [youth] of great beauty by the Bab al-Taq [in Baghdad]. He said, "O God! place this [youth], whom Thou hast created so comely, in my service!" When the time came, the Christian [youth] came and said, "O shaykh! teach me the *shahada!*" [Junayd] taught [him] the *shahada*. The youth embraced Islam and went on to become one of God's friends.[49]

Junayd said, "One night, I saw Iblis—upon whom be a curse—in a dream. He was walking through the marketplace naked, and I said, 'O Accursed One, have you no shame before these men?' 'O Junayd!' answered Iblis, 'You call *these* men and reckon them men—whom I toy with night and day as if they were children playing in the street?' 'Who, then, are the [*real*] men?' I said. 'Those who are in the Shuniziyya Mosque[50] are the ones whom I try day and night to injure and on whose account I burn with envy and despair.' When I awoke from [this] dream I went straight to the Shuniziyya Mosque—it was still the middle of the night—and there were three dervishes sitting with their heads wrapped in their patched cloaks. When I entered the mosque, one of them turned and said, 'O [Junayd]! Whatever that accursed one told you, understand that it has no basis, for he is indeed a liar.'"[51]

Junayd was once asked, "What [benefit] do [Sufi] *murid*s derive from [godly] storytelling?" and he replied, "Stories are one of God's armies, with which He strengthens the hearts of the *murid*s."[52] "Have you doctrinal support (*shāhid*) for this [pronouncement]?" "Yes, [the Qur'anic verse:] *And each thing we relate to you from the tidings of the messengers is that with which we strengthen your heart. [And in these things, there have come to you the truth and an exhortation and a reminder for the believers.]*"[53]

Many sayings concerning Sufism are attributed to Junayd. Regarding tawakkul *he said,* "The reality of absolute reliance on God is that one should become for God what he was not, and that God should be as He has always been."[54] *When asked for a definition of a spiritual knower* ('arif), [Junayd] said, "The spiritual knower is he who tells you of your secret while you remain silent."[55] Junayd was asked about Sufism: "[It is] purifying the heart of the things that are agreeable to created beings, separating oneself from one's natural disposition and extinguishing one's human characteristics, avoiding the promptings of the *nafs*, taking up spiritual qualities, cleaving to knowledge of what is real, using what is foremost for the eternal, admonishing the entire Muslim community, serving God truly, and following the example of God's Messenger regarding the *sharīʿa*."[56] *On another occasion, when they asked Junayd to define Sufism,* he said, "Sufism is employing every exalted natural disposition and abandoning every base natural disposition."[57] *Junayd also emphasized the scriptural basis of Sufism, saying,* "Our knowledge is regulated by the Qur'an and *hadith*; he who does not heed the Qur'an or write *hadith* or live in accordance therewith is not guided by it."[58]

Junayd and the Complementary Nature of Jihad

The theologian Ibn Qayyim al-Jawziyya (d. 751/1350) attributed the following interpretation of Qur'an: 29:69 to Junayd, "And those who have struggled *against their passions* with regard to Us *in repentance,* verily We will guide them by our paths *of purity.*"[59] Ibn Qayyim al-Jawziyya explained Junayd's words as meaning: "No one can successfully undertake the outer jihad against his enemies save for him who has carried out jihad against these enemies inwardly, and he who is victorious against [his inner enemies] will be victorious against his [outer] enemies. And as for him [whose passions] are victorious over him, his enemy will likewise vanquish him."[60]

It is said that there was a *sayyid* (i.e., a man descended from the Prophet) whom they called Nasiri. He decided to undertake the Hajj. When he arrived in Baghdad, he went to pay his respects to Junayd. Junayd asked, "Whence comes the *sayyid*?" "From Gilan." "Of which sons [of the Prophet's household] are you descended?" "I am a descendant of the Commander of the Faithful 'Ali."[61] [Junayd] said, "Your forefather wielded two swords: one against the unbelievers, and the other against his *nafs*. O *sayyid*, you who are one of 'Ali's sons, which of these two swords do *you* command?" When the *sayyid* heard [these words], he wept much and fell at Junayd's feet and said, "O Shaykh, my Hajj is here—show me the way to God!" [Junayd] said, "This, your breast, is God's holy precinct; as much as you are able, you must not allow any stranger to enter the holy precinct." "So be it." [said the *sayyid*].[62]

Junayd and the Military Jihad

It is related that [Junayd] had eight *murid*s who were among his most special and for whom any thought [from him] sufficed. It occurred to them that they ought to go on jihad. The next day Junayd summoned a servant and said, "Make preparations for jihad." So [Junayd] and the eight *murid*s went to the Land of the Byzantines (Rūm) to wage jihad. When they formed ranks, a mighty warrior strode forth from among the unbelievers and martyred all eight *murid*s. Junayd said, "I [looked up and] beheld nine camel litters suspended in the air, and the spirit of each one of the martyred *murid*s was placed in a litter. There remained one empty litter, and I said, 'Surely that one is mine,' and I entered the thick of the battle. That warrior who had slain my companions strode forth and said, 'Abu'l-Qasim, that ninth litter is *mine!* Go back to Baghdad and be the people's spiritual guide. But [first], expound Islam to me.' [The warrior] became a Muslim, and, with the very sword with which he had slain the eight *murid*s, he killed eight unbelievers; then he became a martyr. Junayd said, "They placed his spirit in the ninth camel litter, and then they vanished."[63]

Junayd said, "I went forth one day [to take part in] a military expedition. The commander of the army sent me something for [my] maintenance. I was loath to accept it, so I dispersed it among the poor *ghazi*s. Several days passed, and I prayed the noon prayer and then sat reflecting on [the commander's gift], regretting having accepted and dispersed it. Then sleep overcame me, and I beheld palaces constructed with great embellishment and comfort. So I asked about them, and was told, 'These [palaces] are for the wealthy who dispersed [wealth] among the *ghazi*s.' I said, 'Is there something for me among them?' 'Yonder palace,' and they indicated a great palace among the most lavish and greatest palaces. 'Why did I merit such favor over all the others?' 'They gave money in expectation of reward [in the hereafter], and this was their recompense, whereas you distributed money with apprehension, fearing [God] and holding yourself responsible, in regret. Thus,

God—exalted—multiplied [your recompense] on account of the righteousness of your intent.'"[64]

The Death of Junayd

One of the Sufis said, "I was with Junayd when he died, and he recited the entire Qur'an. Then he began reciting *Surat al-Baqara*.[65] He recited seventy verses and then he died—may God have mercy upon him."[66]

It is also said that just before he died, Junayd knotted his fingers in his prayer beads so that his four fingers were knotted, and his forefinger was omitted. With complete majesty he uttered, *In the name of God, the compassionate, the merciful*, closed his eyes, and gave up the ghost. When the time came for washing [his body], the corpse washer tried to apply water to the shaykh's eyes, an unseen voice said, "Take your hand from the eyes of Our friend, for the eyes that shut while saying Our name will only be made to open upon meeting Us!" [The washer] then attempted to open the fingers [clutching the prayer beads], and the voice said, "Those fingers that became knotted in Our name will not open save by Our command!"[67]

When they raised Junayd's bier, a white dove perched on the corner, and however much they tried to shoo [the dove] away, it would not leave. Then [the dove] spoke, "Trouble not yourselves nor me, for my claws are fastened to the bier by the nail of love. I have perched [here] because today [Junayd's] body belongs to the archangels, and were it not for your clamor, his body would have already ascended aloft like a white falcon."[68]

One of the Sufi shaykhs related, "I dreamed that they said, 'Rise, for the caliph of the Muslims has died!' I rose and went to Baghdad but saw no sign [of the death of the caliph]. I went to one of the Sufi shaykhs and said, 'They showed me in a dream that the caliph of the Muslims had died, but now I see no sign [thereof].' The [shaykh] began to weep and said, 'Your dream is indeed true, for our shaykh Junayd—may God have mercy on him—has died, and it is he who is the caliph of the truth.'"[69]

Another Sufi said, "I saw Junayd in a dream and asked, 'What has God done with you?' [Junayd] replied, 'All those acts of worship and indications were nothing; the wind bore them away and nothing was gained—save for those two *rak'at*s of prayer I performed at night.'"[70]

Abu Ishaq al-Kazaruni

Abu Ishaq al-Kazaruni (d. 426/1035), also known as Shaykh-i Murshid, was an early Sufi in the region of Fars as well as the eponym of the first Sufi order, the Kazaruniyya (also known as the Ishaqiyya or Murshidiyya). He is traditionally remembered for having converted to Islam many Zoroastrians—who, at that time, were still the majority in much of rural Iran.[71] Indeed, though his mother and father had embraced Islam, his grandfather remained a Zoroastrian. Like many early Sufis and Sufi archetypes, Abu Ishaq was known for his piety and asceticism as well as for his learning in the traditional Islamic sciences. Hujviri described him as having many followers and great authority.[72] The Persian Sufi poet Khwaju Kirmani (d. 750/1349) considered himself a follower of the shaykh and praised him in his poetry.[73] The Kazaruniyya Sufi order eventually spread as far as India and China, where the fourteenth-century traveler Ibn Battuta, who visited Abu Ishaq's tomb while in Fars, remarked that it was common for Muslims traveling by sea to make a vow to Abu Ishaq for their safety.[74] As for his involvement in the military jihad, the hagiography devoted to Abu Ishaq's life and wondrous deeds, *Firdaws al-murshidiyya fi asrar al-samadiyya,* devotes many pages to the depiction of the shaykh inspiring the Muslims of Kazarun to undertake military campaigns against the Byzantines.[75]

Regarding the primary sources for the life of Abu Ishaq al-Kazaruni as presented hereunder: anecdotes regarding Abu Ishaq's childhood and first steps on the Sufi path are from *Firdaws al-murshidiyya, Tadhkirat al-awliya', Fawa'id al-fu'ad,* and the *Shiraz Nama.* Anecdotes of his dicta, exempla, *mujahada,* and death are from *Firdaws al-murshidiyya* and *Tadhkirat al-awliya'.* Anecdotes of the military jihad are exclusively from *Firdaws al-murshidiyya.*

Abu Ishaq's Childhood and Introduction to the Sufi Path

It is said that the night the shaykh came into existence, a light like a great pillar with beams [of light] was seen from the house, reaching the heavens, and beams of that light were traveling in all directions. The shaykh's father and mother were Muslims, but his grandfather was a Zoroastrian.[76]

[When Abu Ishaq was a boy], there were two teachers from whom the shaykh—may God hallow his secret—learned the Qur'an. And both were learned and accomplished. One of the [Qur'an] reciters was named Abu Tammam and was from Basra; the other reciter was named Bu 'Ali Muhammad b. Ishaq b. Ja'far, and he was from Syria—God's mercy upon them both. Bu 'Ali established a school in the Sarvak mosque in the wilderness below Kazarun. A great throng flocked to Bu 'Ali and studied the Qur'an. [Abu Ishaq]—may God hallow his dear spirit—would go and learn the Qur'an from him; however, his father forbade him from learning the Qur'an, saying, "O light of your father's eyes, go and learn a trade so that you can earn a living, for we are poor folk, and a trade is therefore indispensable." The shaykh—may God hallow his secret—replied, "Father, I am already doing what you bade me [do] and will learn a trade that is indispensable." Thus, Shaykh-i Murshid—may God hallow his dear spirit—would rise at dawn each day and go to Bu 'Ali and study the Qur'an, and another group would go and learn the Qur'an, but the shaykh would arrive before them all. Someone from that group said, "Tomorrow, I will arrive before Abu Ishaq so that I may have the first [lesson]." At dawn, he rose and went to the [Qur'an] school. It so happened that God—exalted—made sleep overcome him, and he lay down and went to sleep. The teacher Bu 'Ali entered the mosque and saw him sleeping, and at that moment, Shaykh-i Murshid—may God hallow his dear spirit—arrived and began studying. That man was awakened by the sound of the shaykh's reading the Qur'an, and he said, "O teacher, the first lesson is mine since I arrived earlier!" Bu 'Ali said, "If you had been awake the first lesson would have been yours, but since you went to sleep, you were absent, and Abu Ishaq arrived. The lesson is his, and he is the first."[77]

[Abu Ishaq] said, "In the beginning, when I was studying the religious sciences, I desired to follow a shaykh on the Sufi path and serve [him] and cleave to the path of that shaykh. I sought divine favor by performing two *rak'at*s of prayer, touching my [fore]head to the prayer rug, and [saying], 'O God! Advise me about these three shaykhs; which of them ought I to follow?' They are: Ibn Khafif, Harith al-Muhasibi, and Abu 'Amr ibn 'Ali—may God have mercy upon them.' I fell asleep and dreamed that I saw an old man with a camel laden with books. [The old man] said to me, 'These books belong to Shaykh Abu 'Abdullah-i Khafif, and he has sent them all to you.' When I awoke, I knew that I was to follow [Ibn Khafif]." Later, [Ibn Khafif's disciple] Husayn-i Akkar—may God have mercy upon him—came and placed the books of [Ibn Khafif] before [Abu Ishaq]. "The truth [of this] increased, and I chose to follow the path [of Ibn Khafif].'"[78]

Another source relates that when Abu Ishaq was still a boy, he was weaving a rope one day—for his father was a weaver—when Shaykh Ibn Khafif passed by him and gazed upon him to see what he could see in his countenance. Ibn Khafif then said to Abu Ishaq, "Come; be my *murid!*" Abu Ishaq was astonished and replied, "What do I know about being a *murid?*" Ibn Khafif said, "Place your hand in mine and say, 'I've become your *murid.*'" So Abu Ishaq did as the shaykh bade him, grasped his hand, and became his *murid.*[79]

It is said that [Abu Ishaq's] father said, "You're poor and can't afford to show hospitality to every traveler who arrives, lest you become destitute." Abu Ishaq said nothing. When a group of travelers arrived during the month of Ramadan, however, and there was nothing to offer them—and dinnertime was nigh—a man suddenly appeared with ten loads of baked bread, currants, and figs and said, "Feed the poor and travelers with this food." When [Abu Ishaq's] father beheld this, he left off admonishing [his son], took heart, and said, "As much as you are able, continue serving mankind, for God will surely not forsake you."[80]

Dicta, Exempla, and Mujahada *of Abu Ishaq*

It is related that, at first, Abu Ishaq—may God hallow his dear spirit—would sometimes eat meat but later he forswore it and would not eat it. Ahmad b. Behruz said, "I heard Shaykh-i Murshid—may God hallow his dear spirit—say, 'The reason I forswore meat was this: I was on the Hajj and arrived in Basra. One day, I was in the company of a group of shaykhs—may God's mercy be upon them all. When it was time to eat, they brought some cooked meat; they ate of it, but I did not do as they did. Later, when I returned home, I desired meat. They brought some cooked meat before me, and I was hungry and wished to eat it. When I was about to eat some [of the meat], I said to myself, "You wouldn't eat meat when you were among [those] men; instead you feigned that you did not eat meat. Now that you are alone you wish to eat meat and enjoy yourself." After that, I ceased [eating meat] and swore to God that I would never eat meat again.'"[81] He also forswore dates and sugar and would likewise not eat of them. Once, when he was sick, the physician [tending to him] prescribed sugar; however, no matter how hard they tried, [Abu Ishaq] would not eat [any sugar]. And he would never drink water from the ditch belonging to Khurshid the Zoroastrian, who was governor of Kazarun.[82]

Concerning the wonders attributed to Abu Ishaq, the Qur'an reciter Abu 'Abdullah Muhammad b. Ahmad related, "The shaykh—may God hallow his dear spirit—said to his companions, 'When you are with your kinsfolk, and they bring you something to eat or give you something, do not eat it save in the presence of your companions.' Abu 'Abdullah said, "Each Friday following the noon prayer, I would ask the shaykh's leave to visit my mother. My mother would often set food before me, but I would forbid myself [to eat of it] in accordance with the shaykh's admonition. Until one Friday, when I prayed and then asked the shaykh's leave and went to my mother's. My mother placed several dates before me and said, 'Eat, for I've brought these dates for you!' I told her of the shaykh's command. She said, 'Eat just two or three dates out of love for me; the shaykh won't find out!' So I ate one date for my mother's sake. Then a violent feeling of disgust seized my stomach, and I refused to eat any more. When I came back to the shaykh and greeted him, the shaykh—may God hallow his secret—returned the greeting and said, 'What did you do at your mother's, and what did you eat with her?' I told the shaykh I had eaten nothing. The shaykh—may God hallow his dear spirit—turned to me and said, 'So you didn't eat a date?' When the shaykh said this, my heart was overcome by [feelings of] awe and reverence for him, and I knew that he possessed miraculous knowledge and that nothing was hidden from him. I asked forgiveness and thenceforth I did not eat anything save in the presence of my companions."[83]

Regarding Abu Ishaq's wilaya, Mawlana Taj al-Din Bukhari, who was one of Abu Ishaq's murids, related, "The greatness and grace of Shaykh-i Murshid—may God hallow his dear spirit—were such that if his glance fell upon an unbeliever, he would become a Muslim forthwith; if [it fell] upon a sinner, he would repent of his sins; if [it fell] upon a tyrant, he would forswear tyranny; if [it fell] upon a godly man, he would become mighty; and [the shaykh's] blessed glance was a supreme agent of transformation (*kimiya'*)."[84]

The companions of Abu Ishaq related that "Once during springtime, Shaykh-i Murshid—may God hallow his dear spirit—had gone to the wilderness with a group of *murids*. When the time for the forenoon prayer arrived, Shaykh-i Murshid—may God hallow his dear spirit—performed the forenoon prayer[85] and then took a short nap. The companions removed a short distance from the shaykh and kept vigil over [him]. Suddenly they beheld a black snake coming with a narcissus in its mouth. It approached the shaykh and laid that narcissus on his blessed chest so that the narcissus bloom was near the shaykh's nose. [The snake] went away and brought another narcissus. It left several times and returned with a narcissus, which it placed on the shaykh's chest, until there was a bouquet. The companions sat watching and did not stir until the shaykh—may God hallow his dear spirit—woke from his sleep, looked around, and saw the narcissus [bouquet]. He turned to his companions and said, 'Who brought these? For I have never seen such fragrant narcissus.' The companions told him what had happened. The shaykh—may God hallow his dear spirit—said, 'Whoever loves God, no doubt all created beings love him.'"[86]

Some of Abu Ishaq's *murid*s related, "One day, the shaykh—may God hallow his dear spirit—was speaking to a gathering, and we were present, when suddenly a sparrow came and alighted on the shaykh's hand. The shaykh said, 'Do you know why this sparrow has alighted on my hand? Because it knows that I will not kill or eat it, nor harm it in any way.' [Abu Ishaq] then said, 'Fear not, little sparrow, for I will neither kill you nor harm you; rather I'm going to let you go.' After that, he released the sparrow, whereupon those present wept much, and they were glad." In another [version of this] story, it is related that Shaykh-i Murshid—may God hallow his dear spirit—said, "This sparrow has come to listen to the words of God and His Messenger."[87]

Several pronouncements are attributed to Abu Ishaq regarding the complementary character of striving in God's path. With respect to the military struggle, he said, "We believe that waging jihad is a duty incumbent on the community: this is to say that if some of the Muslims go on a foray against the unbelievers, they fulfill this duty for the other Muslims."[88] *Abu Ishaq also spoke of the spiritual struggle, saying,* "In the beginning, I bade my followers [embrace] poverty and want, and [undertake] mortification of the body and spiritual striving (*mujahada*). They were so harsh on themselves that their food was the grass of the earth that they would gather and eat. And on account of the food they ate being so much grass, the greenness of the grass was visible under their skin. They did not have turban cloth to wind about their heads; rather, they would collect old [strips of] cloth from the road—such as those with which one wraps pot lids—wash them, and then wind them about their heads."[89]

Abu Ishaq al-Kazaruni and the Military Jihad

When Shaykh-i Murshid—may God hallow his dear spirit—made Islam manifest and brought down the fire temples of the Zoroastrians,[90] the Zoroastrians and fire worshipers were rendered weak, wretched, and hopeless. With each day, the Muslims were overcoming the unbelievers, just as Shaykh-i Murshid—may God hallow his dear spirit—in the beginning of the affair used to say, "Today, one can count the Muslims among the unbelievers, but there will come a day, when the Muslims will triumph, such that one may count the unbelievers among the Muslims, owing to [their being] so few." And thus it was that when the Muslims overcame the unbelievers, they began coming in groups and embraced Islam at the hand of the shaykh—may God hallow his dear spirit—until it happened that all the Zoroastrians of these environs became Muslims. Following this, the shaykh—may God hallow his dear spirit—continually exhorted the Muslims to undertake a military campaign[91] until a group of the folk of Kazarun came before Shaykh-i Murshid and asked leave to equip a host for a military campaign and go to the border (*thaghr*), to wit, the place where the unbelievers are on the further side, and the Muslims on the hither side. They also asked the shaykh to appoint one of his companions to lead their host, and [they pledged] not to disobey him. The shaykh—may God hallow his dear spirit—granted their request. And after that, every Friday, Shaykh-i Murshid—may God hallow his dear spirit—would ask [the Muslims to contribute toward the *ghazis*'] sustenance, and in this way, he collected an abundance of gold, silver, and other things for [the *ghazis*]. He appointed from among his companions Abu 'Abdullah Muhammad b. Judhayn to be their military commander.[92]

One Friday, [the *ghazis*] all gathered with their weapons so that the shaykh—may God hallow his dear spirit—might deliver a sermon to them. Muhammad b. Ibrahim and several of the shaykh's companions said, "That Friday, when the *ghazis* had resolved to undertake a military campaign, they came with their weapons, and Shaykh-i Murshid—may God hallow his dear spirit—was preaching to them and encouraging them [in their endeavor]. Shaykh-i Murshid—may God hallow his dear spirit—was so swept up with them in the endeavor and doing his utmost [on their behalf] that he snatched an unsheathed sword from the hand of one of the *ghazis* and flew into a passion. He began leaping about, brandished the sword over his head, and said in an awe-inspiring voice, 'By the Lord whom I worship in His oneness! If I were to behold anyone at this moment who associated partners with God—exalted—I would sunder his head from his body with this sword, although I have never killed so much as a sparrow!' When the shaykh—may God hallow his dear spirit—had spoken these awe-inspiring words, the door that was nearest to him split asunder, owing to his majesty, and the sound of the door's splitting reverberated throughout the mosque. When those in attendance beheld this, they let out a cry and wept considerably, and a group of the soldiers rose and turned to God in repentance. When the shaykh—may God hallow his dear spirit—had finished his sermon, the soldiers rose, bade the shaykh farewell, and sought his blessing, and then set out for the border to fight with the unbelievers. When they met the unbeliever host, they arrayed themselves for battle, beat on their drums, and attacked forthwith. They slew the unbelievers and routed them—it was a memorable campaign and a famous battle for them—and they plundered [the unbelievers], taking much booty and many slaves.[93] They returned safely [to Kazarun] and came before the shaykh, booty-laden, owing to the blessings and [spiritual] might[94] of Shaykh-i Murshid—may God hallow his dear spirit."[95]

[And so it was that] each year, Shaykh-i Murshid would organize provisions for [the *ghazis*] and send them forth on a military campaign. He himself would remain in [Kazarun] and render them assistance and support by means of his [*wilaya*]. No word they uttered was in vain, and wherever they were in distress, he would come to their assistance and render them aid. Thus, it was that, once, he had sent the army of Islam to Rūm to fight the unbelievers, while keeping watch over their affairs. One day, Shaykh-i Murshid—may God hallow his dear spirit—suddenly rose, took hold of his staff, and ascended to the roof of the mosque. He flew into a passion and began swinging the staff that he held in his hand about his head, as if he were battling a military host, while his companions watched. When some time had passed, the shaykh left off [fighting] and became himself once again. His companions questioned him and said, "O shaykh! What was this affair?" Shaykh-i Murshid—may God hallow his dear spirit—replied, "At that moment, the host of

Islam had become captives in Rūm at the hands of the unbelievers, and they were beseeching me for assistance, so I rendered them aid and succor." His companions recorded the time of this event. After the host of Islam came back from fighting the unbelievers, the shaykh's companions asked them to relate their story. [The *ghazis*] said, "When we met the unbeliever host and formed ranks before them, the unbeliever host was great, and we were few, but we were stout-hearted and strove against them. We battled [them] on all sides and slew them, but they were so many that one hundred unbelievers opposed each one of us. They attacked all at once and surrounded the Muslims, and we feared that they would soon destroy us. We called out to the shaykh and besought him to render us aid and we prayed for his grace and succor. Thereupon, we beheld a horseman possessed of grandeur and might who had come to render us aid. He stood before the ranks, facing the unbelievers with unsheathed sword. He flew into a passion and smote the heads, hands, and feet of the unbelievers, and not one of the unbelievers had the mettle to oppose him—he was sundering heads of unbelievers from their bodies [just as easily] as if they were cucumbers. In [the space of] an hour, he defeated the entire unbeliever host and routed and pursued them. He then withdrew, and we did not know [who he was]. After that, we achieved victory over the unbeliever host, slaying many of them." When they had heard this story, the shaykh's companions looked [at what they had recorded], and it was the same time that the shaykh—may God hallow his dear spirit—had used his staff on the roof of the mosque and routed the unbelievers—may God hallow his dear spirit.[96]

Regarding Abu Ishaq's death, it is said that he succumbed to fever in his old age while returning from a funeral in the city and died after four months of sickness. Three days before he died, however, he assembled his companions to advise them so that they could continue leading the Muslims of Kazarun. At this time, he also appointed Khatib Abu'l-Qasim (d. 442/1050) as his successor. The day that [his] death was near, at the time of the evening prayer, the shaykh—may God hallow his dear spirit—said to Khatib Abu'l-Qasim, "Arise! Go and lead the people in prayer so that they do not miss the communal prayer." When Khatib Abu'l-Qasim descended from the [shaykh's] room, so as to lead the prayer, the shaykh—may God hallow his dear spirit—recited *Ayat al-Kursi*[97] and the *shahada,* passed his blessed hand over his face, and rested it on his chest; [then] he closed his eyes and died.[98]

[After] Shaykh-i Murshid—may God hallow his dear spirit—died, every year, the folk of Kazarun would take up the shaykh's drum and standard and would go forth on a military campaign. One year, an entire army set out from Kazarun on a military campaign, and the shaykh's successor [Khatib] was with them, and they were all under his command. The caliph of Baghdad had also assembled a host and was going on a military campaign. When [the two hosts] met on the way, they made common cause and marched to one of the cities of the unbelievers. They surrounded the city and besieged the inhabitants. They spent several days [in this manner] but were unable to do anything to [the unbelievers], for they had a secure wall and fortress. If the Muslims brought forth a catapult, the unbelievers would also place a catapult in opposition to it; if a host of Muslims mustered before them, [the unbelievers] would muster a host to face [the Muslims] and would resist them. No opportunity presented itself [to the Muslims]. After a time, the caliph grew weary [of this] and wished to return [to Baghdad]. [With this in mind,] he took counsel with Khatib and the folk of Kazarun. Khatib said, "We mustn't give up until this evening, when I will devise a plan and seek assistance from the spirit of Shaykh-i Murshid, and perhaps Shaykh-i Murshid—may God hallow his dear spirit—will guide us, and tomorrow we will decide what we must do." That evening, Khatib devoted himself to worship and asked the shaykh's spirit for help, and Shaykh-i Murshid—may God hallow his dear spirit—instructed him [how the Muslims could find] the way in [to the city]. The following morning, Khatib went before the caliph and said, "Shaykh-i Murshid has instructed us regarding what we must do." "Please explain," said the caliph. "The solution is that the soldiers must take up trays of tin, copper, or iron, as well as all manner of tambourines and drums—anything that may be beaten—and make ready their weapons. They must not light any fires and must remain still and make no sound until our folk [begin] beating their drums. When they beat the drums, in the same manner, everyone [of your soldiers] must rise from his position and begin beating whatever he has placed before him [for this purpose] until our folk cease drumming. After that, we will make for the city, and it may be that God—exalted—will send us victory." Once Khatib had spoken these words, the caliph bade [the plan] be communicated among his army, and it was announced just as Khatib had bidden. Each of the soldiers brought forth something to beat upon, and when night fell, contrary to custom, they did not light a fire, and they made no sound. They sat clutching their weapons, and each of them had placed a [percussive implement] before him from among the pots and pans and trays and drums and the like that they had procured.

At dawn, Khatib arose and took up his drum and began beating it wildly. When the caliph's soldiers heard the sound of the drum, they arose from their positions and all at once began beating whatever they had placed before them. As long as the shaykh's successor beat his drum, they also beat theirs. There was a tumult, and an earthquake shook the city on account of the din of their drumming, for there were several thousand men beating their implements at the same time until morning. The unbelievers were bewildered and confused.

At daybreak, the Muslims attacked in one fell swoop and took the city from the unbelievers, whom they made their prisoners: some they slew; others they put to flight. Once [the Muslims] had defeated the unbelievers and taken the city from them, they pillaged their wealth and possessions and took much plunder and many slaves from among them and made the unbelievers their servants. After that, they went out [of the city] and divided up the spoils that they had taken. When they wished to return home, the caliph of Baghdad asked Khatib how he had devised this plan and what the wisdom was in it, and Khatib replied, "It was [through] the aid and assistance of Shaykh-i Murshid—may God hallow his dear spirit. I saw that the army of Islam was mighty and had all the strength [necessary], and yet it was unable to do anything against the unbelievers. I realized that there were many Christian monks in this city and that it was their custom to gather in their monastery, and at their gatherings they would busy themselves with prayer, supplication, and acts of devotion. I came to understand that it was their supplicatory prayers and zeal that were keeping us [from taking the city]—since every prayer, supplication, and act of worship performed at dawn must receive an answer.[99] Thus, I saw that the solution was to cause a great disturbance so that they would forsake one another and not devote themselves to worship, prayers, and supplications. I devised a plan to do something that would disrupt them at dawn, which is their time of worship and gathering, and would allow us to [attack] them. It so happened that when they heard the awful din, [the like of] which they had never heard before, all at once they ceased their litanies, their thoughts became scattered, and their supplications and zeal regarding us were cut off—consequently we were victorious over them." Then the Muslims, who had taken one of the monks captive, went and asked him, "How did it happen that you surrendered the city and became [our] captives?" The monk explained the events to them just as Khatib had related them. The Muslims rejoiced, beat the drum of good tidings, and returned in safety to their homeland with spoils.[100]

Chapter 3

SUFI *MUJAHID*S OF THE CRUSADES AND THE MONGOL INVASION: THE TWELFTH AND THIRTEENTH CENTURIES

In the twelfth and thirteenth centuries, the eastern lands of the Abode of Islam experienced the two great calamities of the Crusades and the Mongol invasion of Central and Western Asia. These two events would profoundly affect Muslim society, for they resulted in changes to the political, dynastic, and economic landscape of much of the Muslim world.

The impact that the Crusades and the Mongol invasion had on Sufism proved to be no less remarkable, and the many historical and hagiographical accounts of Sufis who lived through the upheaval of this period attest to this, as do the developments that occurred in Sufi practice and the organization of Sufi brotherhoods.

The Crusades would last nearly two hundred years, beginning in 1096 with Pope Urban II's call for an armed pilgrimage to take back the Holy Land and ending with the Mamluk capture of Acre in 1291. The Mongol invasion of Central and Western Asia lasted more than forty years, beginning in 1219 with the destruction of Khwarazm and culminating in the sack of Baghdad in 1258, and wrought a degree of bloodshed and desolation never hitherto seen. Only their defeat by the Mamluks at the Battle of Ain Jalut in 1260 stopped the relentless Mongol hordes from invading the western Muslim world.

The Crusades were the first successful Christian offensive against the Muslim presence in the Levant since the Muslim armies under Khalid ibn Walid had defeated the Byzantines and taken the Holy Land, capturing Damascus in 634 and Jerusalem in 637.[1] The First Crusade saw the capture of such important cities as Antioch, Edessa, and Tripoli and led to the founding of the Kingdom of Jerusalem. Although Muslims fleeing the Levant for Baghdad besought the Muslim rulers in the East to raise an army to fight the Crusaders, little was done initially to check their expansion.[2]

When the Muslim counterattack finally began, in the twelfth century, it was for reasons other than defending the Abode of Islam from the Christians of Western Europe. At that time, the Seljuks of Mosul wished to establish an empire in Mesopotamia and Syria, and the Crusaders stood in the way of this ambition.[3] The Seljuks, thus, became the first to wage offensive warfare against the Crusaders, albeit for less-than-pious reasons. They were, however, successful in this endeavor, managing to take Aleppo in 1128 and Edessa in 1144.

Despite the worldly aims that inspired the initial counter-Crusade of the Seljuks, by the mid-twelfth century the Muslims of Western Asia had grasped the gravity of the threat that the Crusaders posed to the Abode of Islam and endeavored to undertake its defense. During the rule of Nur al-Din Zengi (d. 569/1174), the Muslims of Greater Syria successfully revived the military jihad and began to fight the Crusaders in earnest.[4] The jihad against the Crusaders would continue under Nur al-Din's successor, Salah al-Din (d. 589/1193), traditionally known as "Saladin" in Western accounts, who became the first Sultan of Egypt and founded the Ayyubid dynasty. Salah al-Din was able to unite Syria and Mesopotamia, after having taken Damascus, Aleppo, and Mosul, and would finally end Crusader occupation of Jerusalem in 1187.[5] Although the period of the Crusades would continue for another century, the Muslims succeeded in gradually retaking most of the territory held by the Crusaders.

In many ways, Sufism flourished during this period. Under the Seljuks, Sufi institutions (i.e., the *khanaqah* and the *ribat*) began to proliferate west of Baghdad. Nur al-Din and Salah al-Din continued this support of the Sufi orders begun under the Seljuks, building *khanaqah*s in Damascus, Jerusalem, and Egypt.[6] Moreover, one upshot of the leadership vacuum that the Mongol invasion created was the crystallization of important Sufi orders and their assumption of community leadership during this time of crisis.[7] Furthermore, following the Mongol invasion and the founding of the Mongol Ilkhanid dynasty, Sufis would also play an important part in the Islamization of the Mongols in Persia.[8]

Sufis undoubtedly helped defend the Abode of Islam from the invading Crusaders and Mongols, and hagiographies and chronicles composed both during and after this turbulent era reflect the Sufi role in resisting these invaders. In one example, from an Arabic chronicle of Jerusalem and its environs that includes hagiographical anecdotes of God's friends, the Sufi shaykh Abu Thawr is said to have taken part in Salah al-Din's capture of Jerusalem in 1187, during which the shaykh rode a bull (hence his cognomen, *Abu*, "father [of]," *thawr*, "bull") and fought the Crusaders from its back.[9] Another example, Aflaki's hagiography in Persian of the Mevlevi order, relates that Rumi journeyed miraculously to Syria and back to fight the Mongols.[10]

The lives of God's friends in this chapter—Najm al-Din Kubra, 'Abdullah al-Yunini, 'Abd al-Rahman al-Nuwayri, and Rumi—offer meaningful examples of how the hagiographical tradition portrayed Sufi *mujahid*s during the era of the Crusades and Mongol conquests. Certainly, some of these stories are purely legendary (e.g., Rumi's miraculous journey to Syria to fight the Mongols) and must be read as attempts to show God's friends as stalwart defenders of the faith while underscoring their *wilaya* and wondrous deeds in this respect. Others, such as that of Najm al-Din Kubra, may have some historical basis, though this is difficult to deduce without other corroborating sources. Nonetheless, these stories of God's friends bespeak the significant role that Sufis played as protectors of Muslim communities and exemplars of godliness and courage during the wars and social instability that obtained during this era.

Najm al-Din Kubra

Najm al-Din Kubra (d. 618/1221) is the eponym of the Kubrawiyya Sufi order, which developed in Central Asia and spread thence to Western Asia, India, and eventually as far as China. He was born in the Oasis of Khwarazm, located in present-day Uzbekistan and Turkmenistan, and his tomb is located in Kunya Urgench (Gurganj).[11] Najm al-Din composed a number of important Sufi treatises, in which he emphasized the mystical experiences of the Sufi wayfarer: in particular the dreams, visions, and images encountered during the Sufi's spiritual journey.[12] As is the case with the description of many early Sufis, the hagiographical tradition describes Najm al-Din Kubra as an exemplary *muhaddith* who scrupulously adhered to the Prophet's *Sunna*.[13] He is also said to have traveled widely for the purpose of performing the Hajj and visiting Sufi shaykhs.[14] Most premodern sources relate that Najm al-Din Kubra died while fighting the Mongols during their siege of the city of Khwarazm.[15]

Regarding the primary sources for the life of Najm al-Din Kubra as presented hereunder: the narrative of his origins and awakening is from *Nafahat al-uns*. The anecdotes of his exempla and wondrous deeds are also from *Nafahat al-uns*, and the story of his jihad and martyrdom during the Mongol conquest of Khwarazm is from *Mir'at al-janan*.

The Spiritual Awakening of Najm al-Din

Before he began treading the Sufi path, it is said that Najm al-Din studied hadith *in Tabriz with Muhiyy al-sunna.*[16] He was studying the book *Sharh al-sunna* (*Explication of the Sunna*). One day, when he had neared the end [of the book], he was reading while seated in the presence of his teacher and a group of religious authorities, [when] a dervish, whom he did not recognize, entered. As soon as he beheld [the dervish], a profound change so overcame him that he was [no longer] able to read. "Who is this man?" asked [Najm al-Din]. "He is Baba Faraj-i Tabrizi and he is [reckoned] among the beloved of God—may He be praised—and those whom He has called," they replied. The shaykh was restless that night. At dawn, he went before his teacher, [saying] "Arise, and let us visit Baba Faraj!" The teacher and his companions consented. At the door of Baba Faraj's Sufi hospice there was a servant by the name of Baba Shadan, who, when he saw the group, went inside and asked leave [of Baba Faraj to let them enter]. Baba Faraj replied, "If they go in this manner to God's court—may He be exalted—they may enter—tell them to come in!" Shaykh [Najm al-Din] said, "When I was vouchsafed the glance of Baba [Faraj], I understood the meaning of his words; everything I had concealed I brought forth, and I placed my hand on my breast. The teacher and his companions approved, and we then came in and sat before Baba Faraj. After a little while, Baba [Faraj's] state changed, and an exaltedness was manifested in his countenance. When the sun began to shine, the clothing he had worn was in tatters. When he returned to himself after a while, he rose and clothed me in [his tattered] clothes, saying, 'This is not the time for you to be studying in a classroom; it is time for you to go out into the classroom of the world.' My state changed, and my inner [being] was sundered from everything other than God. When we left [the hospice], the teacher said, 'Only a little of *Sharh al-sunna* remains, study it for [just] two or three [more] days and you will know the remainder [of the book].' When I went to my lesson, I beheld Baba Faraj enter, and he said, 'Yesterday, you passed through one thousand stations of certain truth (*'ilm al-yaqin*), [but] today you are going back to [studying outer] knowledge?' I forsook my lessons and devoted myself to spiritual exercises and seclusion (*riyadat u khalvat*). Mystical knowledge and unseen emanations began to come forth. I said to myself, 'It would be a pity if [these mystical phenomena] were lost.' So I began writing them down. I [then] beheld Baba Faraj enter through the door, and he said, 'Satan is confusing you; do not write down these words!' I cast away my pen and ink and cleared my mind of everything."[17]

Anecdotes and Exempla of Najm al-Din

Regarding the origin of Najm al-Din's nickname, al-Kubra, it is said that during his youth, when he was studying the [traditional Islamic] sciences, Najm al-Din would dominate anyone with whom he argued or disputed, and for this reason they called him "The Great Calamity" (*al-Tamma al-kubra*).[18] That nickname held, [but then] they dropped "the Calamity" and nicknamed him [simply] "The Great."[19]

Najm al-Din was also known as "Shaper of Saints" (*Vali-tarash*), owing to the power of his blessed glance when he was overcome by spiritual ecstasy (*wajd*), for upon whomever his glance fell, the same would attain *walaya*.[20]

As regards the wondrous power of Najm al-Din's glance, it is related that one day a traveling merchant, [thinking] to amuse himself, entered [Najm al-Din's] Sufi hospice. The shaykh [was at that moment] experiencing a powerful [mystical] state, and his glance fell on the merchant, who forthwith attained *walaya*. Najm al-Din asked [the merchant], "What land are you from?" "From such-and-such land," said [the merchant]. Najm al-Din wrote him an authorization of guidance so that [the merchant] might guide people to God in his own land.[21]

One day, the shaykh was sitting with his companions when he saw a falcon pursuing a sparrow hen in the air. Suddenly the shaykh's glance fell upon the sparrow, and she turned around, caught the falcon, and brought it before the shaykh.

Another time, Najm al-Din was relating and explaining the *sura* of the Companions of the Cave.[22] Shaykh Sa'd al-Din Hammu'i[23]—may God, exalted, have mercy on him—who was one of the shaykh's *murid*s, thought to himself, "Is there anyone among [the Muslims] whose companionship could make an impression on a dog?" [Najm al-Din] discerned [the *murid*'s thought] by means of the light of his inner understanding (*firasat*), rose, and went to the door of the hospice, where he stood [as if waiting for someone]. Suddenly a dog appeared and stood [before the shaykh], wagging his tail. [Najm al-Din's] glance fell upon the dog, which thereupon found grace and was enraptured and overcome [by the shaykh's *wilaya*]. The dog turned away from the city and made for the graveyard, [where] he prostrated himself. Then they discovered that wherever the dog went, fifty or sixty other dogs would gather around him in a circle standing paw to paw and making no sound. The dogs would not eat and would remain standing out of respect. In the end, [the dog] died, [and Najm al-Din] bade [his companions] bury him and erect an edifice over the grave.[24]

The Military Jihad and Martyrdom of Najm al-Din

When the Mongols reached Khwarazm,[25] Shaykh [Najm al-Din Kubra] assembled his companions, who numbered more than threescore. The sultan—Muhammad Khwarazmshah—had already fled [the realm]; however, the Mongols believed Sultan Muhammad to still be [there] and entered Khwarazm [to avenge his grave insult to them].[26]

Najm al-Din summoned several of his aforementioned companions, among whom were Sa'd al-Din Hammu'i, Shaykh Radi al-Din 'Ali Lala, and his nephew 'Ali b. Muhammad with a group of knowers [of God]—and said, "Arise and return to your homelands! For a fire has been kindled in the East that will burn [everything in its path] till it nears the West. This is a great calamity, the like of which the Muslim community has [never before] experienced." Some of his companions said, "If your grace were to utter a prayer of supplication to God, perhaps He would repel this [calamity] from the lands of the Muslims." "This is irresistible fate from God—exalted," said the shaykh. "Supplicatory prayer is of no use and cannot drive it away." His companions then besought [him to flee with them, saying], "We have horses—ride with us and leave forthwith!" [Najm al-Din], however, replied, "I will be killed here, and God has not given me leave to go out of [the city]; make ready to leave for Khurasan!" So his companions left. When the [Mongol] unbelievers entered the city, the shaykh called on his companions whom he had not bidden to depart to pray together. Then he said, "Arise in the name of God, and let us fight in His path!"[27]

Najm al-Din went home, donned his shaykh's *khirqa*, girded his loins, and [proceeded to] fill both [sleeves] of his robe with stones; then he took up his spear, and went forth. When he came face to face with [the Mongols], he began throwing the stones at them until all that he had were spent, while [the Mongols] shot volleys of arrows at him, wounding him. He began whirling and dancing; one of the arrows pierced his breast. [Najm al-Din] drew the arrow [from the wound] and cast it heavenward. The blood flowed from his breast, and he began singing a poem in Persian: "If it be Thy will, slay me with reunion or with separation; I am finished with them both—Thy love is enough for me...." Then he died and was buried in a Sufi hospice. May the mercy of God—exalted—be upon him.[28]

It is said that at the time of his martyrdom, [Najm al-Din] had captured the unbeliever standard. After his martyrdom, ten men could not wrest [the standard] from the shaykh's grasp, and in the end, they [had to] cut it from his hands.[29]

'Abdullah al-Yunini—The Lion of Syria

Shaykh 'Abdullah al-Yunini (d. 617/1221), known as Asad al-Sham—the Lion of Greater Syria—was from the village of Yunin, near Baalbek in Lebanon. 'Abdullah al-Yunini exemplified both the military jihad, in which he is said to have participated many times, and the spiritual jihad (*mujahada*).[30] A simple hospice (*zawiya*) was established for 'Abdullah in his hometown, which many people would visit, seeking the shaykh's blessing.[31] In his conduct, 'Abdullah al-Yunini displayed the characteristic internal and external piety of the Sufis—he epitomized the fundamental Qur'anic precept of enjoining what is righteous and forbidding evil, and he was known for his many wondrous deeds and mystical states.[32] 'Abdullah is also described as engaging in *dhikr* throughout his life, ever remembering God.[33] After his death, 'Abdullah al-Yunini's tomb became a place of pilgrimage.[34]

Regarding the primary sources for the life of 'Abdullah al-Yunini as presented hereunder: the anecdotes of his exempla and wondrous deeds are from *al-Dhayl 'ala al-rawdatayn*, *Mir'at al-zaman*, *Mir'at al-janan*, and *al-Bidaya wa'l-nihaya*. The anecdotes of his military jihad are from *al-Dhayl 'ala al-rawdatayn* and *Mir'at al-zaman*, and the story of his death is from *Shadharat al-dhahab*.

Exempla and Wondrous Deeds of 'Abdullah al-Yunini

It is said that 'Abdullah al-Yunini led a life of rigorous asceticism and relied solely on God for his daily bread. He was a paradigm of self-mortification and the spiritual struggle (*riyadat wa-mujahadat*), as well as wonders and intimations (*karamat wa-isharat*). He would rise for no one, glorifying God, and he would say, "It is not proper to rise for anyone save God." He put nothing aside [for his maintenance], and he would not touch with his hand a dinar or a dirham. He was a righteous renunciant and scrupulously pious and all his life he wore nothing save a homely linen cloak and a cap of sheepskin worth half a dirham.[35] In the summer, he would not don anything more than a shirt, and in the winter, he would wear [only] a hide over it.[36] His servant, 'Abd al-Samad, related, "He would take leaves from the almond tree [under which he would sleep], rub them [between his hands], and swallow them."[37]

As for where 'Abdullah al-Yunini lived, it is related that he would sometimes dwell in the mountains of Lebanon.[38] He would come during the winter to the springs of Fasiriya, near Damascus, for the warmth of the water and to perform his ritual ablutions. Near the springs, a small mosque was built for him in which he would take shelter, and the inhabitants would go out from Damascus to visit him.[39]

The hagiographical accounts of 'Abdullah al-Yunini include anecdotes of wondrous events attributed to his wilaya. The judge of Karak, in the Beqaa, Jamal al-Din b.

Ya'qub, related, "One day, I was near the white bridge by a mosque there during the hot season, when Shaykh 'Abdullah came and dismounted from a bull to perform his ritual ablutions. A Christian [merchant] was crossing the bridge with his donkey laden with wine. The donkey stumbled on the bridge, and the load of wine fell. There was no one on the path. The shaykh came up from the river and called to me, saying, 'Come, legist (*faqih*)!' So I came. 'Give me a hand!' he said. So I helped until we had raised the load back onto the donkey, and then the Christian went on his way. I said to myself, 'To think that the shaykh would do something like this!' I followed after the donkey to its destination. Then [the Christian merchant] came to the vintner's shop, unloaded [the wine], and [the vintner] opened the wineskins, and inspected [the wine] to measure it out, but, lo, [the wine] had turned to vinegar! The vintner said to [the Christian merchant], 'Confound you, this is vinegar!' [The Christian merchant] wept and said, 'By God, it was wine [only] an hour ago, and I know the reason [for this].' Then he tied his donkey at the [vintner's shop] and returned to the mountain. The shaykh performed the afternoon prayer in the mosque near the bridge and then sat down praising God. The Christian entered and said, 'O master! I bear witness that there is no god but God,' and thereupon, he became a Muslim and embraced poverty."[40]

With regard to the jihad of speaking a just word to a tyrant, it is said that al-Amjad,[41] ruler of Baalbek, would come to visit ['Abdullah al-Yunini], who would greet him and say, "O Mujayd, you continually behave as a tyrant, and you do this, and you do that" [al-Amjad] would then ask [the shaykh's] pardon.[42]

'Abdullah al-Yunini and the Military Jihad

It is related that ['Abdullah al-Yunini] was brave and had no regard for whether [the number of] enemy] men were few or many, and his bow [weighed] eighty rotls.[43] He never missed taking part in a military expedition in Syria; he wished to die a martyr and would hurl himself into the thick of battle.[44]

His servant, 'Abd al-Samad, related, "When al-'Adil[45] entered the territory of the Franks and reached Safita[46] and Uraymah, meanwhile, the shaykh was in his *zawiya* in Baalbek and said to me, 'Go to [our] trusted friend 'Abdullah and ask for his mule.' So I fetched [the mule] for him, and he mounted it, and I went forth with him. We stayed the night in Yunin and then we got up at midnight and came to al-Muhdatha before dawn, and I said to him, 'Do not speak here, for this is the hiding place of the Franks.' Then, however, the shaykh raised his voice and exclaimed *Allahu akbar!* which echoed from the mountains—I [nearly] died of fright. The shaykh then dismounted, performed the dawn prayer, and mounted [the mule]. The sun rose, and the birds were not flying in that land; then a white host suddenly appeared from the direction of the Krak des Chevaliers, and [the shaykh] thought it must be the Knights Hospitaler, so he said, '*Allahu akbar!* How blessed Thou art from day to day!' and drove [the mule] toward the host while unsheathing his sword. I said to myself, 'A shaykh with a mule under him, and in his hand a sword—heading toward a host of Franks!' After a long spell, they neared us, and lo, it was only a herd of wild asses! [The shaykh] was dejected and his zeal subsided, so I said to him, 'Most praised is your lord! God certainly took notice of you—you sought to meet one hundred [in battle] on a mule!' Then we came to Homs, and the *mujahid* king Asad al-Din[47] met us and presented [the shaykh] with a horse, so he mounted it and entered [the battle] with them, [in which he] performed wondrous deeds.[48]

The Death of 'Abdullah al-Yunini

When it was Friday, the tenth of Dhu'l-Hijja,[49] he performed the morning prayer in the congregational mosque of Baalbek and bathed before the Friday Prayer. Dawud the muezzin, who would wash the bodies of the dead, came, and [the shaykh] said to him, "Woe unto you, Dawud! See how you'll be tomorrow?" But Dawud did not understand [the meaning of the shaykh's words] and replied, "O master, tomorrow we will be under your protection." The shaykh then ascended to his grotto. He had bidden the dervishes cut away a large stone by the almond tree beside which he was wont to sleep—so they cut it away. The shaykh rose and performed the morning prayer and then went up with his prayer beads in his hand while the dervishes were cutting away the stone. The sun rose and they finished cutting away the stone while the shaykh was sleeping with the prayer beads in his hand. A servant came from the palace on an errand and saw [the shaykh] sitting asleep and he did not dare to wake him, but this went on for too long for him, so he said, "O 'Abd al-Samad! I can't sit longer than this." So ['Abd al-Samad] approached [the shaykh] and said, "Master!" But [the shaykh] did not speak, so he stirred him, and he was dead. A cry went out, and the ruler of Baalbek came and beheld him in that state, and he said, "Let us build for him an edifice with him in this [wondrous] state." But they replied, "Following the *Sunna* is of primary importance." Then Dawud the muezzin came and washed him by the almond tree, and that was on Saturday, and [the shaykh] had passed his eightieth year. His grave is visited in Baalbek—may God have mercy upon him.[50]

Abu'l-Qasim 'Abd al-Rahman al-Nuwayri—The Eloquent Martyr

Several hagiographical sources relate anecdotes regarding The Eloquent Martyr (*al-shahid al-natiq*), 'Abd al-Rahman al-Nuwayri, whose custom it was to go to war against the unbelievers,[51] and who died while fighting the Crusaders at Damietta, in Egypt, in 1250.[52] 'Abd al-Rahman al-Nuwayri was from al-Nuwayra in Egypt[53] and belonged to a family known for its learning and leadership.[54] He was a respected jurist known for his forthrightness,[55] and the family tradition of Islamic legal scholarship continued with his descendant Shihab al-Din al-Nuwayri— whom Ibn Battuta mentions as one of the prominent learned residents of Mecca and Medina.[56] Safi al-Din ibn Abi'l-Mansur ibn Zafir, author of the hagiographical *Risala*, recalled seeing 'Abd al-Rahman in Lower Egypt during the Crusades and mentions that the most upright and godly men of that era would come to pay their respects to the shaykh.[57]

The primary source for the life of ʿAbd al-Rahman al-Nuwayri as presented hereunder is the *Risala* of Ibn Zafir, though one quotation from al-Munawi's *al-Kawakib al-durriyya* is also included, following the main narrative.

Among those I saw in Egypt[58] was the great shaykh and jurist ʿAbd al-Rahman al-Nuwayri. He was highly esteemed and concealed by his learning [and was vouchsafed] many wonders (*karamat*). Anyone who spent a day in his company would behold a wonder.

Once, a Maghribi man, who had come from the Maghrib, saw [ʿAbd al-Rahman al-Nuwayri], and he was thereby robbed of his senses. The shaykh understood and taking him aside said, "Do not reveal what you have seen!" [The man], however, was unable [to restrain himself] and informed [those around him] that he used to always see Shaykh ʿAbd al-Rahman al-Nuwayri with Shaykh Abu Muhammad Salih in Asfi, in the Far Maghrib.[59] And this is the sentence I mentioned [above], which suffices [to show] that no one spent time in his company without beholding a wonder.[60]

A man from Bahnasa[61] who had become a companion of [al-Nuwayri] told me, "We sat with him once and mentioned *samaʿ* and said to [al-Nuwayri], 'Master, do you consider *samaʿ* a legitimate [practice]?' 'Yes,' the shaykh replied, 'provided that it is [practiced by those sensible of its true purpose].[62]' We asked him, 'Are you among them, master?' 'Yes,' he replied. 'We wish to listen with you.' So [the shaykh] bade someone come and sing. [The singer] began humming softly before [the shaykh] and we beheld [the shaykh's] color change. Then he said, 'Each of you has a desire [for something special to eat].' One of us desired honey, another wished for cream, and so on. Behind [the shaykh] there stood a cupboard from which he began to withdraw whatever it was that each man desired." This is the end of the story, which the [man from Bahnasa] related. The meaning of the story is that when the [mystical] state came over [al-Nuwayri], and his color changed, he manifested its presence [to them] by extracting from the unseen plane of existence whatever they asked for. [This is] because they were unable to comprehend what had come over him, so he manifested its effect to them in a way that was appropriate [to their level of understanding].[63]

The Military Jihad and Martyrdom of al-Nuwayri

When the *ghazi*s were assembled in Damietta, the *faqih* ʿAbd al-Rahman al-Nuwayri said to his companions, kinfolk, and sons, "Whoever wishes for martyrdom, let him make up his mind about it!" He went forth, taking his sons with him, and they came to Cairo and stopped over at the Ghayn Mosque,[64] and I visited him during that time as I had seen him before that.

When [al-Nuwayri] arrived in Damietta, he pitched his tent on the field of battle. When the Franks advanced to the field and routed whomever [they found] on it, [some of the *ghazi*s] fled. The shaykh and his son, however, remained in their tent until the Franks entered and slew them.

Sometime later, after the Muslims had defeated [the Franks] and concluded a temporary peace with [them], a merchant journeyed from al-Nuwayra to Acre and displayed his wares [there]. A Frank approached the merchant and bought [all the goods]. [The Frank] said, "Come with me to get the money for your goods." So the Muslim merchant went with the Frank to his home and entered it with him. But when the Muslim [merchant] found himself alone with his money in the house of the Frank he became afraid. The Frank was sensible [of his fear] and said, "O Muslim, fear not! Like you, I, too, am a Muslim." Then [the Frank] recited the *shahada* and said to him, "It was I who killed 'Abd al-Rahman al-Nuwayri: I entered his tent and struck his neck until he died. Then I said to him after he had died, 'O priest of the Muslims! You say in your Qur'an: *Reckon not dead those who have died in God's path, but rather alive with their Lord, receiving their daily bread.*'[65] I spoke these words in mockery," said the Frank. "Then [al-Nuwayri] opened his eyes and said with a resounding voice, 'Indeed, yes, *alive and receiving their daily bread!*' Then [the shaykh] spoke no more. After I had seen and heard what I heard, unbelief (*kufr*) was removed from my heart, and I embraced Islam by his hand. I hope that God will forgive me through [the intercession] of [al-Nuwayri's] blessing and because I embraced Islam by his hand. I have [al-Nuwayri's] Qur'an and sword, and when I saw you, I said to myself, 'This man is from his town.' I wished to acquaint you with my condition and his condition. Perhaps you can determine the value of the sword and Qur'an and take [the money from me] to give to his heirs—may God be pleased with him.'"[66]

Concerning the Sufism of 'Abd al-Rahman al-Nuwayri

The hagiographer al-Munawi described 'Abd al-Rahman al-Nuwayri as "The great mystic of consequence (*al-'arif al-kabir al-sha'n*) [who] was prodigious in his *mujahada* and asceticism and exemplary in preservation and restraint and an expounder of the Sufi way."[67]

Rumi

Jalal al-Din Muhammad Balkhi (d. 672/1273), better known in the West as Rumi, scarcely requires an introduction, for he is by far the most famous of Sufi poets, and his poetry has been translated into multiple languages.

Although his epithet, *Rūmī*, refers to his adopted home of Konya, in the Sultanate of Rūm, in Anatolia,[68] Jalal al-Din was born in Central Asia, in the town of Vakhsh, in present-day southwestern Tajikistan.[69] *Balkhi*, the epithet by which Rumi is known in Persian, refers to the nearest important city at the time of his birth.[70] Rumi must have also lived in Balkh as a boy, however, for we know that his father, Baha' al-Din Valad (d. 628/1231), was a Hanafi religious scholar who made his living there teaching in a *madrasa*.

At some point during Rumi's childhood, his father decided to move the family from the region of Balkh to Konya, in Anatolia. The reason for the move is traditionally given as Baha' al-Din Valad's foreknowledge of the coming Mongol invasion of Central Asia and the inevitable destruction of Balkh. After the death of his father, Rumi became a *murid* of Burhan al-Din Muhaqqiq (d. 637/1239/40) of Termez, who guided him on the Sufi path. Rumi followed Burhan al-Din for nine years, which included spending a significant amount of time in Syria.

Rumi was a prolific poet who composed hundreds of *ghazals* as well as his famous *Mathnavi-yi ma'navi*, and his poetry may be seen as a continuation of the Persian Sufi poetic genres that his predecessors Sana'i (d. early sixth/twelfth century) and 'Attar had developed. His *Mathnavi-yi ma'navi* has been called "the Qur'an in Persian,"[71] and it seems that Rumi himself presented it as a kind of *tafsir*.[72] In addition to his poetry, Rumi composed an important treatise on Sufism titled *Fihi ma fihi*.

Rumi also had a lasting influence on the development of Sufi practice following the Mongol invasion, as the Mevlevi Sufi order, which crystallized around him and his descendants, would become an integral part of Ottoman culture and would remain influential for five centuries following his death.

As regards the inner and outer struggle of God's friends, the hagiographical tradition relates that Rumi exemplified both *mujahada* and jihad, and his poetry and prose likewise discuss and portray the complementary essence of this struggle.[73]

The primary sources for the life of Rumi as presented hereunder are *Manaqib al-'arifin*,[74] *Valad Nama*, *Zindagi nama-yi Mawlana*, and *Nafahat al-uns*. Hagiographical details are from all three sources; the story of his military jihad is from *Manaqib al-'arifin*.

Rumi's Childhood and Introduction to Sufism

The stories of Rumi's childhood depict a boy endowed with spiritual precocity and profound insight. It is said that at the age of five, [Rumi] would suddenly leap to his feet in great agitation, to the extent that the *murids* of Baha' al-Din Valad would take hold of his waist. This was on account of the spiritual images and forms of the unseen realm that would manifest to him: to wit, recording angels, god-fearing jinn, and the elect among men who are concealed by the vaults of God,[75] just as in the beginning the angels close [to God] would appear to [God's] messenger, and Gabriel to Mary, and the four angels to Lot and [Abraham]—peace be upon them. The sultan of the religious scholars [Rumi's father, Baha' al-Din Valad] spoke soothing words, saying, "They are of the unseen world; they show themselves to you to bestow favors and have brought singular unseen gifts." And such states and [spiritual] intoxication would continue to come over him.[76]

The following anecdote is traditionally ascribed to Rumi's father, Baha' al-Din Valad: Jalal al-Din Muhammad [Rumi] was six years old in the city of Balkh, when one Friday, he and several other children were walking along the roofs of our houses together. One of the children said to another, "Let's jump from this roof to that roof." [Rumi] said, "Such behavior befits cats, dogs, and other animals. It would be a shame for a human to be involved in these [acts]; however, if you have the strength, come, and let us all fly heavenward." And in that moment, he vanished from the children's sight. The children cried out [in their astonishment], and after a short spell, [Rumi] returned—[but] his color and eyes had undergone a change. [Rumi] said, "That moment when I was speaking to you a host clad in green robes took me from your midst and caused me to wheel around the heavens, where they showed me manifold heavenly wonders. When the sound of your crying and wailing rose up, they brought me back to this place."[77]

Regarding Baha' al-Din Valad's decision to leave Balkh for the Hejaz, it is related that he heard God's voice telling him to leave Balkh at once[78]:

When, because of the folk of Balkh, Baha'-i Valad,	that eternal king, became afflicted,
Suddenly words from God came to him, saying,	"O incomparable king of kings of the axes mundi,
Since this group injured you,	and afflicted your pure heart,
Go forth from among these foes,	so that We may send them chastisement and woe."
When he heard these words from God,	he put aside his anger.
He resolved to go to the Hejaz,	since that secret became realized in him.
He was journeying when the tidings reached him,	when the outcome of that secret became manifest.
The Tatars waged war against that folk;	the host of Islam was routed.
They took Balkh, lamentation and woe followed;	they slew an untold number of that folk.
They destroyed the great cities;	God has one thousand kinds of punishment.

Thus did Baha' al-Din learn that God had sent the Mongols to punish the unrighteous folk of Balkh, just as He had done in the past to the wicked folk who had not heeded His prophets and messengers.[79]

It is said that during the time that they were journeying to Mecca, they met Shaykh Farid al-Din 'Attar in Nishapur, and the shaykh gave [the boy Rumi] his book the *Asrar Nama* (*Book of Secrets/Mysteries*), and [Rumi] would keep the book with him always.[80]

Among the wondrous deeds attributed to Rumi, it is related that when [his father] Baha'-i Valad had come to stay at the Mustansiriya *madrasa* in Baghdad, he would ask for water every night at midnight, and [Rumi] would get up from his bed and go to fetch water. When he would reach the door of the *madrasa*, it would open without a key at the bidding of the [Divine] Opener, just as it did for Joseph the Upright,[81] and he would then go fill a jug with water from the Baghdad estuary and bring it to his father, and the door would shut once more.[82]

After the death of his father, Rumi became the murid of Burhan al-Din Muhaqqiq. As to how this happened, it is said that when Burhan al-Din, who had come to Konya seeking his former teacher Baha' al-Din, learned of his teacher's death and saw Rumi for the first time, he told the boy, "You have surpassed your father one hundred times over in all the religious sciences and certain knowledge; however, your father attained perfection in outer knowledge (*'ilm-i qal*) and had consummate inner knowledge (*'ilm-i hal*). From this day forward, I wish you to seek inner knowledge, which is the knowledge of the prophets and friends of God. It is called [divine] knowledge (*'ilm-i laduni*) on account of [the Qur'anic verse]: *[And they found a servant from among our servants] on whom we bestowed [mercy from Us, and we taught him] knowledge belonging to Us.*[83] This mystical meaning came to me from my shaykh; receive it from me as well so that you may be your father's heir in every way, both outwardly and inwardly, and become just like him." So [Rumi] consented to all that he indicated and took [Burhan al-Din] to his own *madrasa* and served him for nine whole years.[84]

Under Burhan al-Din's guidance, Rumi engaged in *riyada* and *mujahada* for five of those years.[85] When divine knowledge had been revealed to his incomparable essence, he betook himself by means of *riyada* and *mujahada* to the highest stations of *walaya* and became worthy of the secrets of oneness, and the confidant of the celestial treasures, God's caliph on earth, Khizr—upon whom be peace—revealed his many-splendored aspects of grace to [Rumi].[86] Whenever [Rumi] encountered a difficulty in [the apprehension of] these divine mysteries [Khizr] would serve as his guide and would reveal [their meanings] to him and sit with him, and they would concern themselves with mysteries and intimations.[87]

It is said that when [Rumi] was in Damascus, a group of [the Sufis] saw Khizr—upon whom be peace—in the room in the Barraniyya *madrasa* in which [Rumi] dwelled. That room is named after Khizr—upon whom be peace—and the people go there on pilgrimage to pray regarding their needs.[88]

Dicta, Exempla, and Wonders of Rumi

It is said that [Rumi] was once expounding mystical knowledge and truths by the side of a stream, and the frogs in the water were making such a racket with their croaking that [no one could] hear. [Rumi]—may God hallow his venerable secret—cried out and with complete majesty addressed the frogs: "If you have something better to say in this regard, then speak, and we will be silent and listen to you!" They immediately became silent, and it was some time before anyone heard the sound of the frogs again.[89]

It is related that [Rumi] was walking along [a path] in Konya built for pedestrians lest they would fall in the mud, when [he came upon] a dog sleeping on the path. He halted, and all his companions [also] halted. Someone came forward and saw that a dog was asleep on the path. Out of respect for the shaykh, he chased it away. This upset Rumi, and he said, "Why did you disturb the dog's rest? One must imitate the perfection of kindness [the Prophet Muhammad showed] to all creatures."[90]

Once, [Rumi] noticed that one of his companions was sad and heartsick, [so] he said [to him], "All heartsickness is the result of cleaving to this earthly world with one's heart. When you become free of this world and know yourself a stranger, and when you know that every color you see and everything you taste [is transitory] and that you are going to a different place, your heartsickness will cease."[91]

Rumi and the Military Jihad

The pride of the companions, Jalal al-Din Qassab—may God have mercy on him—who was one of [Rumi's] former *murid*s, was a man replete with worldly grace and elegance. It was his custom to buy Arabian foals, which, having raised them, he would sell to grandees and noblemen, thus, he always had a stable of fine horses. [Jalal al-Din Qassab] related, "One day, a great agitation from the divine realm came over [Rumi], and for forty whole days he wandered about with his blessed turban tied below his neck in Arab fashion. All at once, I saw [Rumi] come in through the door, bathed in sweat and with an awe-inspiring mien. Like one helpless, I bowed my head and remained [in a state of] amazement. [Rumi] commanded [me], 'Saddle that excellent horse.' Having placed the saddle [on the horse] with [the help] of three young servants and with countless efforts and a tether, I brought [the horse] before [him]. [Rumi] mounted the horse and set off in the direction of Mecca. I asked whether I could also accompany [him], [Rumi] responded, 'Render assistance through your high-minded intention.' That evening, I saw him return, covered in dust, and the great horse was emaciated and spent. The following day, I saw him return, and he asked for another, but better, horse. He mounted it and rode away. He returned at the time of the evening prayer, and the Arabian horse was [likewise] weak and emaciated, but I didn't dare utter a word. On the third day, he returned and having mounted another steed, rode off. He returned again at the time of the sunset prayer, dismounted, entered the house, sat down completely relaxed, and spoke [the following line of poetry]:

Good tidings, good tidings, O ye joyful folk!	For that dog from Hell has gone back to Hell.

[He then recited the Qur'anic verse] *The folk that oppressed were eliminated—Praise be to God, Lord of the worlds.*[92] I was [so overcome] with awe that I was not able to ask the why and wherefore of the situation. Several days later, a great caravan from Syria arrived, and [those traveling with the caravan] brought tidings that the Mongol army had placed the city of Damascus in dire straits." They say that this was Hulagu Khan, who put Baghdad to the sword in the year 655 (1258) and slew the caliph. In the year 657 (1260), he attacked Syria and took Aleppo. They say that Kitbuqa with a great host advanced toward Damascus.[93] During that terrible time, when the [Mongol] army had surrounded Damascus, the inhabitants of Damascus witnessed [Rumi], who had come to render aid to the host of Islam on [the battlefield]. They defeated the Mongols, who were utterly routed and left having suffered great losses. The narrator of these tidings says that "From the joy of hearing this news I became happy and went to [Rumi] to tell him of what had occurred in Damascus. He said, 'Yes, Jalal al-Din!

That horseman who was victorious over the army,	who is the sultan of discernment to the men of the faith?'"

[Rumi's] companions all cried out and made a commotion, and there was excitement and rejoicing among the world's inhabitants. And news of this wonder and the might of [Rumi] spread far and wide, and those who loved him rejoiced.[94]

The Death of Rumi

It is said that Rumi died in Konya following an illness, suddenly, on a Sunday in winter, on the fifth of Jumada al-Akhir, in the year 672 (December 17, 1273), while [he was] expounding mystical knowledge and truths, at the time of the westering sun, the sun of his glory set in the world of holiness. All at once a lamentation rose from the lowly and the noble, rich and poor, strangers and acquaintances, Muslim and Christian. Clothing was rent, and eyes became moist, and dust was on every head. Doors and walls quaked on account of the great clamor and lamentation, and the earth was stained with the tears of blood. Hearts, wounded and sad, mourned everywhere. With burning heart and eyes full of tears from distress, the following lines of poetry were recited[95]:

That sun of the celestial spheres has entered the earth, why would I not cover my head in dust?
The spring dove having flown from the meadow, why would I not cry out in cloudlike lamentation?
The world-illuminating lamp has gone to its death, why would my day not become nightlike on this day?

Chapter 4

SUFI *MUJAHIDS* OF AL-ANDALUS AND AL-MAGHRIB: THE TWELFTH THROUGH SEVENTEENTH CENTURIES

The Muslim conquest of North Africa occurred during the Umayyad period in the late seventh century, bringing both Islam and the Arabic language to the indigenous Berber-speaking population.[1] Several decades later, in 711, Arabicized Muslim Berber warriors, led by Tariq ibn Ziyad (d. early second/eighth century), began the conquest of southern Spain and thereby introduced Islam and Arabic to the Iberian Peninsula.[2] Islamic urban civilization developed rapidly in the region over the next hundred years—'Abd al-Rahman I (d. 172/788) made Cordova the capital of the newly established Umayyad Emirate of Spain in 756, and Idris II (d. 213/828), son of Idris I (d. 175/791), who founded the Idrisid dynasty, built Fez, in Morocco, in 808.[3] These cities flourished as early centers of culture and learning in the Islamic West and would in time see the arrival of Sufism from the East.

Sufism first came to the Islamic West in the early eleventh century with pilgrims returning from the Hajj, who had been introduced to the various Sufi practices and doctrines in Egypt and the holy cities of Mecca and Medina. After its establishment in the urban centers of Maghribi Islamic culture, Sufism began to spread throughout North Africa and Spain.[4] In Spain, especially, theoretical and practical Sufism throve. The first Sufi of consequence to bring Spanish Sufism to North Africa was Abu Madyan al-Andalusi (d. 594/1198).[5] The Sufism of Abu Madyan emphasized the Sufi's duty to guide the Muslim community, a role for which the Sufi's spiritual discipline and indifference to worldly desires made him ideally suited.[6] Other influential Hispano-Arab Sufis included Ibn 'Arabi (d. 638/1240) of Murcia, who was one of the greatest Sufi thinkers of any era, and Ibn 'Abbad al-Rundi (d. 792/1390) of Ronda, who in all likelihood was the first to introduce Shadhili teachings in Morocco, which would be central to the development of Maghribi Sufism.[7]

Sufism did not initially fare well politically, especially under the Berber dynasties of the Almoravids (1040–1147) and the Almohads (1121–1269), who came to dominate much of Spain and Morocco after the Spanish Umayyad Caliphate ended in 1031. These dynasties, though in some respects influenced by Sufi practice and ideas, tended to see the popularity of Sufism as an ideological threat.[8] With the rise of the various North African dynasties (i.e., the Marinids,

Wattasids, and Sa'adians) who succeeded the Almohads, however, Sufi friends of God began to play an ever-greater role in Muslim society and the defense of the Abode of Islam.

In the twelfth century, the Spanish Christians began the Reconquista in earnest, inspired by their newfound strength, the Crusades in the East, and as a reaction to the jihad of the Almoravids. These Christian holy warriors succeeded in gradually winning back the Iberian Peninsula.[9] With the fall of Granada, in 1492, Muslim rule in the peninsula came to an end, and many Iberian Muslims left for nearby North Africa, settling in Fez, Tlemcen, Tunis, and other urban centers.

In the aftermath of the Reconquista, first the Portuguese and then the Spanish began harassing and attacking the Muslims of North Africa, partly out of zeal for continuing their Crusade, but also for economic reasons, as the coasts of the Maghrib were the gateway to the trade routes with sub-Saharan Africa.[10] And these two threats ensured that the Muslims of North Africa would continue to fight the Spanish and Portuguese on the *thughur* throughout the sixteenth and seventeenth centuries.

During the period of the Reconquista and the above-mentioned military and economic expansion of the Portuguese and Spanish in North Africa that followed, Sufi shaykhs would take part in, and sometimes lead, the defensive jihad against the Christian invaders, while also assuming roles of authority in rural communities, where they and their *zawiya*s were often the only source of stable Muslim leadership.[11] Though European sources have traditionally depicted "marabouts" (i.e., God's friends in North Africa) as backward, rustic holy men, recent scholarship has shown that the majority of these Sufi friends of God were from urban areas, were literate, and were often respected religious scholars who followed the Maliki school of Sunni jurisprudence and the sober Sufi path of Junayd.[12]

The hagiographical sources for the stories of God's friends of the Maghrib and al-Andalus in this chapter differ in some respects from those of the Eastern Islamic world; in particular, the lives in these sources tend to be shorter, concentrating on the deeds and learning of their subjects as paradigms of Islamic ideals (i.e., *rijal* anthologies) rather than relating wondrous birth-till-death narratives in the manner of the *manaqib* genre.[13] Moreover, in portraying the learning and piety of God's friends, the *rijal* sources often highlight their role as ideal *mujahid*s, who exemplify courage, selflessness, and austerity while fighting in God's path. The emphasis on their martial activity is probably due to several factors, which include the historical reality of ongoing war with the Spanish and Portuguese, as well as the influence of the earlier, Eastern hagiographical tradition, which depicted *mujahid* friends of God such as Ibrahim ibn Adham and 'Abdullah ibn al-Mubarak. Thus, history and religious idealism are intertwined in many of these hagiographical narratives.

As for the history of this period, there are abundant reliable sources that document the role of Sufis in the jihad against the Portuguese and Spanish invaders. The most influential of these friends of God include Muhammad al-Jazuli (d. 870/1465), Muhammad ibn Yajjabsh al-Tazi (d. 920/1514), Muhammad ibn al-Mubarak al-Aqqawi (d. 924/1518),[14] and 'Abd al-Rahman al-Tha'alabi (d. 875/1479).[15] Muhammad al-Jazuli deserves special attention, as it was he who defined what would come to be the ethos of Sufism in Morocco from the fifteenth century onward.[16] For example, like his predecessor Abu Madyan, whom we mentioned above, Muhammad al-Jazuli taught that it was the duty of Sufi shaykhs to teach the local populace by means of admonitions and precepts that everyone could understand.[17] The Sufism of the Maghrib was well suited for this didactic role in that it emphasized a code of conduct based on essential Islamic piety and practice rather than esoteric theoretical concerns.[18] This pragmatic Sufism is at least in part the result of the predominance of Shadhili doctrine in North Africa, which stressed the necessity of believers submitting to the authority of one of God's friends rather than seeking mystical unification with God.[19]

With respect to the duty of the military jihad in Islam, these friends of God proclaimed its centrality to the ethos of the faith. For example, al-Jazuli insisted that fighting in God's path was essential to being a Muslim.[20] His spiritual descendant, Muhammad ibn Yajjabsh al-Tazi, likewise wrote that *mujahids* exemplified true Islam and, moreover, emphasized that Sufis were the paradigmatic *mujahids*, for they did not fear death.[21]

The Sufi *mujahids* in this chapter include the relatively well-known historical figure Muhammad al-'Ayyashi as well as obscure friends of God such as 'Abdullah al-Arkushi and 'Umar al-Tanji—both of whom appear in only one hagiographical source. In the case of Abu'l-Hajjaj al-Mughawir, whose deeds seem to have been quite popular if one considers the many anecdotes and stories about him, there are abundant hagiographical sources but little in the way of historical corroboration. As for the remaining two friends of God, 'Ali ibn 'Uthman al-Shawi and Muhammad al-Bahluli, both of whom lived during the sixteenth century, there are relatively few historical or hagiographical sources. Regardless of the abundance or paucity of sources, however, or whether these friends of God appear in the historical record or are merely legendary, they represent a hagiographical tradition spanning five hundred years and two continents and bear witness to the importance of Sufis in premodern Muslim culture of the Maghrib and al-Andalus. Like the other lives described in the previous chapters, the hagiographical lives of these six friends of God embody the ideal of the Sufi *mujahid* in that they portray Sufis overcoming the lower self through *mujahada,* admonishing and encouraging rulers regarding their religious duties, and bravely and selflessly fighting the enemies of Islam in battle.

Abu 'Abdullah Muhammad al-Arkushi

Little is known regarding the life of God's friend Abu 'Abdullah Muhammad al-Arkushi (d. mid-sixth/twelfth century?) other than the anecdotes that al-Sadafi relates in *al-Sirr al-masun*, which is the sole source for his life and deeds as related hereunder. His *laqab* (nickname) indicates that he was from Arkush (present-day Arcos de la Frontera, in Spain), which had been a Berber Taifa kingdom from the early eleventh century until the Almoravid conquest of the southern Iberian Peninsula in the mid-twelfth century.[22] Tahir al-Sadafi relates that Abu 'Abdullah al-Arkushi embodied the essential characteristics of God's friends, led an exemplary life, followed the Sufi path, and lived to a ripe old age.[23] Several wondrous deeds are attributed to him, including his bloodless victory over a Christian military host.

Abu 'Abdullah Muhammad al-Arkushi in al-Sirr al-masun

Tahir al-Sadafi related that, "I parted from him—may God have mercy upon him—[he having] attained perfection among men, and [having] reached a ripe old age. He [never] did what was forbidden, nor did he stray from duty, and he trod only the [Sufi] path. I witnessed one of the wonders that God bestowed on him; a voice cried out in one of the realms of al-Andalus, 'O *mujahid*s in God's path! The Day of Reckoning [is upon us], for the spears of the Christians have reached the city walls!' The people were roused one and all, prepared themselves, bolted the city gates, and then ascended to the fortifications and took up their battle positions. [The Muslims] looked out, and [saw] the open country brimming with [their] cursed foes. Suddenly, one of the city's gates opened, and a leader of the Muslims went forth with many horses and halted before the gate with his soldiers. The townsfolk watched from the fortifications. When the unbelievers noticed him, they all turned toward him and gave a loud cry [swearing] to capture [him and his soldiers]. Now this Abu 'Abdullah [al-Arkushi] was one of those who were on the fortifications. The townsfolk cried out to him, 'O Abu 'Abdullah! Do you not see the distress the Muslims are in and the triumph of [our] foes? Supplicate God on our behalf!' So [al-Arkushi] uttered some words to himself, which he did not reveal, and then climbed one of the towers of the fortifications. He began waving his cloak at the enemy, [crying] 'Go away and disperse!' And, by God, I have never seen a host disperse [like this one] or a gathering disunite and scatter in such a flash or nearly so.

Someone who went on the Hajj with [al-Arkushi] told me that when the party of [Hajj] travelers stopped for the night in the wilderness on one of the days [of their journey], they needed to prepare their food, but they found no fire and nothing with which to kindle a fire. [Al-Arkushi] found the traces of a campfire, which had been kindled long before, and placed a stick of wood in the cold ashes, which then caught fire, and the smoke rose up. The people in the caravan made a fire from it, prepared their food, and then continued on their way.

One of the emirs of [al-Arkushi's] town prepared a great feast, for which he seized the livestock belonging to the townsfolk to slaughter. This Abu 'Abdullah [al-Arkushi] had an ox, which [he used to] plow the land where he grew his food, and the emir took [this ox] by force along with all [the other animals]. While they were making off [with his ox], [al-Arkushi] recited [the Qur'anic verse] *We ransomed him with a great blood sacrifice.*[24] [The emir's servants] herded al-Arkushi's ox together with the other animals into the emir's stables, where they proceeded to slaughter them and then prepared the food. [Al-Arkushi's] ox, however, roamed among the emir's horses, and a mule [belonging to the emir] took the ox's place and was slaughtered along with the other [animals]. The following morning, they found the mule's head among the heads [of the slaughtered animals] and [al-Arkushi's] ox alive. They told the emir the story, and he understood that he had behaved unjustly and greatly regretted [what he had done]. He sent [the ox] back to [al-Arkushi] and sought his forgiveness and blessing. No one ate any of the meat that had been slaughtered for that feast, on account of its dubiousness, for it had been mingled with the meat of the mule.

I parted from [al-Arkushi]—may God honor him—[and he was still] living, but I know not what God has done with him."[25]

Abu'l-Hajjaj al-Mughawir

As his *laqab*, al-Mughawir,[26] indicates, the friend of God Abu'l-Hajjaj Yusuf al-Mughawir (d. 619/1222) was a renowned *mujahid* who spent twenty years of his life wayfaring in the lands of unbelief and fighting in the path of God.[27] He was also well known for his *walaya* and *tawakkul*.[28] The various hagiographical sources name him Abu'l-Hajjaj, Yusuf, and, in one instance, simply al-Mughawir.[29] He was originally from Cordova.[30] The extant sources reckon al-Mughawir among the many Sufis and pious men who journeyed to Egypt during the era of the Crusades, where, according to one source, he is said to have resided in Qena, in Upper Egypt, with his shaykh, Abu'l-Hasan ibn al-Sabbagh (d. 612/1215).[31] Although Abu'l-Hajjaj al-Mughawir was known primarily for his prodigious wayfaring and zeal for jihad, the hagiographical sources also relate anecdotes that tell of his wondrous deeds and rigorous *mujahada*, as well as his strange adventures.

The primary source for the life of Abu'l-Hajjaj Yusuf al-Mughawir as presented hereunder is the *Risala* of Ibn Zafir. Two additional anecdotes not related in the *Risala* are also included: the anecdote of al-Mughawir weeping from Ibn 'Arabi's *al-Futuhat al-makkiyya*, and the anecdote of al-Mughawir confronting a tyrannical local emir from al-Sadafi's *al-Sirr al-masun*. Other hagiographies, including al-Munawi's *al-Kawakib al-durriya* and Ibn al-Mulaqqin's *Tabaqat al-awliya'*, relate anecdotes of al-Mughawir that are based on those of Ibn Zafir's *Risala*.

al-Mughawir in Ibn Zafir's Risala

The singular and venerable shaykh Abu'l-Hajjaj Yusuf al-Mughawir—may God be pleased with him—was from Cordova and was the follower of many godly men of al-Andalus, in Seville and other [cities]; among them was Shaykh al-Ghazzal.[32] [In this regard,] Shaykh al-Mughawir told me, "Shaykh al-Ghazzal used to say to me, 'O Yusuf! You do not belong to me; you belong to a man whom you will meet toward the end of your life, in the East'"—that is, Egypt.

Shaykh al-Mughawir said to me, "There is no place on earth that this foot has not trodden." And he pointed to his foot, [meaning] his wayfaring and many peregrinations.

I saw many men [of the Sufi way], but I never saw anyone, other than him, who outwardly manifested oneness, which is manifested inwardly in the others. His outward demeanor was not affected by external occurrences, neither extreme heat nor bitter cold, nor hunger nor satiety, nor abuse, [nor] praise, nor blame. He once dwelled in Aswan in [a state of] rapture (*akhdha*), which he endured for forty days—wrapped in nothing but a cloak—and never stirred a limb. I asked him about his inner state during those forty days of rapture, "How was it?" He replied, "I [passed] back and forth from the [way of] Muhammad to the [way of] Moses." That is, he would alternate between beholding God and conversing with Him.

When [al-Mughawir] met Shaykh Abu'l-Hasan ibn al-Sabbagh toward the end of his life—he was roughly eighty years old—he took shelter with him and rested and informed [Abu'l-Hasan] of all his states. The shaykh praised [al-Mughawir] and witnessed that he was one of [God's] Seven Pillars [on earth].[33] And he experienced two [states] of rapture with [Shaykh Abu'l-Hasan]: one for seventeen days, and one for fifteen days. The shaykh then told his companions about him, saying: "God has apprised this [man] al-Mughawir of my knowledge, which is a great testament, for a man's knowledge is his deepest secret with God—may He be praised."[34]

Among the [stories] [al-Mughawir] related to me about himself [is the following]: "I used to spend several years waging war (*mughawiran bi'l-harb*) and several years wayfaring, during which I would enter the land of the unbelievers for [various] matters for the sake of which I was bidden to enter. And at my will, if I wished to be seen, I would be seen, and if I wished that I not be seen, I would not be seen. Thus did I receive a true command from God—may He be praised—that I enter the land of unbelief so that I might meet a most righteous man (*rajul siddiq*). So I entered the land [of unbelief] and revealed myself [to the unbelievers], who then took me prisoner. The man who captured me rejoiced; then he bound me and took me to the market to sell me—and this was the path I was commanded to follow. Someone mounted on a worthy steed bought me and made a pious gift of me to the church that I might be a servant in it. I served in this capacity for several days, when [those who served the church] brought many carpets, censers, and perfumes. I asked them, 'What's all this about?' 'It is the king's custom to visit the church once a year, and the time for his visit has come, so we are preparing and decorating it for him. No one must remain inside [when the king] enters to worship alone.' When [the servants] locked [the church] I remained inside and hid from them, and they did not see me. The king arrived, and they opened the doors; [the king] entered by himself, and they closed the doors behind him. The king walked through the church, inspecting it [to make sure no one else was there], and all the while I was watching him, but he didn't see me. When [the king] was satisfied [that he was alone], he approached the altar and then, facing the *qibla* (direction of Mecca), uttered *Allahu akbar!* in preparation for praying. Then [I heard a voice] telling me, '*This* is the man whom We wished you to meet.' So I came out and stood behind him until he had finished praying. The king then turned, and seeing me said, 'Who might you be?' 'I'm a Muslim like you,' I responded. 'What has brought you here?' said [the king]. 'You have,' I said. [The king] came up to me and asked me about myself, so I informed him that I had been commanded to meet [him] and that my path [to him] could not have proceeded otherwise. [I told him] how I [had been captured], and then made a servant of the church, [all] in order that [our] meeting might occur. [The king] was delighted with me and confided to me his inner spiritual state, and I [mine] to him, and I found him to be among the godliest of men. I then said to him, 'How do you fare among these unbelievers, considering what you are concerned with inwardly?' 'O Abu'l-Hajjaj, there are many advantages to my being among them, the like of which I would not have were I among the Muslims.' 'Such as?' I asked him. 'My [belief in God's] oneness and my submission [*islam*] [to God], as well as the sincere deeds [I do] for God alone, that no one knows anything about. I eat licitly, as [my food falls under the war-time statute] (*fay'*), and thus there is nothing doubtful about it. I help the Muslims [in ways] that would be impossible even were I the greatest of kings, [e.g.,] defending them, keeping the hostility of the unbelievers from reaching them, and by killing [unbelievers] and spreading corruption among them. I will show you some of my deeds among [the unbelievers].' Then we bade each other farewell, and he said to me, 'Return to what you were doing.' So I hid myself and was concealed from those who might see me. Then the king went out and seated himself near the church doors and said to [his servants], 'Bring before me those who serve the church!' So they brought a group before him and said, 'This is the patriarch, and this is the cantor, this is the monk, this is the supervisor of pious endowments, and this is the collector of tithes.' [The king] asked, 'Who, then, looks after [the church]?' 'So and so,' they said, meaning the man who gave me to the church as a pious endowment; 'he bought a prisoner and gave him to serve [the church].' Then the king became quite angry and said, 'You were all arrogant regarding serving the house of the Lord, for you made a [ritually] unclean man who is not of the [Christian] community to serve the house of the Lord.' [The king] then had all of them beheaded in order to prove his zeal regarding the house of the Lord. Then he bade them bring me into his presence and I appeared before them, and they approached me, and he said, 'This is the servant who deigned [to serve the church], in contrast with those who disdained it, [he is to be] honored and compensated and given a mount, and [he is to be] set free [in order that he may return] to his own land and folk.' And they did [as he commanded], and I departed from them."

[Al-Mughawir] said to me: "During my travels I once happened on an island where none save monkeys dwelled, and I spent a day wandering among them. There I saw a she-monkey with a he-monkey asleep at her side and with his head on her thigh, and she was picking lice from his hair. All at once, another he-monkey came to her from afar and gesticulated to her, so she moved the monkey's head from her lap and went to [the other he-monkey]. The he-monkey proceeded to copulate with her, then she returned to her place and laid the [first] monkey's head on her thigh again as it had been. When the monkey awoke, he smelled the scent of copulation from the other monkey, so he flew into a rage and began shouting. Then the other monkeys, hearing his shout, gathered around her while he was shouting and stoned her to death. I was in awe at the application of divine law—even among monkeys—inspired by God—may He be praised."

[Al-Mughawir] related to me, "I was wayfaring in the Long Land"—that is, the Land of Alfunsh,[35] in the West—"when I met 'Abdullah al-Mughawir, who dwelled in Alexandria. So we greeted each other, and then he said, 'O Abu'l-Hajjaj! I have a tale to tell you about what happened [to me] in this place.' 'Tell me!' I replied. 'I was once in this waterless desert, when, lo, a troop of the soldiers of Rūm were coming toward me. I gave up any hope of living, so I turned toward Mecca and began praying, so that should they kill me, I would be killed while praying. When they reached me, they beheld me as a stone and leaned their spears against my head. Then one of them said to the others, "We often come to this place and yet we've never seen this stone here!" They stood there for an hour, then they took up their spears and left.' So I asked him, 'O my brother 'Abdullah, when you were setting out [on the Sufi path] did you think well of stones?' 'Yes, I went forth wayfaring with [the desire] to seek, as well as with purity and righteous intention. I saw some stones that seemed to me to be friends of God, which were concealing themselves from me in the guise of stones. I wept and kissed them, and I sought the help of God—may He be praised and exalted—through them.' 'God has blessed you for your good thoughts regarding them,' I told him, 'for He made you a stone so as to save you, and this confirms the outer meaning of the *hadith*: *If one of you should think well of a stone, God will bless you through it.*'"

[Al-Mughawir] related to me, "I was once in Egypt, when I received a command from God—may He be praised—saying, 'Go to Mecca!' in order that I might obtain there a certain knowledge that would come to me the moment I entered [the hallowed precinct]. So I set out wrapped in a robe tied at my chest, with a ewer in my hand and clogs on my feet—this was not during the months of pilgrimage. I journeyed up hill and down dale by myself, night and day, until I reached Mecca. I entered the hallowed precinct through the Bani Shayba Gate, and the knowledge for which I had journeyed came to me—I accepted it completely and left forthwith through the Gate of Abraham and returned to the wilderness and thence back to Egypt in the same manner as I had left."

He stayed for nearly twelve years in the *ribat* of Shaykh Abu'l-Hasan [Ibn al-Sabbagh], in Qena, in [a state of] consummate uprightness, undertaking acts of devotion. I heard only remembrance of God from his tongue outwardly, for he was overcome by his presence with God and his continuous [state of] spiritual ecstasy (*wajd*).[36] And whoever beheld him remembered God. And whenever his close companions in poverty, to wit, his brethren, gathered around him, they would engage in remembrance of God, each according to his state, and if anyone passed to a [degree] of *dhikr* that was beyond his state, Shaykh al-Mughawir would say to him, "Return to the presence [appropriate to your state]! Where do you think you're going?" If ever anyone mentioned a fault to another or one of the shortcomings of existence before [al-Mughawir], he would say, "Render it beautiful, my friend; render it beautiful!" For he beheld only the beauty [of God].

One day, he was sitting in his *zawiya* when a young reciter [of poetry] passed by the door. [Al-Mughawir] was experiencing a state of ecstasy and said to [the youth], "Halt and recite!" The youth, who was one of the kitchen servants, responded, "I'm busy," and continued on his way. Forthwith he lost his voice, and his throat began to feel hoarse, so that if he wished to speak, he was unable to do so. [The youth] then went to the house of Shaykh Abu'l-Hasan [Ibn al-Sabbagh] and complained to [the shaykh] of what had befallen him. The shaykh said to him, "Return to the *zawiya* of al-Mughawir, stand [before it], and recite whatever it was that he bade you recite." "O Shaykh, how can I recite when I'm in this state?" "Go!" said the shaykh. So the youth went and stood by the door of al-Mughawir's *zawiya*, determined to speak, and his tongue was loosed. Al-Mughawir then came out of the *zawiya*, and he was moved by his ecstatic state for an hour; then he grew calm.[37]

The Jihad of Speaking a Just Word to a Tyrant

In al-Sirr al-Masun, *al-Sadafi relates the following story of how al-Mughawir once admonished a local governor:* Some of the Sufis said: "In one of the regions of al-Andalus there was a wayfaring man for whom God made what is far near and made his feet traverse the wildernesses swiftly. He is known as al-Mughawir and is alive to this day, renowned in every land and locale. He would divide his year between the Hajj and jihad and would go forth from his home at the beginning of the year for these two endeavors and return to [his home] at the end of [the year], and he carried out both [religious duties]. [It is said] that he went forth one year for this purpose and when he returned, he found that one of the [local] emirs had taken up residence in a house belonging to him and forcibly appropriated his property. When he came to the door of his house, he found horses, and slaves, and something he was not familiar with. 'Who's in this house?' he asked. 'One of the emirs.' He entered [the house], taking the emir by surprise and still clad in his tattered wayfarer's clothes and with the traces of the road on him. The emir looked at him and decided that he was no one of any consequence and [began reproaching him], saying, 'Woe unto you! Who might you be, and what brought you [here]?' 'And who might *you* be, and what brought *you* [here]?' answered [al-Mughawir]. The emir then said to those around him, 'Throw him out!' 'Who's going to expel me from *my* house?' said [al-Mughawir]. 'I make my allegation [regarding my property] against you to God's Messenger—may God bless him and grant him salvation.' [Having spoken these words,] he left the house and went to stay at the home of a friend [while] he prepared for jihad and the journey [that this would entail]. When it was night, he heard a knock on the door, so he looked out, and there [stood] many servants with a light, summoning him, and he complied. They said, 'The emir says, "Come at once so that I may speak with you".' So [al-Mughawir] went with them and came to the house, [where] he was brought before the emir and there found him crying out for help in a section of the house and weeping copious tears. 'The house is yours,' said [the emir]. 'Take it, and may God bless you in it. Give me leave to move out of it.' So [al-Mughawir] did so, and the emir packed up, and he and his folk departed, and he surrendered the house to [al-Mughawir] and it became his property again."[38]

Ibn ʿArabi's Description of al-Mughawir

It is said that al-Mughawir was among those who weep as a result of having witnessed God's self-disclosure (tajalli). *In this regard, Ibn ʿArabi related,* "As for those who weep, I have never seen any save one—the renowned Yusuf al-Mughawir in the year 586 (1190) in Seville. He accompanied us and manifested his states to us, [showing] great sadness, and his tears never subsided."[39]

Shaykh ʿUmar al-Tanji

The only source for the life of shaykh ʿUmar of Tangier (d. sixth/twelfth or seventh/thirteenth century) is al-Badisi's hagiography, *al-Maqsad al-sharif*, from the early fourteenth century. *Al-Maqsad al-sharif* describes ʿUmar al-Tanji as a friend of God who was both mild-mannered and possessed of discernment; it also extols the redemptive power attributed to the shaykh's supplicatory prayer and relates that he devoted himself to teaching the Qurʾan. He exemplified *waraʿ* and was known for his assiduity in praying and fasting, as well as for speaking little.[40]

The Military Jihad of Shaykh ʿUmar al-Tanji in al-Maqsad al-sharif

As regards ʿUmar al-Tanji's military endeavors, al-Badisi related that he said, "I set out for al-Andalus as a *ghazi* and went forth with a raiding party. A great host took us by surprise and took the majority of the raiding party captive. Some of [the *ghazi*s], however, concealed themselves, and I was among those who hid in a stationary war skiff—my legs were sticking out from [the skiff]—so I could do nothing but [wait] to be captured. The horses of the [enemy] passed by me, yet no one saw me. A troop halted near me, and they had hounds, which they loosed to search for [me]. The hounds approached until they were licking my feet—then they went away from me. God—exalted—concealed me, while I was reciting Surat Ya Sin [Qurʾan 36:9: *And We have placed an obstruction before them and an obstruction behind them, and we have placed a covering over them so that they see not*]. When night fell, I left and began walking, and God—exalted—concealed me until I reached the land of the Muslims."[41]

ʿAli ibn ʿUthman al-Shawi

Several North African hagiographies relate anecdotes about Abu'l-Hasan ʿAli ibn ʿUthman al-Shawi (d. 940/1534). Although the anecdotes are few, they describe him as a renowned friend of God and attribute both inner knowledge and manifold wonders to him.[42] The sources also portray him as a fearless *mujahid* and relate that he died a martyr in the Battle of Humar, near Asila.[43] The following anecdotes of his life are from Ibn ʿAskar's *Dawhat al-nashir*, with the exception of the final anecdote, which is from al-Hudaygi's *Tabaqat*.

'Ali ibn 'Uthman al-Shawi in Dawhat al-nashir *and* Tabaqat al-Hudaygi

Ibn 'Askar related that *"*'Ali b. 'Uthman al-Shawi was a client of the [Berber tribe of] Bani Yarutan. He—may God have mercy on him—was one of God's friends, and miracles and wonders arose from him, and he learned [the Sufi path] from Shaykh Abu Muhammad 'Abdullah al-Ghazwani—may God benefit him. Shaykh [al-Ghazwani] would call [al-Shawi] 'sun of the forenoon.' He possessed a most wondrous voice, such that when he would recite the Qur'an or mention God's name no one could refrain from listening to him. He died a martyr—may God be pleased with him—in the Battle of Hudmar [*sic*], which took place during the forties between the Christians and the general 'Abd al-Wahid b. Talha al-'Arusi near [the town of] Asila. More than one of those who were present at the battle and who are to be trusted and who testified to the truthfulness of one another's words, told me that, 'When [the Muslims] attacked, Shaykh Abu'l-Hasan [al-Shawi] strode toward the Christians with his sword in hand, all the while reciting the *burda* of the imam al-Busiri[44]—and that was the last anyone knew of him. When [the Muslims] returned the following day to bear their slain [from the battlefield], there remained no trace of [al-Shawi], though they found a fragment of his cloak among the Christians, which bore the mark of a stab wound in the breast.'"[45]

As for the fate of al-Shawi's body, Shaykh 'Abd al-Rahman Muhammad al-Fasi related that "He died a martyr, and [thus his body] was raised aloft [to heaven]."[46]

Muhammad ibn Yahya al-Bahluli

The hagiographical sources describe Muhammad ibn Yahya al-Bahluli (d. 943/1536/7) as a Sufi, man of letters, legist, and *mujahid* who lived in what is now northern Morocco during the period of the Wattasid dynasty.[47] Muhammad al-Bahluli followed the *Sunna* scrupulously, and he is said to have advised the Wattasid sultans in their jihad against the Christians of Spain and Portugal who threatened the Abode of Islam in North Africa. He was also renowned for his zeal in waging jihad himself, as well as for the splendid poetry that he composed, which included poems urging his fellow Muslims to undertake jihad against the Christian invaders. The life of al-Bahluli presented hereunder is from Ibn 'Askar's *Dawhat al-nashir*, with the exception of the two lines of poetry quoted in the narrative, which are based on the version found in al-Tazi's *Jami' al-Qarawiyyin*.

al-Bahluli in Dawhat al-nashir

Among them [i.e., the friends of God] was the upright man, the Sufi and *mujahid* Abu 'Abdullah Muhammad b. Yahya al-Bahluli; this shaykh was among those who pursued the duty of jihad incessantly, and he was granted success in [this endeavor]. He [composed] venerable odes and poems, and so on, concerning [jihad]. He was a contemporary of Sultan Abu 'Abdullah Muhammad b. al-Shaykh al-Wattasi (d. 932/1526) known as "al-Burtughali."[48] Whenever [al-Bahluli] would come to the sultan, he would encourage him [to undertake] military campaigns and would help him in whatever way he wished in that [endeavor]. When the aforementioned sultan died, his son Sultan [Abu'l-'Abbas] Ahmad (d. 956/1549) became the ruler, and he was obstructed by the nobles from the region of Sus,[49] who revolted against him. He made peace with the neighboring Christians in the northern coastal lowlands and their sultan [the king] of Portugal.[50] [News of the truce] reached [Shaykh al-Bahluli], and he promised himself that he would not receive the aforementioned sultan nor would he go to him, nor would he accept from him what his father [Abu 'Abdullah Muhammad] had designated for him of the *jizya*, [which] the *Dhimmis*[51] in Fez [had to pay], to provide for the shaykh's sustenance. Shaykh al-Bahluli abided by [his promise] until death came to him. When he was in the throes of death, and his companions were gathered around him, one of them said to him, "O Sidi! I must inform you that the sultan has ordered a military expedition [against the unbelievers] and he has followed through with [this endeavor], and the people have borne this out, and the Muslims are strongly [supportive], and thus [the matter] proceeds." The shaykh opened his eyes, and his face beamed with joy and happiness. He praised and magnified God, then he gave up the ghost, glad of [the tidings].

Shaykh al-Bahluli [composed] many splendid *zajal*s and short poems that urged jihad, among which [are the following lines]:[52]

> Set out on jihad—may God watch over thee—following the path of right guidance to the nations, if they but understood.
> On account of al-Andalus I remain furious. Were it possible, I would gird my loins [for battle] at night.

Among other things worth mentioning, the honorable jurist Abu'l-'Abbas Ahmad al-Daghuri al-Qasri related to me that "Shaykh Abu 'Abdullah [al-Bahluli] used to say, 'We have never undertaken a military campaign but that I beheld the Prophet there—peace be upon him—and he would inform me of what would happen to me and my companions in that campaign.'"

A spirited story regarding his character: Once, [al-Bahluli] had left with his companions to wage war [with the unbelievers] in northern Morocco, when he found out that his wife, the daughter of the shaykh and friend of God Abu Zakaria b. Yahya b. Bakkar, had passed away. The townsfolk and their imam, Shaykh Ghazi b. al-shaykh Abi 'Abdullah Muhammad b. Ghazi, prayed for her in the Qayrawiyyin Mosque [of Fez]. Shaykh [al-Bahluli] arrived at the graveside during her funeral, and the townsfolk wished to bury her. [Shaykh al-Bahluli said, "Don't be in such a hurry!" He drew near [to the grave] and then he and his companions prayed for his wife a second time. The townsfolk came up to him and censured him for having performed the funeral prayer a second time with the group. [Shaykh al-Bahluli] replied to them offhandedly, "Your first prayer for her was in vain, [for you performed it] without an imam." "How could that be, O Sidi?" He then said [to them], "Being a man is one of the requisite conditions for being an imam, and that is lacking in your friend, for whoever has never girded himself with a sword to fight in God's path and has not wielded it, and thus has not known war the way our Prophet—upon whom be peace—did, and thus may not be described [as possessing any of the characteristics embodied] by the Prophet's conduct, cannot therefore be considered a male imam. Indeed, by God, your imam [must be reckoned] among the women!" He died—may God have mercy upon him—[in A.H. 943]—and God knows best—in Fez—may God have mercy upon him.[53]

Muhammad al-'Ayyashi

The hagiographical tradition of North Africa relates many anecdotes about the friend of God Muhammad b. Ahmad al-'Ayyashi (d. 1051/1641). Though little is known concerning his birth and childhood, Muhammad al-'Ayyashi is said to have spent his youth in the town of Salé, near Rabat.[54] The hagiographical sources describe him as a respected religious scholar, a godly *mujahid,* and a renowned horseman.[55] Much is made of Muhammad al-'Ayyashi's role in the military jihad, and in this regard the hagiographical sources describe him as the chief *murabit* of his era,[56] who devoted himself to waging jihad on the frontier with the Christians.[57] In addition to the hagiographical depiction of Muhammad al-'Ayyashi as a friend of God, the historical sources recount several of his military exploits. The most notable of these was the successful attack that he led on the Spanish fleet at al-Ma'mura, on the northwestern coast of Morocco. After defeating the Spanish fleet, he fortified the town of Salé and was then able to extend his control as head of a confederation of the local tribes thence all the way to Taza.[58]

The primary sources for the life of Muhammad al-'Ayyashi as presented hereunder are al-Ifrani's *Nuzhat al-hadi bi-akhbar muluk al-qarn al-hadi* and al-Hudaygi's *Tabaqat al-Hudaygi.* Other sources include: al-Qadiri's *Nashr al-mathani li-ahl al-qarn al-hadi 'ashar wa'l-thani;* al-Ifrani's *Safwat man intashara min akhbar sulaha' al-qarn al-hadi 'ashar;* and Abu Salim 'Abdullah b. Muhammad al-'Ayyashi's *al-Rihla al-'Ayyashiyya.*

Muhammad al-'Ayyashi's Introduction to the Sufi Path and Jihad

He became acquainted with the godly friend of God and great shaykh Sidi 'Abdullah ibn Hassun (d. 1013/1604), from whom he learned the Sufi way. He cleaved to [Ibn Hassun] and served him, and he was among [the shaykh's] most favored companions, such that one day, [when] some of the local tribal elders brought a horse to [Ibn Hassun], the shaykh said, "Saddle it and make it ready [for a journey]." When the horse was ready, [the shaykh] said, "Where's Muhammad al-'Ayyashi?" "Here I am, Master!" said [al-'Ayyashi]. [The shaykh] said [to him], "Mount, by the power of God, for your horse is your [destiny either in] this world or the next." [Muhammad al-'Ayyashi] drew back and hesitated out of shyness and deference, but the shaykh insisted [that he mount] and grasped the steed with his blessed hand, saying, "Ride to Azammur and alight among the sons of Bu 'Aziz and prepare for jihad! There is no doubt that you will return to the town"—meaning

Salé—"and have great renown." The shaykh then placed his hand on [al-'Ayyashi's] head and, weeping, commended him to God and bade him farewell. Then [al-'Ayyashi] rode [to Azammur] and alighted where [his shaykh] had instructed him.[59]

Muhammad al-'Ayyashi and the Military Jihad

[Muhammad al-'Ayyashi] did not cease striving and waging war against the unbelievers, and thus his fame spread.[60] Whenever Sidi Muhammad [al-'Ayyashi] would send spoils and prisoners from the victories God granted him to Marrakesh, his fame increased, and the people would discuss and spread news of [his deeds]. For this reason, the heart of the sultan[61] was bitter, and his anger toward [al-'Ayyashi] grew, and thus he sent his general Muhammad al-Sanusi with four hundred horsemen to seize and kill him. But God—exalted—caused the general [to feel] in his heart compassion toward [al-'Ayyashi] when he learned that [al-'Ayyashi] was innocent of what he was accused of, and therefore he sent him [a message] in secret, [saying,] "Save yourself, for you are betrayed!" So [al-'Ayyashi] left with forty horsemen and foot soldiers, making for Salé. When al-Sanusi reached Azammur, he found no trace of [al-'Ayyashi], and he made a show of taking great pains to search for him and punished a party of those charged with searching for [al-'Ayyashi] for [having allowed him] to escape.[62]

For that reason, [al-'Ayyashi]—may God be pleased with him—went away to Salé, where he found the townsfolk in distress, for the Christians of [al-Ma'mura] harassed them. So [al-'Ayyashi] came to the aid of Islam, elevated God's word, and ordered the extinguishing of the fires of unbelief and the annihilation of [the unbelievers]. He launched incessant attacks against [the Christians] until he weakened them, and their forces fled in the border regions of Larache and al-Burayja and the surrounding areas.[63]

The [news] reached him—may God be pleased with him—from a student of jurisprudence that jihad was not permissible unless the Commander of the Faithful ordered it. So [al-'Ayyashi] asked the jurists of Fez [their opinion in this matter]. The jurists—al-Imam Sidi 'Abd al-Wahid b. 'Ashir, Sidi al-'Arabi al-Fasi, Sidi Ibrahim al-Hilali, among others—wrote to him, [saying,] "[The religious duty of] fighting the unbelievers does not depend on the existence of the sultan—or any other ruler—[for in this case,] the Muslim community takes the ruler's place."

The sultan asked Muhammad al-'Ayyashi to end [his jihad], but [the shaykh] refused, and instead gathered together all the tribal chieftains encompassing the area from Marrakesh to Taza. So [al-'Ayyashi] made a pact with the chieftains that [thenceforth] they would always appoint him [to lead any jihad] when necessary.[64]

[Muhammad al-'Ayyashi]—may God be pleased with him—was very zealous on behalf of Islam, and when he settled in Salé, some of [the townsfolk] who held a grudge against him made a pact with the Christians to be in league with them against him and the Muslims. So [al-'Ayyashi] sent [an inquiry] to the religious scholars of Fez [asking whether it was permissible] to kill them. [He also discovered that these same townsfolk] were [providing food to] the Christians by [secretly] delivering the harvest to them by night. He rebuked them, and they rebelled. The religious scholars issued a *fatwa* [in which they ruled that it was, indeed, permissible] to kill any [Muslim] who behaved in this manner. So [al-'Ayyashi]—may God be pleased with him—continued fighting (*mujahidan*) and guarding the borders, defending the lands of Islam, until a group of men from Khalat betrayed him and slew him in a place called 'Ayn al-Qasab on the ninth of Muharram in the year 1051 (April 20, 1641).[65]

Among the wonders [vouchsafed al-'Ayyashi]—may God be pleased with him— it is related that he went forth to carry out a raid on al-Burayja in the year 1049 (1639/40). He found the Wadi of Boulaouane[66] so full to the point [of overflowing] that no one could ford it, while he was hoping to attack the unbelievers unawares. He feared that if he tarried, the nobles would inform [the unbelievers], so he leaped into the wadi, saying, "In the name of God," and his companions followed after him. The water did not reach the stirrups of their horses—and the people were amazed by this great wonder.[67]

The Death of Muhammad al-'Ayyashi

Regarding the death of his father, the son of Muhammad al-'Ayyashi—Abu Salim 'Abdullah b. Muhammad al-'Ayyashi (d. 1090/1679)—related a wondrous encounter: "There was a [Maghribi] man from al-Qasr, in Blessed Medina, during the year in which the upright friend of God and *mujahid* Sidi Muhammad b. Ahmad al-'Ayyashi died. He came to me one day and said, 'I saw my sister in a dream, and I beheld a man seated on the ground with his hand cut off, and the blood was flowing. So I asked [the injured man], "who are you?" and he replied, "I am Islam. They cut off my hand in Salé'." I said to him, 'It seems to me from your dream that the godly man and *mujahid*, who was in Salé, must have been killed.' Later at the end of the year, the pilgrims from the Maghrib [coming for the Hajj] brought us tidings of the death of [Muhammad al-'Ayyashi]—may God be pleased with him."[68]

Chapter 5

SUFI *MUJAHID*S OF THE INDIAN SUBCONTINENT: THE ELEVENTH THROUGH SEVENTEENTH CENTURIES

Islam first arrived in the Indian subcontinent during the Umayyad period when Muhammad ibn Qasim (d. 95/715), at the head of an Arab Muslim army, conquered Sindh, in 712.[1] Muhammad ibn Qasim is traditionally portrayed as a just conqueror, who at least in some cases dealt equitably with the Hindu and Buddhist population that did not convert to Islam, declaring them *mushabih Ahl al-Kitab*[2] and allowing them to worship and maintain their temples, provided they paid the *jizya*.[3] The later sultans of Delhi also generally followed this policy of treating Hindus as *Ahl al-Kitab*.[4] Nevertheless, throughout the premodern period of Muslim rule in India there were those among the religious scholars who advocated harsher treatment of Hindus—including the renowned theologian, reformer, and Naqshbandi Sufi Ahmad Sirhindi (d. 1034/1624), who lived during the Mughal period.[5] In reality, however, such a policy would have been impractical, given that the great majority of India's inhabitants never converted to Islam.

The question how Islam spread throughout the Indian subcontinent has long intrigued historians, and many have assumed that the sword was the primary agent of conversion. Scholarship of the last two decades has shown, however, that conversion to Islam was a much more complicated process, involving political, cultural, and economic factors.[6] This is not to say, of course, that the succession of Muslim conquerors who arrived in the Indian subcontinent were all as broad-minded as Muhammad ibn Qasim—for example, Mahmud of Ghazna's conquest of Somnath was by all accounts bloody and undertaken primarily for spoils.[7] In any event, although the arrival of Islam in the subcontinent was by and large the result of military conquest, it does not necessarily follow that the subjugated indigenous population who converted to the new faith did so owing to coercion.

As for the advent and development of Sufism in the Indian subcontinent, this is far too vast a subject to cover adequately in a brief chapter introduction; therefore, what follows must be understood as an attempt to highlight only those aspects of Indian Sufism essential to our topic of Sufi *mujahid*s in hagiography.

It appears likely that Sufism first arrived in India around 1200 with the invading Turkic Muslim armies, and—at least according to traditional sources—many of the first Sufis came to India as warriors.[8] The tombs of these early Sufi warriors are found throughout the subcontinent and remain the loci of a continuing tradition of religious and devotional activity for many Muslims.[9] As with the other Sufi hagiographical traditions we have considered, the legends and anecdotes that developed around these early Sufi warriors embody paradigms of piety and the ideals of the selfless *mujahid*, as well as the wondrous characteristics of God's friends. The historicity of many of these accounts, however, is difficult to prove, as hagiographies were often composed decades, if not centuries, after their subjects lived.[10] In this regard, it is worth noting that the majority of the sources used in the composition of the lives of God's friends in this chapter date from the Mughal period (1526–1858), though there are several exceptions, a fact that must be borne in mind when reading the lives of Abu Muhammad Chishti (d. 410/1020) and Shah Jalal al-Din Mujarrad (d. 746/1346).

Notwithstanding the legendary nature of many Sufi-warrior narratives in Indo-Muslim culture, Sufis did play a significant role in the conversion of Hindus to Islam, especially in the centuries that preceded the Mughal period, though this was generally accomplished through various forms of proselytizing rather than by the sword.[11] The social role of Sufis was undoubtedly their most important contribution to Indo-Muslim culture over the centuries following the initial conquests. This included their role as mediators of Islam to non-Muslims through folk literature and *'urs* festivals at Sufi tombs.[12] Sufis also fulfilled the social role of reformists for the Muslim population; for example, Sufis dwelling in urban centers where Muslims were concentrated often played a significant part in upholding fundamental Sunni Islamic practice based on the *shari'a* and the Five Pillars.[13]

Unlike what transpired in Western and Central Asia, which saw the emergence of the first Sufis in the pre-*tariqa* phase of Sufism, in India Sufism unfolded entirely in the context of the Sufi orders during the thirteenth and fourteenth centuries.[14] The majority of the Sufis who founded orders in India were originally from Western and Central Asia. The two Sufi orders explicitly mentioned in connection with the friends of God who appear in this chapter are the Chishtis and the Naqshbandis.

The Chishti order developed as exclusively Indian, though its founder, Mu'in al-Din Chishti (d. 627/1236), was originally from Central Asia, where he had studied before arriving in Lahore and then finally settling in Ajmer.[15] The Chishti order dominated spiritual life in Muslim India during the pre-Mughal period,[16] and the success of the order was due in part to its ability to adapt to the Indian religious environment and incorporate aspects of practice that were familiar to Hindus, Buddhists, and Jains.[17]

Although the Naqshbandi order, which arose in Central Asia, arrived in the subcontinent considerably later than the other orders, it would play a significant role in Indian religious and political matters during the seventeenth and eighteenth centuries.[18] As we have mentioned, Sufi orders often differed from one another with regard to doctrine and practice, as well as in their willingness—or unwillingness, as the case might be—to have dealings with temporal rulers, and this was also true in India. Sufis of the Naqshbandi order, for example, were often involved in the affairs of temporal rulers and carried on a tradition of taking an active role in political and military matters in order to uphold orthodox Sunni Islamic practice and secure the well-being of the Muslim polity.[19] The life of Baba Palang Push, with which this chapter closes, exemplifies the willingness of the Naqshbandis to take part in religiously sanctioned military campaigns.

Sufi hagiography also has a long history in the subcontinent; indeed, the eleventh-century Sufi 'Ali Hujviri of Ghazna (popularly known in the subcontinent as Data Ganj Bakhsh), author of *Kashf al-majub*, which, as we have mentioned, was the earliest well-known Sufi treatise composed in the Persian language, is buried in Lahore, where his tomb continues to be an important place of pilgrimage. Hujviri's treatise, though not a hagiography, does incorporate many hagiographical anecdotes, and it exerted a significant influence on the Persian hagiographical tradition as it unfolded during the centuries that followed.

Here we ought to pause briefly to note the importance of the Persian language in Indian Islam before considering the Indian Sufi hagiographical tradition. Persian first came to the subcontinent with the Ghaznavid Muslim conquerors, in the eleventh century. Although the Ghaznavids were of Turkic origin, they had adopted the Persian language and court culture of their predecessors the Samanids (whom they had served as slave soldiers) when they seized power and established the capital of their new dynasty in Ghazna. The Ghaznavid Sultan Mahmud, the early conqueror of northern India whom we mentioned above, was a great patron of the Persian language, which by the eleventh century had become the vehicle of Islamic culture throughout the Eastern Islamic world. Under the Ghaznavids (eleventh and twelfth centuries), their successors the Ghurids (1192–1206), and the subsequent Turkic Muslim dynasties of the Ilbaris (1206–90), the Khaljis (1290–1320), and the Tughluqs (1320–1413), Persian was established as the language of the court, as well as of literature and poetry in Muslim India. For this reason, the majority of Indo-Muslim Sufi hagiographies are composed in Persian.

Important examples of Indo-Persian Sufi hagiographies include *Siyar al-awliya'* (fourteenth century), *Siyar al-'arifin* (early sixteenth century), *Gulzar-i abrar* (seventeenth century), *Khwajagan-i Chisht* (seventeenth century), and *Akhbar al-akhyar* (seventeenth century).[20] Another important genre of Indo-Sufi literature that is relevant to any discussion of hagiography in the subcontinent is the *malfuzat*, the conversations and pronouncements of a given Sufi friend of God as recorded by his followers. The earliest and best-known example of *malfuzat*, *Fawa'id al-fu'ad*, contains the conversations of the Chishti friend of God Nizam al-Din Awliya' (d. 725/1325), which the poet Amir Hasan (d. 725/1337) composed with editorial input from Nizam al-Din.[21] Another significant example of the *malfuzat* genre is *Lata'if-i Ashrafi* (fourteenth century), which collects the conversations of Shaykh Sayyid Ashraf Jahangir Simnani (d. 808/1386). All the above-mentioned hagiographies and *malfuzat* have served as sources for the stories of God's friends related in this chapter.

With regard to hagiographical depictions of Sufis as warriors in the subcontinent, it is likely that some are more or less accurate, or at least accurately portray a certain ethos of Sufi jihad. Others, however, are more complicated and ought not to be taken at face value. In particular, we would do well to remember the symbolic function of hagiographical portrayals of Sufi friends of God as warriors. As an example of the former (i.e., the quasi-historical depictions of Sufi warriors), we may cautiously accept the anecdotes regarding Baba Palang Pūsh as reflecting the historical reality of Sufi shaykhs accompanying Muslim armies as spiritual guides and urging them on in their battles against unbelievers. As an example of the latter (i.e., the symbolic Sufi warrior anecdotes), we must understand the narrative of the conquest of Sylhet, in Bengal, by Shah Jalal as symbolizing the break between the region's "Hindu past and its Muslim future."[22] We may likewise view the anecdotes regarding Abu Muhammad Chishti's military and wondrous deeds during Sultan Mahmud's raid on the temple of Somnath, in Gujarat, as symbolizing the role of Sufis in spreading Islam in the subcontinent while also serving to portray the Chishti Sufi order as a fundamental part of Indian Islam. Another example of hagiography symbolizing historical events or circumstances may be found in an anecdote concerning Mu'in al-Din Chishti, the aforementioned founder of the Chishti order. The anecdote relates that when Mu'in al-Din settled in Rana Sagar, there were still many Hindu temples (*but khana*) in the area, and when he saw them, he foretold that with the help of the Prophet they would soon be destroyed. After Mu'in al-Din took up residence there, every day his servants would slaughter a cow and eat the flesh thereof. When the unbelievers found out about this, they became wroth and, burning with anger, decided that this was as good a time as any to attack the Muslims and drive them out. With this in mind, they took up swords, cudgels, and slings and went to the place where Mu'in al-Din was. There they surrounded him with the intention of harming him. Now, Mu'in al-Din was praying and did not heed the unbelievers' presence. His servants, however, became alarmed and informed the shaykh of the dire situation. Having completed his prayers, Mu'in al-Din rose, took a handful of earth in his hand, and, reciting the Verse of the Throne,[23] cast it at the armed unbeliever mob. The body of anyone whom the dust touched immediately withered, and the remaining unbelievers were vanquished.[24]

This anecdote is found in *Khwajagan-i Chisht: Siyar al-aqtab*, a hagiography of the Sabiri branch of the Chishti order, which Shaykh Allahdia Chishti (d. mid-eleventh/mid-seventeenth century) composed during the reign of Shah Jahan (1627–58). That era saw a Hindu revival, with Rajputs in the Mughal army and Hindu officials in the Mughal secretariat.[25] Moreover, the controversial reign of Akbar, which ended in 1605, had been one of religious tolerance for all Indians under Mughal rule, including religious and administrative innovations that many Muslims found objectionable. (For example, Ahmad Sirhindi, whom we mentioned above, was inspired to admonish Mughal officials largely on account of these innovations.) It is therefore possible that Allahdia Chishti's depiction of Mu'in al-Din's confrontation with the Hindus reflects the contemporary concerns of Muslims regarding Hindu power while also underscoring the friend of God's *wilaya*.

The hagiographical accounts of Abu Muhammad Chishti, Shah Jalal al-Din Mujarrad, Sayyid Muluk Shah, and Baba Palang Pūsh embody Muslim piety and in some cases symbolize the arrival of Islam in the subcontinent while upholding the ideal of Islam's early *mujahid* ethos. These stories of Indo-Muslim friends of

God differ considerably from one another in certain aspects—for example, the "miracle mongering" in the life of Abu Muhammad Chishti as compared with the more sober depictions of Shah Jalal al-Din and Baba Palang Pūsh. Notwithstanding such differences, all four hagiographical narratives share basic similarities with one another, as well as with the other hagiographical accounts that we have read in *Sufi Warrior Saints*, while shedding light on some historical and social aspects of Islam's unique history in the Indian subcontinent.

Abu Muhammad Chishti

Abu Muhammad (d. 411/1020) was from the town of Chisht, near Herat in modern-day Afghanistan, and is traditionally considered one of the spiritual forebears of the Chishti Sufi order. The hagiographical sources portray him as exemplifying *mujahada* and supererogatory piety as well as detachment from worldly concerns. The Sufi hagiographical tradition relates that Abu Muhammad led a band of Sufi *ghazis* in Sultan Mahmud of Ghazna's raid on the Hindu stronghold of Somnath.[26] During the ensuing battle, it is said that the shaykh saved the Muslim host from defeat by means of his *wilaya*.

The primary source for Abu Muhammad's life as related hereunder is the seventeenth-century Indo-Persian hagiography *Khwajagan-i Chisht*.

Abu Muhammad Chishti in Khwajagan-i Chisht

That mine of fidelity, that friend of the *qibla* of *walaya*, that bright *ka'ba* of guidance, that jewel of the mine of truth and rightness, Hazrat Nasih al-Din Shaykh Abu Muhammad Chishti—may God hallow his dear secret—who was worthy in all actions and adorned with sundry wonders and qualities, was a friend of God from birth, and possessed of great authority and high rank. His *laqab* is Nasih al-Din. He lived seventy years, and he received the *khirqa* from his father, the Axis of the God-fearing, Hazrat Qidwat al-Din Shaykh Abu Muhammad Chishti—may God hallow his dear secret. On whomever his glance fell, the same would forthwith become a consummate friend of God.

The righteous mother of that venerable [friend of God] related that "When Shaykh Abu Muhammad was but four months in my womb, I heard the sound of felicitous speech [uttering] 'There is no God, save God, and Muhammad is the messenger of God.' I informed his father [of this], and he said, 'May this be good tidings to me and you, for a blessed child and friend of God will come into existence from your womb.'"

One day, his illustrious father was sitting near [Abu Muhammad's] mother, when he turned to her and addressed her belly, saying, "Peace be upon you, O friend of God and my successor!" A voice came from her womb that no one understood. The righteous mother said to her husband, "It is not yet known whether the child will be a boy or a girl, and yet you speak in this manner." [Her husband] replied, "God—may His might be glorified—has indicated the good tidings and made a promise to me. I have also read on the Preserved Tablet that a son would be born to me and that he would be a friend of God from birth."[27]

It is related that the night of [Abu Muhammad's] birth was the night of 'Ashura,[28] and at that same moment his father beheld [the Prophet] Muhammad—upon whom be peace and upon his kin and Companions—in a dream. [The Prophet] said, "You are blessed, Abu Ahmad, for in your house a son has been born. You must give him my name and greet him [on my behalf]." When Abu Ahmad awoke, he saw the boy had been born. They had scarcely placed Hazrat Shaykh Muhammad in the [bath] water, when the seven felicitous words "There is no God, save God, and Muhammad is the messenger of God"[29] left his mouth. His illustrious father performed the ritual ablutions again and spoke [the traditional Muslim greeting] "Peace be upon thee!" The boy returned [the greeting], saying, "Peace be upon thee, our shaykh! Tell me what your dream was this evening."[30] [Abu Ahmad] whispered in his son's ear that, "[The Prophet]—upon whom be peace—has sent his greetings to you." The boy prostrated himself in prayer, and [his father] Shaykh Abu Ahmad likewise prostrated himself on his prayer rug, calling out to God, "Make this boy Thy friend!" An unseen voice responded, "I have answered your prayer, Abu Ahmad, and I have accepted your boy as My own."

It is related that the night he was born was 'Ashura, and when the day was done, he had not drunk any milk, so his mother told his father, who explained, "Your son is a friend of God from birth; thus, he follows the [way of] the prophets and friends of God and therefore keeps the 'Ashura fast." And thus, when [the new day began] at dinner time, he drank [his mother's] milk. One day, his honorable mother was giving him milk, when—as he was drinking the milk—he began to laugh exceedingly. His mother was greatly surprised and informed his father, who explained, "Satan had come to make your son cry, so God—exalted, may His might be glorified—bade the angels drive him away and hinder him [from his intention]. When that Accursed One found that he had no power over [our son] and became dejected, [our son] was overcome with laughter."

[Abu Muhammad's] mother related, "From the time Abu Muhammad was born till he was two and a half, he would turn his eyes toward heaven whenever it was time for one of the five daily prayers and say, 'There is no god, save God' countless times. Each time, a heavenly light would illuminate the boy's blessed countenance, and the entire house shone therewith, and sometimes, when there was no lamp, the house was lit from his forehead, such that, if a needle were lost, it could be found easily by the light [emanating from] his forehead."

It is said that when he was two and a half, he began to eat little, so his mother complained about it to his father. Abu Ahmad explained, "[Our son] is a dervish, and eating very little is the perfection of the dervishes; thus, they make a habit of eating little from the outset." It is also said that when Abu Muhammad was four years and four months of age, they took him to school. All at once, the following words appeared on his slate from the unseen: *In the name of God, the compassionate, the merciful; teach me the Qur'an, Lord. Make it easy, not hard, and increase my knowledge and understanding, Lord, and cause it to turn out well.* Thus, in a short time, he had read the Qur'an and learned the religious sciences and attained the perfection of men. So at age four, he began leading the Friday prayer, and at age seven, he went into seclusion (*khalvat*).

During that time, whatever he uttered with his blessed tongue, it would be so, and the caliph of the time, as well as all the people, came to rely completely on [Abu Muhammad]. Anyone who hastened to him with a wish would find his desire achieved. For thirty years, his ritual purity was unbroken, save [when visiting] the privy. Any unbeliever who came into his presence became a Muslim forthwith, with the result that no unbelievers remained in Chisht. Any Muslim who came before him would experience a complete spiritual unveiling. When he was twenty-four years old, his illustrious father left on a journey, and [Abu Muhammad] became his viceregent. He sat upon the prayer rug, and the majority of sultans from near and far, as well as famous men, came to him in willing friendship.

It is related that he would mostly perform his prayers [hanging] upside down in a well, and sometimes his blessed side would not touch the earth. He would busy himself day and night with self-mortification and worship until he attained [the station] of the shaykhs of the era and God's servants for all time. When the time for his illustrious father to pass to the next world drew nigh—he was seventy years of age—[his father] made him his *murid,* bestowed the *khirqa* on him, and seated him in his stead. [His father] admonished him, [saying,] "Choose poverty and penury, associate with the poor and indigent, and shun this world and worldly folk so that you may be poor." Shaykh [Abu Muhammad] accepted all [his father's] counsel and remained twelve years [in seclusion] in his room, and after seven days, he broke his fast with a single date.[31]

It is related that one day during his childhood, on his way to school, [Abu Muhammad] met Khizr—upon whom be peace—who hailed him and said, "May this be good tidings to you, Abu Muhammad! For the Glorious Lord has bade me teach you outer as well as inner knowledge." [Abu Muhammad] kissed his feet and said, "O master, whatever is commanded, so be it." So Khizr—upon whom be peace—taught him the Great Name [of God] and revealed every kind of divine knowledge and spiritual learning to him. [Afterwards,] he returned home. His mother asked, "What did you learn today? Bring me your slate so I can see [your lessons]." [Abu Muhammad] replied, "O mother, no slate could hold what I learned." So his mother brought the Qur'an that was in the house to him, but he said, "Mother, keep the Qur'an with you, for I will recite it from memory." His mother did as he asked, and then he immediately proceeded to recite the entire Glorious Qur'an from beginning to end. His mother, astonished, gave thanks to God.

It is related that one day, the Axis of the God-fearing [Abu Muhammad's father] was listening to *samaʿ*. The *qawwali* singers were in attendance and singing poetic verses.[32] When he had reached a state of ecstasy (*tavājud*), he looked upon [his son] and said to him, "Join [me] in audition!" [The boy did so] and [fell into a deep state] of rapture and remained in [a state of] ecstasy for a long while. Then, having swooned, he fell [to the ground] and [continued] to engage in uninterrupted *samaʿ* for seven days. When it was time for prayer, he would bid the *qawwali* singers stop playing, perform the prayer, and then return to *samaʿ*. During this time, [Abu

Muhammad remained unconscious. Finally, his father commanded the *qawwali* singers to cease [playing] in order that his dear son might return to himself. So the singers were silent, and Abu Muhammad came to after a while and, opening his eyes, gazed heavenward, saying in Arabic, "Speak, speak!" Forthwith a sweet melody was heard from the unseen world, and indeed no one had ever heard the like of such lyrics. All those present listened well. [Abu] Muhammad returned to *sama'*, and all those present did likewise. They remained in a state of continual audition for three days, listening to that unseen melody. When they returned to themselves, Abu Muhammad fell at his father's feet and exclaimed, "Master, this opening of doors that occurs during *sama'* is not to be found through any other endeavor—not even were one to engage in the most trying and rigorous *riyada* and *mujahada* for one hundred years could one attain the station that results from one audition." [His father then admonished him,] saying, "The secret of *sama'* must be concealed, for it is beyond the capacity of the poor common folk. If I were to reveal its secrets, all those on earth would be afflicted [with longing for] *sama'* and would seek for no other gift from God—mighty and exalted."

It is said that [Abu Muhammad] was once sitting on the bank of the Tigris River, stitching his Sufi cloak, when the caliph's son approached him [on horseback]. The youth dismounted, kissed the ground before the shaykh, and sat down respectfully. [Abu Muhammad began to admonish him,] saying, "[The Prophet]—upon whom be peace—commanded that should an old woman go to bed hungry in a king's realm, she would seek justice from that king on the Day of Reckoning." "Since God—may He be praised and exalted—has placed the kingship in your hands, if the poor and needy are wretched, you must not ignore [their plight], lest tomorrow you regret it." When [the shaykh] had finished his admonishment, the caliph's son called for some money (from what was allocated to kings for their expenses) to be brought to him and then laid it at Abu Muhammad's [feet]. The [shaykh] smiled and said, "O Prince, as none of [God's friends] have accepted this, neither will I accept it, for the power of our poverty is better than Solomon's kingdom." The caliph's son insisted, but Abu Muhammad replied, "O Prince, God—may He be praised and exalted—has opened the door of the unseen treasury to his servants, so they have no need of your offering." The caliph's son persisted, so, in the end, Abu Muhammad turned his face heavenward and addressed God, saying, "Lord, show this [young man] the beneficence Thou showest to Thy friends!" All at once, the fish of the Tigris raised their heads above the water, and each fish held a gold dinar in its mouth. [On beholding this,] the caliph's son was overcome with wonder and fell at the shaykh's feet, where he remained for an hour. [The youth] then received [the shaykh's] leave to depart, and he left—without [Abu Muhammad's] having accepted any of his offering.[33]

It is related that when Sultan Mahmud Sabuktigin [of Ghazna] went to raid Somnath, he saw [Abu Muhammad] in the battle, as he also was coming to [the sultan's] aid. Thus, at the age of seventy, he went thither with a company of dervishes. When they arrived, the shaykh selflessly waged jihad against the idolaters. One day, the idolaters gained the upper hand, so the army of Islam sought refuge in the woods. Now, [Abu Muhammad] had a senior *murid* back in Chisht by the name of Muhammad Kaku. [Abu Muhammad] cried out, "O Kaku, [come to our aid]!" Forthwith, Kaku appeared and furiously fought [the unbelievers] until the army of Islam achieved victory. At the same time, the folk of Chisht beheld Kaku take up the mill hopper and begin beating the walls and doors of the mill therewith. When the townsfolk asked him the meaning of [his astonishing deed with the mill hopper], he related this story to them.³⁴ After the conquest of Somnath, Sultan Mahmud, having seen with his own eyes that Abu Muhammad had rendered him aid both inwardly and outwardly, believed more than ever [in the shaykh's power] and prostrated himself before the shaykh as soon as he arrived.³⁵

Shah Jalal al-Din al-Mujarrad

The lesser jihad and the greater jihad were his destiny

Shah Jalal of Sylhet (d. 746/1346) is the most renowned friend of God in present-day Bangladesh,³⁶ where he is popularly associated with the spread of Islam in the region.³⁷ Many wonders and glorious deeds are attributed to him, and it is traditionally believed that he was blessed with an inordinately long life. It is said that Shah Jalal died at the age of one hundred and fifty, that he had seen the Abbasid caliph al-Musta'sim bi-Allah in Baghdad, and that he was in Baghdad when the Mongols executed the caliph, in 1258, after having sacked the city.³⁸ Shah Jalal was known for the austere life he led in the hills surrounding Sylhet, where he engaged in *mujahada* and *riyada*.³⁹ Little is known about Shah Jalal's early life, save that he was originally from Central Asia (hence the epithet *Turkestani* that is appended to his name in some sources) and that he was a spiritual successor of the friend of God Shaykh Ahmad Yasavi (d. 561/1166).⁴⁰ The sources, both hagiographical and other, present Shah Jalal as the epitome of the Sufi understanding of jihad as a complementary spiritual and military endeavor.

The primary sources for the life of Shah Jalal Mujarrad as related hereunder are the hagiographies *Gulzar-i abrar* and *Thamarat al-quds*, and the travel narrative (*rihla*) of Ibn Battuta.

Shah Jalal in Gulzar-i abrar *and* Thamarat al-quds

He was a native son of Bengal and the successor of Sultan Sayyed Ahmad Yasavi. One day, he presented a request to his *pir* of shining essence. The request was that, just as by the light of the master's guidance he had attained some degree of success in the greater jihad, [he hoped] likewise to achieve his heart's desire regarding the lesser jihad with the help of [the master's] wish-granting power. Everywhere there might be an Abode of War, by striving to [bring it into the Abode of Islam], he hoped to attain the rank of *ghazi* and martyr. The shaykh consented and bade seven hundred of his own elite companions accompany [Shah Jalal].⁴¹

Through the might of God, wherever they battled unbeliever warriors (*harbiyan*), they unfurled the banner of victory, and God made the *ghazi*s victorious over them. It is even more wondrous that, [during the time that Shah Jalal and his *ghazi*s] roved far and wide [in the Abode of War] they had no daily bread, save for the booty [from their conquests], which allowed them to live quite well. Whenever they obtained low-lying land and livestock, [Shah Jalal], having given these to one of his elite companions, would appoint him [to remain there] and teach [the inhabitants] Islam.[42]

So, in the end, [Shah Jalal] came to the village of Sylhet, in the province of Bengal,[43] with three hundred and thirteen men.[44] Raja Gour Govinda, who was lord of one hundred thousand foot soldiers and several thousand horsemen, was the ruler. [The raja] thought little of this group [of Muslims], for they could not compare with his great host. When the battle was hanging in the balance, the meaning of the divine words *How many a small band overcame a large band with God's permission?*[45] was made manifest, and, the idol-worshipping king having fled, [the *ghazi*s pursued him and sent] him to Hell. In this way did the land [of Sylhet] fall into the hands of the *ghazi*s.[46]

[Following their victory over the raja,] Shaykh [Shah Jalal] Mujarrad gave all [the *ghazi*s] a share of the spoils and assigned them land, bidding each of them become a householder.[47]

[Those of the unbelievers] who were spared the sword (*baqiyat al-sayf*) became Muslims, and they took [Shah Jalal] as their king. Once [Shah Jalal] was satisfied that the light of Islam would evermore illuminate the kingdom, he relinquished his rule, having bestowed the kingship on one of his companions and the viziership on another. He embraced solitude and the path of God and dedicated himself to *riyada* and *mujahada*. It is said that the name of the companion to whom he gave the kingship was Sultan Sikandar Ghazi.[48]

Among the wondrous anecdotes from Shah Jalal's life is one that concerns Sikandar Ghazi: [It is said that] Shah Jalal never gazed at a woman's face.[49] One evening, Sultan Sikandar Ghazi was watching a group of singing girls perform, and he was quite taken with one of them. He said to himself, "Although I know that the shaykh [never] looks at a woman's face, I am, in any case, going to be the one to make him look at this singing girl." Having resolved to do this, he went to Shah Jalal and said to him, "O Shah! This night I have beheld something worthy of the shaykh's blessed glance." Shah Jalal said, "Bring it [that I may see] what it is." [The sultan] replied, "It will come tonight."

When night fell, having adorned the singing girl, the sultan brought her into [the shaykh's] view. [The shaykh's] blessed glance fell upon the girl for only a moment, [but] immediately he covered his eyes with his hands and said, "May God—exalted—cause you to drown!" Having spoken these words, Shah Jalal went away. Several days later, [the sultan] wished to go on a pleasure excursion on the river, and so he embarked on a boat. No sooner had he commanded the boat to sail, when all at once a great wind began blowing and sank the boat, drowning [Sultan] Sikandar Ghazi and the singing girl.[50]

Ibn Battuta's Description of Shah Jalal

This shaykh is among the great friends of God and singular men. He [is known for his] many well-known wonders and great deeds, and he is of hoary age. He told me—may God have mercy upon him—that he beheld the caliph al-Musta'sim bi-Allah the Abbasid in Baghdad, and that he was there when [the caliph] was slain. [Shah Jalal's] companions told me after this that he had died at the age of one hundred and fifty and that he continually fasted for forty years and that he would not break his fast until after ten consecutive days and would then break his fast with [only] the milk of a cow he owned. He would remain standing all night and was slender of body and tall with a thin beard. The folk of the mountains had become Muslims at his hands, and therefore he remained among them.

Several of his companions related to me that the day before [Shah Jalal] died, he summoned [his companions] and admonished them to fear God, telling them, "I will leave you on the morrow—God willing—and my successor to you is God, other than Whom there is no other god." The next day, Shah Jalal performed the afternoon prayer, and God took him during the final prostration. Near the cave in which Shah Jalal had lived, his companions found that a grave had been dug, and next to it there lay a winding sheet and aromatic herbs for the shaykh's burial. [The companions] washed [Shah Jalal's body], wrapped it in the shroud, and having prayed the final prayer, buried their shaykh—may God have mercy upon him.

When I traveled [to Sylhet] to meet [Shah Jalal], I was met by four of his companions a full two days' journey from where he lived. They informed me that [Shah Jalal] had told the [Sufis][51] that were with him, "A wayfarer from the Maghrib has come to you—go to meet him." And therefore, they had come at the behest of the shaykh, who heretofore had had no knowledge of me, and yet [this] had been revealed to him. I journeyed with them to the shaykh and arrived at his Sufi hospice outside the cave, [noting that] there was no sign of any other human habitation in the area. The folk of that land, both Muslims and unbelievers, would come to visit him and bring gifts and offerings, which the [Sufis] and visitors would consume. As for the shaykh, he contented himself with the cow with whose milk he would break his fast after ten days, as we have already noted. When I entered the hospice, [Shah Jalal] rose and embraced me and asked me about my country and travels, so I told him about them. He then said to me, "You are a wayfarer [among] the Arabs." Then one of his companions said to him, "And the non-Arabs, O master." "And the non-Arabs," said [the shaykh]. "Treat him with honor." So they led me to the hospice and treated me as a guest for three days.

The day I entered [to visit] the shaykh, I saw [that he had wrapped himself in] a soft woolen mantle, which pleased me, and I said to myself, "Would that the shaykh would bestow [the mantle] on me!" When [on the day of my departure] I entered to take leave [of Shah Jalal], he rose and removed the mantle and placed it on me along with the cap from his head. [Shah Jalal] then donned a patched cloak. The [Sufis] informed me that the shaykh was not in the habit of wearing that mantle and had only donned it for my coming; moreover, the shaykh had said to them, "The man from the Maghrib will ask for the mantle, but a sultan of the unbelievers will take it from him and give it to our friend of God Burhan al-Din al-Saghirji, to whom it belongs and for whom it had originally been made." When the [Sufis] had told me this, I said to them, "I have received the shaykh's blessing, as he has clothed me with his [mantle], therefore I will be sure to never come before any sultan—be he an unbeliever or a Muslim—[while wearing] this mantle." Then I departed.

A long time thereafter, I entered the land of China, where I ended up in the city of Khansa.[52] My companions became separated from me because of the many throngs of people, and the mantle was on me. While I was standing in one of the streets, the vizier and his great retinue chanced to pass by. The vizier's gaze fell on me and he called me over and took me by the hand. He asked me about my arrival and did not leave me until I arrived at the sultan's palace with him. I wished to withdraw, but the vizier would not allow me, and so he brought me before the sultan, who asked me about the sultans of Islam, and I answered his queries. Then he saw the mantle and was struck by its comeliness. The vizier bade me remove the mantle, and I was unable to refuse. The sultan took it and then bade [his servants give] me ten robes, a well-equipped horse, and much money. I was upset because of this, but then I recalled [Shah Jalal's] words that an unbeliever sultan would take [the mantle from me], and I was amazed at [what had happened].

The following year, I visited the palace of the emperor of China, in Khan Baliq[53]; then I went to the hospice of Burhan al-Din al-Saghirji, whom I found reading and wearing the very same mantle. I was astonished and turned the mantle over in my hands. [Burhan al-Din] asked me, "Why are you turning it over when you know very well what it is?" "Indeed! it's the [mantle] the sultan took from me in Khansa." [Burhan al-Din] then said, "My brother Shah Jalal made the mantle for *me* and wrote to me, saying that the mantle would come to me at the hand of such and such a man." He then brought forth the letter, which I read while marveling at the shaykh's foreknowledge. I related to him how the story began, and he replied, "My brother Shah Jalal is [far] greater than that, for he would effect changes in the world without restriction; however, he has since passed on in God's mercy." Then he said to me, "I have been told that he would [journey to] Mecca each morning to say his dawn prayers and that he would perform the Hajj each year, for he would vanish from among the folk [of Sylhet] on the days of *'Arafa* and *'Id al-Adha,* and no one knew whither he had gone."[54]

Sayyid Muluk Shah

Sayyid Muluk Shah (d. ninth or tenth/fifteenth or sixteenth century?) was a friend of God to whom many wonders and deeds were attributed.[55] Sayyid Muluk Shah was from Sindh, a region where Sufism has played a prominent role in the devotional and literary life of the mostly Muslim inhabitants since its arrival in the subcontinent.[56] Regarding the origins of Sayyid Muluk, it is related that his forebears had emigrated from the region of Mazandaran, in Iran, and settled in the environs of Thatta, in lower Sindh. Little is known about him other than that he died a martyr, and the main extant sources provide only scant details of his life.⁵⁷ After his death, his tomb became an important place of local pilgrimage.⁵⁸

Sayyid Muluk Shah in Tuhfat al-tahirin

That knower of Reality, the one supreme in union, the drinker of the wine of certainty, the wayfarer on the paths of divine guidance, the exemplar of justice, cream of generous men, Sayyid Muluk—may God hallow his inner secret—[who] is among the noblemen of Mazandaran. Those who were [known for their] generosity in the past stood back when he arrived in the land.

It is said that [Sayyid Muluk] was once journeying in the countryside [near Thatta] when he heard that two or three yogis, in accordance with a command to disperse the Muslims, were perpetually making war. Wishing to achieve martyrdom and render assistance to his fellow Muslims, he hurried to the place [of battle]. He achieved martyrdom while fighting [the Hindu aggressors].

[Following the battle, the Muslims placed Sayyid Muluk's] body on a bier and raised it upon their shoulders—in the place where his blessed tomb is now located. [Before leaving, however, they decided] to perform the funeral prayer, so they placed [the bier once again] on the ground. It is related that, having finished the prayer, [those in] the funeral procession sought to raise Sayyid Muluk's bier, so as to bear it to the cemetery of Makli,⁵⁹ but, lo, by the power of God, the legs of the bier cleaved fast to the ground. They tried with all their might to raise [the bier], but they could not. [The Muslims] were astonished and spent the [entire] day in that place[, unable to raise the bier]. When night fell, [they understood that it was God's will,] saying, "This very spot is to be [the shaykh's final] resting place." So they buried him there[, where he had achieved martyrdom].

The wonders and deeds of [Sayyid Muluk] are [too many] to be reckoned. Now, on the eleventh of the month of Rabi' al-Thani, a great gathering comes to sit at his noble graveside—may God illuminate his tomb.⁶⁰

Baba Palang Pūsh

Baba Palang Pūsh (d. 1110/1699) was from Ghijduvan, near Bukhara in modern-day Uzbekistan. His epithet, "Palang Pūsh," means "Clad in a Leopard (hide)." Little is known regarding Baba Palang Pūsh's childhood. It is said, however, that he began following the Sufi path as a youth when he persuaded Baba Qul Mazid to accept him as a *murid*. It was Baba Qul Mazid who bestowed the *khirqa* on Baba Palang Pūsh and taught him *dhikr*.⁶¹ Following the death of Baba Qul Mazid, Baba Palang Pūsh served Shaykh Darvish 'Azizan for twelve years, until he reached the stage of perfection, at which time his shaykh allowed him to leave.⁶² Although Baba Palang Pūsh followed the Naqshbandiyya Path of Sufism, it is said that when he went to Tashkent after leaving the wilderness, he was initiated into the Kubrawiyya Path after he beheld in a vision his Naqshbandi spiritual forebears, who gave him their consent in this regard.⁶³ The hagiographical *Malfuzat-i Naqshbandiyya* portrays him primarily as a "military pír"[64] who accompanied the Muslim army of Ghazi al-Din Khan (d. 1121/1710) in his Deccan campaigns, during the reign of the Mughal sultan Awrangzeb.[65] As military *pir*, Baba Palang Pūsh provided spiritual guidance to the soldiers, many of whom were also of Central Asian origin, and would use his great supernatural power to aid them in battle.[66] The primary written source for his life is the hagiography *Malfuzat-i Naqshbandiyya*, composed in Persian by Shah Mahmud Awrangabadi (d. 1175/1762). There is also a much shorter source for his life in the hagiography *Ma'athir al-kiram* of Ghulam 'Ali Azad Bilgrami.[67] Additionally, those associated with the shrine of Panchakki in Aurangabad (in modern-day Maharashtra State, India), where are buried Baba Palang Pūsh and his companion and successor, Baba Shah Musafir (d. 1127/1715), keep alive the oral tradition regarding the deeds of the two Sufis.[68]

Baba Palang Pūsh Embarks on the Sufi Path

Baba Qul Ahmad [Mazid] had [achieved] the rank of axis mundi from the Eternal. He followed the Path of Blame (*malamati*).[69] His speech was reckless and his words unintelligible. At the height of his insensibility, he was fully aware in his remembrance of God. Fate decreed that his spiritual allure should attract that abode of mystical knowledge, that rightly guided successor of the illustrious house of prophethood, star of good fortune, heaven of the Prophet's descendants, Hazrat Baba Shah Sa'id [Palang Pūsh]. In the hope of attaining his desire to become the [*murid*] of that sun of the sphere of wonders [Baba Qul Mazid], [Baba Palang Pūsh] followed his shadow and was not sundered from him for one moment. [Baba Qul Mazid] did not grant this on account of his absolute independence. Nonetheless, as [Baba Qul Mazid's] independence waxed stronger, the desire of [Baba Palang Pūsh] likewise waxed ever stronger. After some time had passed in this manner, [Baba Qul Mazid] entered his blessed room in one of the *madrasa*s in Bukhara and shut the door. [Baba Palang Pūsh] stood outside the door. After quite some time had passed, [Baba Qul Mazid] opened the door and asked, "Who's there?" "The poor man (*faqir*) of your worship (*hazrat*)." Out of kindness and mercy, he opened the door for [Baba Palang Pūsh] and gave him leave to enter the room. [Baba Qul Mazid] then uttered several words as one drunk, after the manner of the *Malamati*s, which [Baba Palang Pūsh] understood as auspicious tidings regarding his affair. [This did not cause] his belief to weaken by even a hair's breadth but rather caused it to wax. Then [Baba Qul Mazid] manifested favor and acceptance regarding the matter of his discipleship and, having placed the hand of guidance on the head [of Baba Palang Pūsh] and clothing him in the dervish's *khirqa*, he taught him the divine [formula] of remembrance of God (*dhikr*), which [Baba Palang Pūsh] performed in accordance with the proper civilities toward the Refuge of Prophecy.[70] [Baba Palang Pūsh] chose to remain in the [shaykh's] grace-bestowing company for a time. When the time of [the shaykh's] death and reunification with God neared, [Baba Qul Mazid] placed [Baba Palang Pūsh] in the service of Shaykh Darvish 'Azizan—Shaykh Darvish 'Azizan and Baba Qul Mazid had been [*murid*s] of the same *pir*.[71]

The Wayfaring of Baba Palang Pūsh and His Meeting with Khizr

When [Baba Palang Pūsh] had received the noble leave of [Shaykh Darvish 'Azizan], he decided to make for Tashkent and wandered in the manner of Majnun in love with the true Layla.[72] Having sundered all ties with worldly folk, he bound himself to reflecting on the beauty that does not fade away.

After some time, Khizr—upon whom be peace—met with him and relayed the auspicious tidings to him, "O fortunate in faith and this world! Your repentance in nakedness has passed.[73] The time has now come for you to clothe yourself in the special robe of nearness to God." Khizr then gave Baba Palang Pūsh a bow and two arrows and said, "A mighty lion (*sher-i qavi*)[74] will come upon you suddenly in this very wilderness, and once you have slain it, fashion a fur cloak for yourself from its skin." Thus, that lion (*hizabr*) of the divine law and leviathan of the sea of divine truth did as Khizr—upon whom be peace—bade him. When he clad his blessed body in the skin of that lion, it was as if the resplendent sun had bestowed the rank of honor on the Sign of Leo. Henceforth, he always clothed his noble body in the leopard skin, and thus he garnered fame throughout the world under the name "Baba Palang Pūsh."[75]

[Baba Palang Pūsh] set out to perform the Hajj, making for the Two Hallowed Cities by way of Iran. When he had traversed part of the distance, he arrived in hallowed Mashhad, where a throng of Shi'ites[76] surrounded him like a pack of dogs in the market that bark in vain when they see a leopard. [Baba Palang Pūsh] attacked them in the manner of a leopard. [The Shi'ites] again tried all together to overcome [Baba Palang Pūsh], but he took refuge in the splendid tomb precinct of Imam Reza[77]—may God be pleased with him—on account of whose aid no harm befell him from them. Witnessing that resplendent tomb brought light to his eyes and happiness to his heart. Having received this great blessing from [Imam Reza], he stayed one night and then proceeded on his way in the morning. He was ennobled in this world and the hereafter by visiting the Holy Cities. He then returned to Transoxiana and the Dome of Islam, Bukhara.[78]

Baba Palang Pūsh and the Defeat of the Qalmaqs

It is said that after Baba Palang Pūsh returned to Bukhara from the Hajj, the nomadic unbeliever Qalmaqs began raiding the realm of Balkh. Yalangtush,[79] who was the vizier of the ruler of that time, Nadhr Muhammad Khan,[80] sought the aid of [Baba Palang Pūsh,] saying, "The Qalmaqs with their many hosts are causing trouble in the lands of this kingdom, and the king has appointed me to confront and repulse them. Will your worship be so kind as to turn your attention [to this matter] and send one of the dervishes to accompany [me] so that by means of your worship's aid, victory may be easily assured in our campaign?" Baba Palang Pūsh appointed a servant [to go with Yalangtush], a mad-seeming [Sufi], whom he employed as a water carrier. Baba Palang Pūsh instructed the dervish, saying, "Go with the emir and occupy yourself with supplicatory prayer (*du'a*)." The dervish replied, "Your worship, I am witless and do not know how to wash my hands and mouth or perform the ritual ablutions well, so what could I know about directing my attention and supplicatory prayer?" Baba Palang Pūsh replied, "Do as I have bidden you!" He then recited the *fatiha*,[81] and sent the mad [dervish] to accompany the vizier. Yalangtush met the [Qalmaqs] in battle; the mad [dervish], meanwhile, had fallen asleep—as was his wont—on a hill behind the host. The enemy host fought fiercely, and [Yalangtush] besought Baba Palang Pūsh [to aid the Muslims], and [the shaykh heard him] by means of his inner sense and called to the mad dervish, saying, "I sent you to render assistance, not to sleep!" Straightaway, the mad [dervish] awoke and beheld Baba Palang Pūsh standing before the Muslim army, commanding him to strike the enemy. So the mad [dervish] picked up some stones, which he held in his hands and under his arm, and attacked the enemy host. Through divine aid, the Qalmaq [army] was defeated and fled. Yalangtush thus achieved a great victory, took much plunder, and then returned. [After the battle, Yalangtush] went before Baba [Palang Pūsh] and, bowing his head, presented a lovely young girl to him as an offering. [Baba Palang Pūsh] gave the girl to the mad dervish, saying, "You have labored much, take your reward!" But the dervish refused to accept her, saying, "Whatever they did, I had no idea and, [in any case,] what use is a girl?" In the end, [Baba Palang Pūsh] gave [the girl] her freedom.[82]

The Military Jihad of Baba Palang Pūsh

It is said that Baba Palang Pūsh was at the fort of Hasan Abdal, in the Punjab, when he undertook his journey to the Deccan to aid the army of Islam in fighting the unbelievers. The reason for this was a wondrous vision. Baba Palang Pūsh related, "At dawn [one morning] at Hasan Abdal, a [vision from] the unseen occurred. The hallowed gathering of the chief[83] of the prophets—upon whom be peace—appeared. Before this, I had seen Abu Bakr Siddiq and 'Umar—may God be pleased with them—standing to the right of [the Prophet], while I beheld 'Uthman and 'Ali—may God be pleased with them—on his left. This time, however, I witnessed all four of the [Prophet's] Companions standing on his left, and on his right stood a man of medium height with hair that was turning gray, and in his hand, he held a naked blade. I tried to kiss the [Prophet's] feet, but he gestured with his right hand and said to me in Arabic, "First pay your respects to Sayyid Hamza!"[84] So I kissed the feet of [Sayyid Hamza], who then called to me, saying, "Muhammad Sa'id!" "At your service!" I answered. "Take this sword (*sayf*) and go to the army of Mir Shihab al-Din in the Deccan!" Sayyid Hamza then placed the sword in my hand. As commanded, I set out for the Deccan, though I did not know in which direction the Deccan lay, [nor did I know] who Mir Shihab al-Din was. [Baba Musafir] related, "When Baba [Palang Pūsh] had recounted what had happened, I prepared what he would need for the journey, and he left the following morning." After several days of journeying, he happened to halt at a mosque that was beside the military camp of Mir [Shihab al-Din]. Baba Palang Pūsh asked whose army it was, and the people told him it was the camp of Mir Shihab al-Din the son of 'Abid Khan, chancellor of the emperor [Awrangzeb].

At that time, Mir [Shihab al-Din] had the rank of [commanding] four hundred [men], and with a contingent of the king's troops and a group of his father's companions he had been commanded by [the emperor] to take a fortress in the Deccan. He was beginning to worry because of the days that had passed and his failure to bring the campaign to a close. That very night, he saw in a dream a man who looked like Baba Palang Pūsh and who asked him, "Why are you anxious?" [Mir Shihab al-Din] told him the truth of the matter, and [Baba Palang Pūsh] took the hand of Mir Shihab al-Din in his blessed hand and led him several steps in the direction of the fortress and said, "This is the way to the fortress gate." When Mir [Shihab al-Din] awoke the next morning, he asked his companions, "Who has seen a dervish like this?" One of them, a man by the name of 'Abduh Chihra Aqasi, replied, "Yesterday, a great man of this description came to the mosque behind the military camp." [When the emir heard this,] he rose and went to [Baba Palang Pūsh] and approached him with reverence and respect. He saw the very same perfect comeliness of [Baba Palang Pūsh] that he had witnessed in his dream. So he took Baba Palang Pūsh back to his camp, and on the following day the fortress was captured. Right after this victory, [Mir Shihab al-Din] was honored by the [emperor] with an increase in rank and the title Shihab al-Din Khan.[85]

With the arrival of [Baba Palang Pūsh], Mir Shihab al-Din Khan's star of good fortune continued to wax, and wherever he faced the hosts of his enemies, even if they were many thousands, he was always victorious over them with only a small contingent. He continued to be honored with increases in his rank until after a time he reached the threshold of seven thousand, which is the [highest rank] of emirs, and was honored with the title Ghazi al-Din Bahadur Firuz Jang[86] and reached a position superior to the other great emirs, who were twenty-two in number and possessed the distinction of having ceremonial music played before their assemblies (*nawbat*).

[Ghazi al-Din Khan] was appointed to lead forty thousand horsemen and to pursue and fight the enemy with his troops separately wherever [the enemy] dispersed. [The soldiers] would see Baba Palang Pūsh going before the army of Islam and shooting arrows at the unbeliever troops. The soldiers, seeing the blessed comeliness [of Baba Palang Pūsh], would take heart—even if their numbers were few—and would hurl themselves at the enemy and gain the victory. When they were returning home [following the battle], one of the soldiers would say, "[Baba Palang Pūsh] was with our band!" Another would say, "He was with us!" while another soldier would say, "[Baba Palang Pūsh] came to our aid!" Following a victory, after the army of Islam had returned, [the townsfolk] would ask [the soldiers], "Which band did [Baba Palang Pūsh] accompany in the battle?" [Baba Palang Pūsh] would say, "I was everyone's companion [in battle]!"[87]

Baba Palang Pūsh Admonishes Sharif Khan

Baba Palang Pūsh betook himself to Northern India (Hindustan) and graced the region of Hasan Abdal with his splendid presence, accompanied by Baba Musafir. Sharif Khan, who had come to Northern India from Central Asia (*Vilayat*) during the reign of Shah Jahan and attained both high rank and the title *khan*, dwelled there. As he had manifested sincere belief in [Baba Palang Pūsh], from time to time [the latter] would visit [Sharif Khan's] home. One day, it happened that [Baba Palang Pūsh's] blessed presence was at the court [of Sharif Khan], where there were also many emirs in attendance, when a dervish who had severed all ties with this world (*majdhub*) entered. Baba Palang Pūsh, who would never rise to show honor to any of these powerful men, rose with the greatest respect for the dervish and seated him higher than any other of those in attendance. This annoyed Sharif Khan, who was [blinded] by transitory, worldly [concerns], and he asked [Baba Palang Pūsh], "In which station do you consider mendicant dervishes [to be] in relation to the [important] men of this world?" That leopard of the wilderness of those without need replied, "You and these powerful men who are with you do not equal one hair of a [dervish's[88] head]." The khan was greatly disturbed [by this response], and Baba Palang Pūsh rose in full majesty and returned to his abode. Three days later, Sharif Khan was going somewhere or other when he came to the downward slope of a hill; suddenly his palanquin toppled over, and he fell out and broke his arm.

Oft have we experienced retribution in this tavern (*dayr*).

Whoever quarreled with the dreg-drinkers fell back.

Thus admonished, Sharif Khan put off going anywhere else and went straight to Baba Palang Pūsh. Having asked forgiveness [of Baba Palang Pūsh], [Sharif Khan] offered two horses that he had [as spare mounts] and three thousand rupees cash as a gift.[89]

Baba Palang Pūsh's Wondrous Journey to Rūm

Mir Isma'il of the men of Tashkent, who was a *murid* of [Baba Palang Pūsh], said, "One day, Baba Palang Pūsh was sitting on a dais, and great emirs, as well as a group of both noble and common folk, were in attendance at the foot of the dais and the flowers were in bloom. [Baba Palang Pūsh] asked for coffee. Shah Khaki, who had been raised by [Baba Palang Pūsh] since childhood, was the coffee cook and made [such] good coffee, that Ghazi al-Din Khan Bahadur would request coffee from [Baba Palang Pūsh] and would drink it with great relish—indeed, his own servants could not make [coffee] so well. Shah Khaki poured a cup of coffee and brought it to [Baba Palang Pūsh]. No sooner did he grasp the cup with his hand than the color of his blessed countenance changed, and he went into such a deep state of meditation that the cup of coffee nearly fell from his blessed hand to the ground. Those in attendance were astounded and did not have the wherewithal to take the cup from his blessed hand. [Then] Hajji Muhammad, who was a special servant and senior companion of [Baba Palang Pūsh] took [the cup] from his blessed hand. After some time, [Baba Palang Pūsh] returned [from the state of meditation], and the people in attendance requested that the Hajji ask [him] what had happened. The Hajji consented, and [Baba Palang Pūsh] said, "What business is this of yours?" The Hajji asked again and received the same response. The third time, the companions [asked] in earnest, and the Hajji pleaded with [him], so he said, "The learned men in the land of Rūm have slandered a dear man among my acquaintances, who has the rank of assistant (*martaba-yi ghawthiyat*), and they have informed the sultan thereof in order to have him killed. That friend called to me for help by means of his inner voice, and so I went thither. Through the grace of God and the Refuge of Prophecy—upon whom be peace—I delivered him from the hands of his enemies." Astonished, those present wrote down on a piece of paper the day, month, and year when this had happened. Whenever anyone arrived from Rūm, they would ask [him about this affair]. After two years, a party [of travelers] arrived from Rūm. When asked [whether they knew anything of this matter,] they said that the sultan there, at the behest of some learned men, had indeed sought to slay a dervish with the rank of assistant dwelling in Rūm. Then a great man appeared from the unseen and by means of persuasion, removed the king's suspicion regarding that dervish, who was thereby saved from calamity. "As we have arrived hither, we see that very same noble soul here!" And they indicated Baba Palang Pūsh. They found that the [date] they had written down accorded with the tidings brought by the party of travelers.[90]

The Death of Baba Palang Pūsh

One of his companions related that, "At the end of [his] life, [Baba Palang Pūsh] became quite ill, and it happened that in that state his consciousness was like a flowing river. He would regain his health, but then the sickness would return. He regained consciousness in this way many times, and this happened thrice in one month." [The companion went on to say,] "Without any doubt it became evident to us that the choice [to continue living or to die] was in our shaykh's hands. One day, [Baba Palang Pūsh] said to us, 'The choice is mine: if I wish to live, I shall, and if I wish to pass from this world, I shall do so.' Then he said, 'This is the proper time to die. I must go.' That [same] day, the army moved camp. On the way, they came to some high ground, and there they placed the palanquin of [Baba Palang Pūsh] under the shade of a tree. This poor servant was in attendance, and [Baba Palang Pūsh] said, 'For some time, I have been a companion to Ghazi al-Din Khan, so I have to see him.' At that moment, [Ghazi al-Din's] messengers arrived and said, '[Ghazi al-Din] is coming to see [Baba Palang Pūsh].' [Ghazi al-Din Khan] came, and even though he had been far from [him], he came as swiftly as he could. [He] came with such speed that it was as if the veins of the earth had contracted. He kissed the feet of [Baba Palang Pūsh] and showed him the courtesy a *murid* shows [to his shaykh]. [Baba Palang Pūsh] bade him sit down, and he sat. [Baba Palang Pūsh] said, 'Till now, I have been charged by the great [friends of God] with praying for your army and rendering it aid, but now I am entrusting you and your army to God.' [Baba Palang Pūsh] then gave [Ghazi al-Din Khan] leave [to depart], and [the latter], weeping, took leave of [Baba Palang Pūsh] and then sent him two thousand rupees as a gift. [Baba Palang Pūsh] recited the *fatiha* and, as his debts were in the amount of two thousand rupees, he bade them give [the money] to his creditors. That same day, after they arrived at the new camp, Baba Palang Pūsh made the journey from this Abode of Perishing [on] Thursday, the seventh of Ramadan, in the year 1110 (March 9, 1699)."[91]

CONCLUSION

The many stories of God's friends that we have read in the foregoing chapters illustrate several significant aspects of both Sufism and the Sufi role in premodern Sunni Muslim culture. While recognizing the differences in Sufi practice and doctrine, especially insofar as concerns the various Sufi orders that developed in North Africa and Western, Central, and Southern Asia, we may state that there are certain fundamental characteristics common to most manifestations of Sufism. In this respect, we will summarize hereunder some of the significant conclusions that may be drawn from the stories of God's friends.

The first is the Sufi belief that Islamic scripture and practice have both an inner and an outer meaning, and that these two meanings are complementary. Many historical Sufis have exemplified this in their scrupulous adherence to the dictates of the *shari'a*, which includes fulfilling all the duties prescribed for believers (e.g., the Five Pillars of Islam) as well as following the inner spiritual (and specifically Sufi) path toward *haqiqa* (i.e., the ultimate reality of God). Likewise, idealized stories of Sufis in hagiography generally depict God's friends following the *shari'a* and fulfilling their outward Islamic duties, as well as embodying the mystical and ascetic practices of Sufism.

The second is the multifaceted role that Sufis have played in Muslim society, which cannot be reduced to their being simply the "mystics of Islam." Even though Sunni Islamic mysticism is generally synonymous with Sufism, and the inner spiritual path of Sufism that seeks union with God may certainly be defined as mysticism, Sufis have fulfilled many important social functions throughout the history of Islam that are not of a mystical character. Sufis have, for example, served as teachers, proselytizers, reformers, and military leaders, and all these roles required their active involvement in the social and, at times, political affairs of their respective societies. Furthermore, their outward deeds were inseparable from the inner spiritual path that they followed, and this accords with the aforementioned complementary nature of Sufi thought and action. This is to say not that Sufism is not a form of mysticism but that the influence of Sufis has throughout history gone far beyond the purely spiritual and theoretical realms Sufis are often assumed to have primarily occupied.

The stories of God's friends in particular demonstrate an important aspect of the social role that Sufis played in premodern Muslim societies as guardians and disseminators of Islamic practice. Although anecdotes of God's friends initially served to vindicate the piety and religious learning of the early Sufis in the face of skepticism and hostility from religious scholars (as did the majority of early Sufi writings, which were at pains to show that Sufism and Sunni Islam were in accord), they would over time develop into an effective vehicle for teaching essential Muslim practice and doctrine. As 'Attar indicated in *Tadhkirat al-awliya*', the words and deeds of God's friends served as an explication of Islamic scripture, thus making them a living *tafsir* for the many believers who heard their stories. God's friends embody Islamic ideals in the same way as heroes in mythology or folklore embody the ideals of the culture to which they belong. In this respect, there is little in the stories of God's friends that conveys the kind of esoteric mysticism one encounters in theoretical Sufi writings, which further underscores the didactic role that these stories played in premodern Muslim societies: the great majority of Muslims would not have been concerned with the arcane mystical concepts and allegories of such writings.

Moreover, the recurrent motifs that define the fundamental characteristics of God's friends also transcend time, language, and geography, for they are found in most of the examples from Sufi hagiography presented herein.[1] These recurrent motifs are yet another indication that the stories of God's friends possessed a certain degree of unity, despite the multiplicity of Sufi orders and practices. It may be that the uniformity of tropes and motifs in these stories owes more to certain trends in premodern traditions of Muslim storytelling than it does to a uniformity in Sufism; however, the role of these stories as didactic vehicles in teaching and reinforcing basic Islamic doctrine and practice, and in some cases proselytization among non-Muslims, is undeniable. Furthermore, although there is a core body of recurrent motifs, Sufi hagiography adapted these motifs to reflect local realities, such as the historical circumstances or the religious communities with which the Muslims of a given region coexisted or fought in times of war (e.g., Zoroastrians in Iran, Buddhists in Central Asia, Hindus in India, and Christians in the Levant, North Africa, and the Iberian Peninsula). The essential character of these motifs and their elasticity with regard to the social, doctrinal, and political circumstances of their narration reflect the historical development of Sufism in general, in that Sufism has shown a remarkable ability to adapt to the needs of Muslim societies wherever it has established itself.

The third fundamental characteristic concerns the elaboration of the doctrine of jihad in Sufism, the complementary nature of which affirms the first conclusion. The earliest Sufi authors elaborated the concept of an inner and outer jihad—no doubt inspired by the threefold definition of al-Raghib al-Isfahani and other Muslim thinkers mentioned in the introduction (e.g., Ibn Nubata and Ibn Rushd): to wit, the jihad against the lower self, the jihad of the tongue, and the jihad of the sword—and as Sufism unfolded, the complementary nature of jihad became a fundamental aspect of Sufi belief and practice. Most Sufi treatises and hagiographies distinguished the two forms of striving, with *jihad* generally signifying the outer struggle against unbelievers (as well as against tyrants within the Muslim community) and *mujahada* signifying the inner struggle against the *nafs* and its passions. The many anecdotes related about God's friends consistently depict them as *mujahid*s struggling against the *nafs* inwardly, outwardly fighting unbelievers in battle, aiding Muslim warriors, and admonishing Muslim rulers. Moreover, as with the recurrent motifs discussed above, these anecdotes are not confined to one particular region of the Muslim world or one period of Muslim history, for they may be found in hagiographical works composed in a variety of languages, spanning a period of seven hundred years, from North Africa to Central Asia to India.

These stories also tell us much about what was considered significant in premodern Muslim culture, especially regarding the *mujahid* ethos, which was central to early Islamic history. As we have mentioned, this ethos originated in *sira* literature (i.e., the earliest biographical narratives concerning the Prophet), portraying the Prophet Muhammad and his Companions in their many battles against the pagan Arab tribes as they fought to establish Islam in the Arabian Peninsula. To accomplish this, the Prophet reinterpreted the old, pre-Islamic Arabian warrior culture of tribal raiding and blood feuds, the aims of which were to acquire camels and booty, as well as to increase fame and defend personal and tribal honor.[2] The Muslim warrior would, instead, fight for the elevation of the new faith; his motives would be pious, and his loyalty would be to his fellow Muslims rather than to his tribe. The astounding success of the Muslim conquests of the Near East, Egypt and North Africa, Iran, and Central Asia, as well as most of the Iberian Peninsula, which occurred during less than one hundred years after the Prophet's death, attests to the efficacy of this religious militancy. The incorporation of the frontier *mujahid* archetypes (i.e., Ibrahim ibn Adham, Ibn al-Mubarak, Ibn Wasi', et al.) and their transformation into the earliest Sufis in hagiography affirm the continuum that existed in the development of *sira* narrative, stories of the prophets, and Sufi hagiographical writing.[3]

Though not a topic commonly addressed in Western studies of Sufi hagiography, God's friends, as depicted in hagiographical anecdotes, often embody this *mujahid* ethos in the bravery and selflessness that they display in battle (e.g., 'Ali ibn 'Uthman al-Shawi approaching the Christian host alone—with sword in hand and a poem in praise of the Prophet on his lips—and dying a martyr), as well as in their exhortation of fellow Muslims battling the enemies of the faith (e.g., Abu Ishaq al-Kazaruni, who encourages the Muslims and helps them organize their military forays into Byzantine territory). They also epitomize the purity of intention of the *mujahid* (e.g., Ibrahim ibn Adham refusing to accept any spoils and imposing the harshest conditions on himself when taking part in military campaigns).

These stories remind us that Sufi jihad is also a spiritual struggle, which God's friends exemplify in their inner battle against the *nafs*. (E.g., Rumi engages in *mujahada* and *riyada* for five years under his *murshid*, Burhan al-Din.) And their success in this struggle, which is the more difficult jihad, renders them ideally suited to accomplish the outer jihad of the sword and the tongue.

We must bear in mind that the majority of these anecdotes regarding God's friends as *mujahid*s are not historical, though they may at times reflect historical Sufi involvement in warfare. Rather, we ought to read them as symbolic representations of the *mujahid* ideal. It is probably for this reason that many Muslim scholars writing in Arabic, Persian, and other languages have emphasized the Sufi role as the paradigmatic *mujahid/ghazi*, as this role has traditionally been a source of pride for Muslims.[4] Examples of Sufis leading the military jihad or fighting in defense of their communities exist in the historical record, especially during the period of European colonialism in the nineteenth and twentieth centuries, and this affirms the historical military role of Sufis, as exemplified by anecdotes of Sufi *mujahid*s in hagiography.

Although the stories of God's friends are not themselves historical records, they do help clarify the Sufi understanding of the complementary nature of the religious duty of jihad. Jihad is not simply "holy war," nor is it solely an inner spiritual struggle. Indeed, the stories of God's friends convey the evolution of the doctrine of jihad in premodern Islamic thought, for they show jihad as a struggle to establish and defend Islam—one that includes using words either to call non-Muslims to embrace the faith or to remind a Muslim ruler of his duties—and as a military struggle when force is deemed necessary. As we have mentioned, these outward struggles are predicated on successful completion of the inner, or greater, spiritual jihad, through which God's friends conquer their *nafs* and its worldly, selfish concerns, thereby rendering their outward jihad selfless and pure.

The reputation of Sufism has suffered in those Muslim lands where some relatively recent interpretations of Islam (e.g., Wahhabism) have become dominant; nonetheless, it is important to remember that for most of Sufism's existence, it has been integral to traditional Sunni Islam and continues to be so for many Muslims. God's friends have never been fringe figures, and the stories told of their wondrous deeds and godly acts have held a prominent place in the hearts of Muslims. Indeed, for many Muslims, Islamic practice and piety have often paralleled the stories of God's friends and the communal devotional activities that take place in the sacred loci of their tombs.

The popularity of the stories of God's friends and their function in premodern Muslim societies underscores the fact that Islam and correct Islamic practice were not solely the domain of religious scholars and jurists, for it is unlikely that the majority of Muslims, many of whom did not know Arabic, learned their faith from treatises and erudite works of exegesis. For this reason, it may be useful to consider the stories of God's friends as sources for understanding premodern Muslim piety and devotion, as they have probably been a more influential vehicle of essential Islamic doctrine than other, more learned, writings of the Islamic textual tradition. This is not to say, however, that these stories were separate from learned religious writings, for they were clearly informed by works of Islamic jurisprudence, exegesis, and *hadith* scholarship, as well as by esoteric Sufi writings. In other words, the stories of God's friends reflect not only the complementary nature of Sufi doctrine and practice but also the complementary relationship between formal religious learning and popular religious narrative traditions.

These stories are valuable for many reasons. They offer a multifaceted view of Sufism that highlights the complementary inner and outer aspects of Sufi doctrine and deeds that we have noted in the portrayal of Sufi jihad in hagiography. The stories of God's friends also contribute significantly to the study of hagiography in general, especially in the ways that Sufi hagiography resembles hagiographical traditions of other religions and, in some cases, has incorporated earlier hagiographical motifs based on the stories of the prophets and *sira* literature of Islamic sacred history.[5] Furthermore, these stories have great literary value and ought to take their rightful place among the classics of premodern Muslim literature. What is perhaps most important, however, is that the anecdotes of God's friends tell us much about how premodern Muslims learned the fundamental beliefs of their faith and experienced its sacred history. It is hoped that by reading these stories, readers—both Muslim and non-Muslim—will gain insight into one of the most significant but often-overlooked sources for understanding Islamic practice and doctrine in a way that is both edifying and entertaining.

GLOSSARY

Ahl al-kitab Literally, "People of the Book": i.e., those belonging to religions with a claim to scriptural and prophetic origins (though toleration of such people does not include validation of their religions from the perspective of Islam).[1] Jews, Christians, Sabians, and Zoroastrians were considered People of the Book and as such were allowed to practice their faiths, provided that they accepted Muslim rule, including (at least theoretically) payment of the *jizya* (*q.v.*, below).

'Arif From Arabic *'arafa*, "to know." *'Arif*, the active participle of this verb, in Sufism signifies a spiritual "knower." Sufi definitions of this term differ to some degree: e.g., "The *'arif* is one who has achieved annihilation in God (*fana'*) but has not yet reached the stage of abiding in God (*baqa'*)."[2]

Aya Verse of the Qur'an; can also mean "sign," "wonder," "exemplar."

Batin "Inner," "inward," "hidden"; from Arabic *batana*, "to be hidden," "to be concealed." In Sufism, the inner meaning or aspect of scripture, words, actions, etc. The opposite of *zahir* (*q.v.*, below).

Dar al-harb "The Abode of War." Theoretically, any land not under Muslim control is at war with the Muslim state, whose aim is to bring all such lands into the Abode of Islam, by means of either proselytization or warfare.

Dar al-Islam "The Abode of Islam": i.e., lands under Muslim rule, where Muslims can freely practice Islam and where People of the Book can practice their faiths under Muslim state protection provided that they accept their subordinate status and (at least theoretically) pay the *jizya* (*q.v.*, below).

Dar al-sulh "The Abode of Truce": lands with which, though not ruled by Muslims, a temporary state of truce obtains. Not recognized by all Sunni legal schools.

Dervish From the Persian word, *darvish*, "poor," "needy." In Sufi writings, "dervish" often denotes a mendicant renunciant Sufi.

Dhikr Remembrance of God; from Arabic *dhakara*, "to remember," "to recall." Sufi *dhikr* generally involves repeating God's name either aloud or silently.

Emir Arabic, "commander," "prince"; from the verb *amara*, "to command," "to order."

Faqir Literally, "poor," "indigent." From the Arabic verb, *faqura*, "to become poor or needy." *Faqir* is often used as a synonym for Sufi, emphasizing the life of poverty and wayfaring the Sufi ideally embraces.

Fatwa A legal opinion issued by a Muslim scholar (or Muslim scholars) in accordance with Islamic jurisprudence. One who issues a *fatwa* is a *mufti*.

Ghazal A genre of lyric poetry; from the Arabic verb *ghazila*, "to woo," "to behave amorously toward [someone]." The *ghazal* would become an important poetic form in Persian (and all literary traditions influenced thereby) and was especially cultivated by Sufi poets.

Ghazi Originally "raider," "warrior"; often synonymous with *mujahid*, though from a legal perspective the *mujahid* is bound to fight solely to protect Muslims and spread Islam, whereas the *ghazi* can carry out raids against non-Muslims for the primary purpose of despoiling them.

Ghazw Originally "raid": military campaign of the early Muslim community; later, religiously sanctioned warfare.

Hadith Tradition or saying attributed to Muhammad or relating his conduct; the body of *hadith* is considered scripture.

Haqiqa From the Arabic root *haqq*, the basic meaning of which is "truth," "real," "right" (also, "God"). In the context of Sufism, *haqiqa* is the ultimate reality of God, toward which the wayfarer progresses on the Sufi path.

Ihsan From Arabic *ahsana*, "to do [something] well." In Sufism, *ihsan* denotes the third stage of the Sufi path, when the wayfarer becomes continuously aware of God's presence. (See *hadith* in the anecdote of Ibn al-Mubarak telling a man to behave as though he sees God before him.)[3]

Imam From the Arabic word for "before; in front of." *Imam* originally designated the man who would stand before the Muslims and lead the Friday prayer. This is still the primary meaning of *imam* in Sunni Islam, though the word can also denote (on the basis of learning) a high-ranking religious authority. In Shi'ism, *imam* designates the successors of the Prophet descended from his daughter Fatima and his cousin and son-in-law, 'Ali.

Islam From the Arabic verb *aslama*, "to submit." Sufis consider *Islam* as having two meanings; the outer meaning is to submit to the laws of the *shari'a*. Abu Sa'id Abu'l-Khayr described the inner meaning of *Islam* as the death of the *nafs* and its worldly desires.[4]

Jihad "Struggle," "fight," "war" to defend or spread Islam (from the Arabic verb *jāhada*). The doctrine of *jihad* as elaborated in the Islamic legal tradition is the duty of Muslims to strive for the universalization of Islam, either by means of persuasion and proselytization or by means of warfare. For the military *jihad* to be legitimate, the caliph or Muslim leader must first invite the unbelievers to embrace Islam. If they refuse—or, in the case of People of the Book, do not accept Muslim rule and payment of the *jizya*—war commences. The rules regarding who may fight as a *mujahid* are complex, requiring among other things purity of intention and the sole aim of spreading God's word. Later jurists elaborated the meaning of *jihad* to include the *jihad* of the heart (i.e., the inner *jihad* against the lower self), the tongue, the hand, and the sword. In Sufism *jihad* generally means the outer *jihad*, of the tongue and the sword, whereas the inner ("greater") *jihad* is referred to as *mujahada*, which is an alternative form of the verbal noun *jihad*. Often translated "holy war," though this term is inaccurate.

Jizya The tax that People of the Book must pay to the Muslim state as one of the requirements for permission to practice their faith.

Kafir "Unbeliever"; from the Arabic verb *kafara*, "to be irreligious," "to blaspheme," "to be ungrateful." This is the term generally employed in premodern texts to refer to non-Muslims. Sometimes translated "infidel."

Khirqa Literally, "rag," "tatter," from Arabic *kharaqa*, "to rend," "to tear": the patched cloak worn by Sufis, often a symbol of initiation if given by a Sufi shaykh to a *murid*.

Kitab "Book" (from Arabic *kataba*, "to write," "to inscribe"). In Islamic sacred history *kitab* can also mean revealed scripture. (E.g., one epithet of the Qur'an is *al-Kitab*, "The Book.")

Maghazi From the same root as *ghazw*. The *maghazi* are the battles and military campaigns that the Prophet Muhammad and his Companions waged against the pagan Arabs in order to make Islam universal in the Arabian Peninsula.[5]

Mufassir One who interprets the Qur'an. (See *s.v. Tafsir*.)

Muhaddith One who undertakes the study and narration of *hadith*.

Mujahada The alternative verbal noun of the verb *jāhada*. (See *s.v. Jihad*) In Sufism, *mujahada* generally denotes the inner, spiritual struggle against the *nafs*. It is often paired with the verbal noun *riyada* (*q.v.*, below).

Murid Sufi initiate or neophyte. (*Murid* is the active participle of the Arabic verb *arada*, "to want," "to strive," "to intend," "to aim.")

Murshid Sufi shaykh who guides the *murid* on the Sufi path. (From Arabic *arshada*, "to guide," "to instruct," "to conduct," "to advise.")

Mushrik Polytheist; from the Arabic *ashraka*, "to make [someone] the partner of God." The related noun *shirk* signifies polytheism or idolatry. A fundamental tenet of Islam is that God has no partners; and neither was He born, nor did He beget.[6]

Nafs In Sufism, the lower self, ego, base self; the seat of worldly desires. The Sufi must overcome the *nafs* through *mujahada* and *riyada*.

Pir Persian: "old man," "elder." The equivalent of the Arabic *shaykh* in Sufism. (For the Sufi meaning, see *s.v. Murshid*.)

Qasida "Ode": the preeminent poetic form in classical and pre-Islamic Arabic poetry, consisting of anywhere from twenty-five to one hundred verses. The two halves of the first verse share the same end rhyme, and the second half of subsequent verses repeats this rhyme. As with other traditional poetic genres, Sufi poets also adapted the *qasida* as a vehicle for expressing Sufi concepts. Ibn al-Farid (d. 632/1235) was the most notable Arab Sufi poet to compose mystical odes.

Qibla The direction of Mecca, which must be faced while praying.

Qur'an The Recitation; from Arabic *qara'a*, "to recite," "to read." God's uncreated word and final message for mankind. Muslims believe the Qur'an is coeternal with God and was preserved on a tablet in heaven until revealed to the Prophet Muhammad over a period of roughly twenty years. The Qur'an abrogates the scriptures of earlier religions (e.g., Judaism and Christianity). A fundamental tenet of Islam is that the Qur'an is inimitable and cannot be adequately translated. The Qur'an may thus be considered the "miracle" of Islam (i.e., God become word) in much the same way as Jesus is the "miracle" of Christianity (i.e., God become flesh).

Ribat In early Islamic history, a frontier outpost where *ghazis* dwelled. In Sufism it denotes a Sufi lodge or hospice.

Rijal From the Arabic word meaning "men" (singular *rajul*). As a genre of North African Sufi literature, it denotes a collection of succinct biographies of God's friends and other pious Muslims.

Riyada Spiritual exercises, self-mortification (from the Arabic *rada*, "to tame," "to break in," "to pacify"); often synonymous with *mujahada* (*q.v.*, above).

Salik "Wayfarer"; from Arabic *salaka*, "to follow [a path]," "to behave [in a certain way]." In Sufism, one who follows the Sufi path.

Sama' "Audition." (From Arabic *sami'a*, "to hear.") Involves listening to music and sometimes either dancing or rhythmic foot stomping (or twirling, in the case of the Mevlevi Sufi order). The aim of *sama'* is to experience *wajd* ("ecstasy"), which involves a visitation from God. The legitimacy of *sama'* was questioned not only by religious scholars but also by sober schools of Sufism. Even those Sufis who did practice *sama'* considered it unwise for non-Sufis to engage in it. (E.g., note the anecdote in the life of Abu Muhammad Chishti in Chapter 5.)

Shahada One of the Five Pillars of Islam: bearing witness that there is no god but God, and Muhammad is His messenger. Recitation of the *shahada* (i.e., profession of faith) is a prerequisite for embracing Islam.

Shari'a The divine law (i.e., the totality of God's revelation), which all Muslims must follow. The sources of the *shari'a* are the Qur'an and *Sunna*. The original meaning is a path leading to water.

Shaykh Arabic: "elder," "old man." (For the Sufi meaning, see *s.v. Murshid*.)

Silsila From the Arabic noun meaning "chain." In Sufism, the *silsila* is the lineage of a given Sufi order, which is traced through its shaykhs to its founder or eponym and ultimately to the Prophet's cousin and son-in-law, 'Ali (with the exception of the Naqshbandi order, which traces its lineage to Abu Bakr, the first caliph and the father-in-law of the Prophet Muhammad).

Sira (plural *siyar*) "Conduct," "way of life." The Prophet Muhammad's military campaigns; also, the biography of the Prophet.

Sufi "Wool wearer." Sufism is generally defined as Islamic mysticism and is described as the inner dimension of Islam. Sufism is not a sect and has developed within the Sunni tradition (with some exceptions). Although Sufism is the inner path of Islam, the role of Sufis in Muslim society has often been of an outward character (e.g., their involvement as teachers, reformers, proselytizers, and warriors).

Sunna The traditional practices and way of life of the Prophet that Muslims follow, which are based on accounts of Muhammad's sayings, deeds, and customary behavior as contained primarily in the *hadith*. From the Arabic noun meaning "customary or habitual practice."

Sura Chapter of the Qur'an, made up of *aya*s. The *sura*s of the Qur'an are, for the most part, ordered according to length from longest to shortest.

Tabaqat Literally, "generations." In Sufi literature, this term refers to a hagiographical collection of lives of God's friends.

Tadhkira From the same Arabic root as *dhikr*, meaning "memoir," "memorial." Often denotes a collection of hagiographical accounts of God's friends (chiefly in Persian or languages influenced by Persian).

Tajalli From the verb *tajalla*, "to appear; to reveal oneself; to be manifested." In Sufism, *tajalli* denotes God's self-disclosure as the ultimate reality behind all things. The verb *tajalla* recalls Quran: 7:143, in which Moses asks God to show Himself to him. God tells Moses to look at a mountain before him and says that if the mountain remains, he shall behold Him. God appears to the mountain and it is immediately leveled.

Tafsir Literally, "explanation"; traditional commentary and interpretation of the Qur'an.

Tariq "Path," "way." In Sufism, it denotes the Sufi path toward *haqiqa* (*q.v.*, above).

Tariqa From the verb *taraqa*, "to travel; follow; take a road; reach" (same root as *tariq*); a term of general significance denoting any Sufi order.

Tawakkul To rely solely on God for one's maintenance—a fundamental Sufi doctrine ultimately deriving from Qur'an 65:3: *And whosoever relies on God, then He is All-sufficient for him.*

Umma "Nation"; specifically, the universal community of Muslims.

Walaya The quality of being a *wali* (*q.v.*, below); friendship or closeness with God.

Wali (plural *awliya'*) In Sufism, one who is close to God or has been chosen by God as an example of his mercy and guidance. Generally translated "friend of God."

Wara' Supererogatory piety. Often exemplified by eating nothing about which there may exist any doubt of its being religiously licit.

Wilaya The power of God's friends to protect and guide the Muslims, often through wondrous means.

Zahir "Outward," "outer." (From Arabic *zahara*, "to appear," "to be evident," "to be manifest.") In Sufism, the outer meaning of Islamic scripture and practice.

Zawiya Sufi hospice or lodge. (Chiefly North African, from the Arabic noun meaning "corner," "nook.")

APPENDIX: THE PRIMARY HAGIOGRAPHICAL SOURCES AND THEIR AUTHORS

Tenth Century

Kitab al-luma'—Abu Nasr 'Abdullah al-Sarraj (d. 378/988) was a Sufi from Khurasan whose *Kitab al-luma'* (The Book of Flashes) is one of the earliest Arabic treatises on Sufism.[1]

Al-Ta'arruf li-madhhab ahl al-tasawwuf—Abu Bakr Muhammad al-Kalabadhi (d. 380/990) was a Sufi from Kalabadh, in Bukhara, whose Arabic treatise *al-Ta'arruf li-madhhab ahl al-tasawwuf* (Introduction to the Way of Sufism) is one of the most important sources for early Sufism.

Qut al-qulub—Abu Talib Muhammad al-Makki (d. 386/996) lived in Basra and Baghdad and composed the encyclopedic manual of Sufism *Qut al-qulub* (Nourishment of the Hearts), which would have a significant influence on al-Ghazali's *Ihya' 'ulum al-din*.

Adab al-muluk—Unknown author (composed ca. late tenth century). The manuscript of this book was discovered in Shiraz, Iran, in the twentieth century. *Adab al-muluk* (Manners of the Kings) is a Sufi handbook in Arabic that contains many anecdotes of early Sufis and proto-Sufis.

Eleventh Century

Tabaqat al-sufiyya—'Abd al-Rahman al-Sulami (d. 412/1021) was a prolific Sufi author from Nishapur, in Khurasan. He wrote a variety of works, including a history of Sufism, which is sadly lost, a *tafsir*, and the foundational Sufi hagiography in Arabic, *Tabaqat al-sufiyya* (Generations of the Sufis).

Hilyat al-awliya'—Abu Nu'aym al-Isfahani (d. 430/1038) was a scholar of jurisprudence and Sufism. His influential Arabic hagiography, *Hilyat al-awliya'* (Adornment of God's Friends) is considerably more extensive than al-Sulami's *Tabaqat*.

Kashf al-mahjub—'Ali Hujviri (d. ca. 465/1072) of Ghazna composed *Kashf al-mahjub* (*Revelation of the Mystery*), which is the best-known early Persian Sufi treatise and was influential in the development and spread of Sufism in the eastern Islamic world, where Persian served as the language of learning.

Tarikh Baghdad—al-Khatib al-Baghdadi (d. 463/1071) wrote his biographical Arabic encyclopedia, *Tarikh Baghdad* (History of Baghdad), as a reference for verifying the reliability of *hadith* transmitters. Nonetheless, *Tarikh Baghdad* is also a valuable source for anecdotes of God's friends.

Al-Risala al-Qushayriyya—Abu'l-Qasim al-Qushayri (d. 465/1072) of Nishapur wrote his Arabic *Risala* (*Al-Qushayri's Epistle on Sufism*) as a compendium of Sufi terminology and principles, which includes many anecdotes of God's friends.

Kitab al-nur—Abu'l-Fadl Muhammad al-Sahlagi (d. 476/1084) of Bistam was a follower of Bayazid and composed *Kitab al-nur* (The Book of Light) in Arabic. Sahlagi's hagiography is the most detailed of the extant sources for Bayazid's life.

Kimiya-yi sa'adat—Abu Hamid Muhammad al-Ghazali (d. 505/1111) of Khurasan was a renowned religious scholar, Sufi, and prolific writer whose influence on Sufism and Sunni Islam cannot be underestimated. He composed his *Kimiya-yi sa'adat* (*The Alchemy of Happiness*) as an abridgement of his most famous and influential Arabic work, *Ihya' 'ulum al-din* (The Revivification of the Religious Sciences), which contains many anecdotes and dicta of God's friends.

Pand-i piran—Unknown author (composed ca. mid-eleventh century). The Persian *Pand-i piran* (Advice of the Sufi Elders) relates many anecdotes and dicta of God's friends.

Twelfth Century

Tarikh madinat Dimashq—Ibn 'Asakir (d. 571/1176) was a *muhaddith* and scholar from Damascus who traveled widely and composed the monumental *Tarikh madinat Dimashq* (History of the City of Damascus), which is a biographical dictionary of notable men who had resided in Damascus and other cities of Greater Syria.

Sifat al-safwa—Ibn al-Jawzi (d. 597/1200) of Baghdad was a Hanbali scholar of law, *hadith*, and history. His history of Sufism, *Sifat al-safwa* (The Way of the Elite), depicted God's friends as following the example of the Prophet's Companions.

Tadhkirat al-awliya'—Farid al-Din 'Attar (d. late sixth/twelfth–early seventh/thirteenth century) of Nishapur is one of the great poets of Persian Sufi poetry. He composed several *mathnavi*s, including *Mantiq al-tayr* (*The Conference of the Birds*), as well as odes, lyric poetry, and quatrains. His *Tadhkirat al-awliya'* (*Memorial of God's Friends*) presents accessible and colorful stories of the lives of God's friends and is a masterpiece of classical Persian literature.

Dastur al-jumhur—Ahmad ibn Husayn ibn Shaykh Kharaqani (d. ca. early eighth/fourteenth century?) was a descendant of the famous early Sufi shaykh Abu'l-

Hasan Kharaqani (d. 425/1033). His *Dastur al-jumhur fi manaqib Sultan al-'Arifin Abu Yazid Tayfur* (Exemplar of the Multitude Regarding the Feats of the Sultan of the Knowers, Abu Yazid Tayfur), which draws on several Arabic sources, presents the deeds and dicta of Bayazid in Persian.

Hazar hikayat-i sufiyan—Unknown author (composed ca. late twelfth century). This fascinating collection of stories in Persian (The Thousand Tales of the Sufis) is a valuable source for anecdotes regarding God's friends.

Thirteenth/Fourteenth Centuries

Fazayil-i Balkh—Va'iz-i Balkhi (d. sixth/twelfth century) is said to have composed *Fazayil-i Balkh* (The Merits of Balkh) in Arabic in the twelfth century; however, the original is lost, and only the Persian translation of 'Abdullah al-Husayni Balkhi (d. early seventh/thirteenth century?) remains. *Fazayil-i Balkh* contains many anecdotes and dicta of God's friends from the region of Balkh.

Al-Dhayl 'ala al-rawdatayn—Abu Shama Maqdisi (d. 665/1268) of Damascus wrote his history of Salah al-Din and Nur al-Din, *Kitab al-rawdatayn* (The Book of the Gardens Twain) of which *al-Dhayl* (The Continuation) is a supplement.

Mir'at al-zaman—Sibt ibn al-Jawzi (d. 654/1256) was the grandson (*sibt*) of the prolific writer Ibn al-Jawzi. (See *Sifat al-safwa*, above.) He was a well-known preacher during his lifetime; however, he is chiefly remembered for his voluminous history, *Mir'at al-zaman* (The Mirror of Fortune), which served as a significant source for later historians such as Ibn Kathir and al-Dhahabi.

Risala—Safi al-Din ibn Abi'l-Mansur ibn Zafir (d. 682/1283) was a Sufi from Lower Egypt, who studied with Sufi shaykhs in Alexandria and Damascus and wrote his hagiographical *Risala*, which relates many fascinating anecdotes of friends of God whom he met during his travels.

al-Maqsad al-sharif—'Abd al-Haqq al-Badisi (d. early eighth/fourteenth century) composed his hagiography, *al-Maqsad al-sharif* (The Noble Aim) regarding the lives of God's friends of the Rif Mountain region of northern Morocco.

Firdaws al-murshidiyya—Mahmud b. 'Uthman (d. after 728/1328) composed the Persian translation of the (now-lost) Arabic hagiography *Firdaws al-murshidiyya* (Paradise of Spiritual Guidance) devoted to the life, deeds, and wonders of Abu Ishaq al-Kazaruni, founder of the first Sufi order.

Fawa'id al-fu'ad—Khwaja Hasan Dihlavi Sijzi (d. 736/1335/6) was a Chishti Sufi and poet. He composed the *malfuzat* (informal talks) of the Chishti shaykh Nizam al-Din Awliya' (d. 725/1325), *Fawa'id al-fu'ad* (Morals for the Heart), in Persian, with input from Nizam al-Din. *Fawa'id al-fu'ad* would have a considerable influence on subsequent Indo-Muslim Sufi literature.

Tarikh al-Islam—Shams al-Din Muhammad al-Dhahabi (d. 748/1348) of Damascus was a renowned historian and religious scholar whose vast *Tarikh al-Islam* (History of Islam) combines historical narrative with biographical notices. *Siyar a'lam al-nubala'* (Biographies of Noble Personages) and *al-'Ibar fi khabar man ghabar* (Lessons in the Annals of Those Who Have Passed), which furnish several anecdotes related herein, are abridgements of his great work.

Manaqib al-'arifin—Shams al-Din Aflaki (d. 761/1360) was a Sufi and hagiographer of Rumi and the early Mevlevi order. His *Manaqib al-'arifin* (*The Feats of the Knowers of God*) in Persian is the most extensive hagiography regarding the life and deeds of Rumi and his disciples.

Nashr al-mahasin/Mir'at al-janan/Rawd al-rayahin—Abu 'Abdullah al-Yafi'i (d. 768/1367) was a scholar and Sufi from Yemen affiliated with the Qadiri Sufi order who traveled widely and wrote several works dedicated to bolstering and defending Sufism, including *Nashr al-mahasin* (Propagation of Good Qualities), *Rawd al-rayahin* (The Garden of Sweet-Smelling Herbs), and *Mir'at al-janan* (The Mirror of the Heart).

Tabaqat al-shafi'iyya—Taj al-Din al-Subki (d. 771/1370) was a religious scholar from Lower Egypt who served as a preacher, judge, and teacher in Damascus. His most celebrated work is the *Tabaqat al-shafi'iyya* (Generations of Shafi'ites), which presents biographies of scholars of the Shafi'i legal school in Sunni Islam.

Al-Bidaya wa'l-nihaya—Ibn Kathir (d. 774/1373) was from Busra, in modern-day Syria, and spent most of his life in Damascus. He was a prominent religious scholar who was a follower of Ibn Taymiyya. Ibn Kathir's greatest work is his history of Islam, *al-Bidaya wa'l-nihaya* (The Beginning and the End).

Tabaqat al-awliya'—Ibn al-Mulaqqin (d. 804/1401) was a Sufi and scholar of the Shafi'i legal school whose biographical Sufi dictionary, *Tabaqat al-awliya'* (Generations of God's Friends), is an important source for Sufism in Egypt at that time.

Fifteenth Century

Nafahat al-uns—'Abd al-Rahman Jami (d. 898/1492) of Herat was a prolific Sufi author and poet of the Naqshbandi Sufi order. His *Nafahat al-uns* (Exhalations of Intimacy) is a vast compendium of Sufi hagiographies in Persian.

Al-Uns al-jalil—Mujir al-Din al-'Ulaymi al-Hanbali (d. 928/1522) was a Hanbali scholar, jurist, and historian from Jerusalem. His *al-Uns al-Jalil bi-tarikh al-Quds wa'l-Khalil* (Sublime Familiarity in the History of Jerusalem and Hebron) is an important source for the history of fifteenth-century Jerusalem.

Sixteenth/Seventeenth Centuries

Dawhat al-nashir—Ibn ʿAskar (d. 986/1578) was a Sufi and jurist from Chefchaouen in the Rif Mountains of Morocco who composed *Dawhat al-nashir li-mahasin man kana bi'l-Maghrib min mashayikh al-qarn al-ʿashir* (The Genealogical Tree of the Proclaimer of the Merits of the Tenth-Century Shaykhs of the Maghrib) regarding the important Sufi shaykhs of his era. Ibn ʿAskar died in the Battle of Wadi al-Makhazin.

Gulzar-i abrar—Muhammad Ghawthi Shattari (d. 1022/1613) was from the city of Mandav, in present-day Madhya Pradesh, India. He became a Sufi of the Shattari order after studying with a Sufi shaykh in Gujarat. His Persian hagiography *Gulzar-i abrar* (The Rose Garden of the Godly) is a valuable source for the lives of God's friends in India.

Thamarat al-quds—Mirza La'l Beg La'ali Badakhshi (d. 1022/1613/14) composed the hagiographical compendium *Thamarat al-quds* (The Fruits of Holiness), concentrating on friends of God associated primarily with the Chishti Sufi order.

Al-Kawakib al-durriyya—ʿAbd al-Raʾuf al-Munawi (d. 1031/1621) of Cairo was a Sufi, religious scholar, and prolific author. He is primarily known for his great biographical dictionary of Sufism, *al-Kawakib al-durriyya fi tarajim al-sufiyya* (The Glittering Stars in the Biographies of the Sufis).

Shadharat al-dhahab—Ibn al-ʿImad (d. 1080/1670) was a Hanbali scholar from Greater Syria who is chiefly known for his biographical dictionary, *Shadharat al-dhahab fi akhbar man dhahab* (Fragments of Gold in the Annals of Those Who Have Gone).

Eighteenth Century

Malfuzat-i Naqshbandiyya—Shah Mahmud Awrangabadi (d. 1175/1762) was the successor of Baba Shah Musafir (d. 1126/1714), the companion and successor of Baba Palang Pūsh. His Persian hagiography is the primary source for the life and deeds of Baba Palang Pūsh.

Tabaqat al-Hudaygi—Muhammad b. Ahmad al-Hudaygi (d. 1189/1775) was a Berber scholar from the region of Sus, in present-day Morocco. He wrote books on a variety of topics, including Sufism, and composed his *Tabaqat* regarding God's friends of the Maghrib.

Tuhfat al-tahirin—Shaykh Muhammad Aʿzam Tattawi (d. late twelfth/eighteenth century) composed his Persian hagiography *Tuhfat al-tahirin* (Gift of the Purified), concerning God's friends of Sindh.

NOTES

Introduction

1. The epigraph to this chapter: Abu'l-Qasim al-Qushayri, *al-Risala al-Qushayriyya* (Beirut: Dar Sader, 2011), 130. Concerning the importance of these stories, the anonymous author of *Pand-i piran* states, "Those who do not heed the lessons and stories of the Sufi shaykhs will soon lose their religion": *Pand-i piran*, ed. Jalal Matini (Mashhad: Bunyad-i Farhang-i Iran, 1978), 5.
2. "Friend of God" is the standard translation among scholars for Arabic *wali* (plural *awliya'*). The Arabic term has a number of possible meanings, many of which are implied insofar as it is used to describe important Sufi figures (e.g., one who is close to God, helper, benefactor, protector, etc.). Although used in the title of this book, English "saint" has Christian connotations such as canonization, which do not apply to the *awliya'*. In Sunni Islam no Muslim hierarchy exists that could officially recognize someone as a *wali*, whereas in the Roman Catholic, Eastern Orthodox, and Anglican Christian churches the process for officially declaring someone a saint (i.e., canonization or glorification) is well established. The verbal and abstract nouns *walaya* and *wilaya* are both associated with the *awliya'*, with *walaya* often denoting friendship or closeness with God and *wilaya* signifying the power of the *wali* as a protector or intercessor. Nevertheless, there is no consensus among modern scholars—nor, for that matter, among the Arab grammarians and Sufis of the premodern period—regarding which form conveys which aspect. For discussion of the *wilaya/walaya* conundrum, see Vincent J. Cornell, *Realm of the Saint: Power and Authority in Moroccan Sufism* (Austin: University of Texas Press, 1998), xxvii–xx; and Ibn Manzur, *Lisan al-'Arab*, XV (Beirut: Dar Sader, 1994): 407. For the sake of consistency in *Sufi Warrior Saints*, *walaya* will henceforth designate friendship with God or "sainthood," and *wilaya* will denote the power and authority of the *awliya'*.
3. Farid al-Din 'Attar, *Tadhkirat al-awliya'*, ed. Muhammad Isti'lami (Tehran: Intisharat-i Zuvvar, 2004), 6.
4. Ibid., 7.
5. E.g., John Renard, ed. and trans., *Tales of God's Friends: Islamic Hagiography in Translation* (Berkeley and Los Angeles: University of California Press, 2009); Paul Losensky, trans., *Farid ad-Din 'Attar's Memorial of God's Friends: Lives and Sayings of Sufis* (New York: Paulist Press, 2009). Likewise, Jeff Eden's fine translation of anecdotes concerning the miraculous deeds of the Central Asian warrior saint Satuq Bughra Khan is especially valuable and germane to the topic of Sufi jihad: Jeff Eden, *Warrior Saints of the Silk Road: Legends of the Qarakhanids* (Leiden: E. J. Brill, 2019).
6. *Ghazi* (warrior) is derived from the Arabic triliteral root /GhZW/. Al-Raghib al-Isfahani, *Mufradat alfaz al-Qur'an*, ed. Safwan 'Adnan Dawudi (Damascus: Dar al-Qalam, 1992), 606, gives the following definition for *ghaza*: "*Ghazw*: to go forth in order to wage war against the enemy." Though often interchangeable with *mujahid* (from the Arabic triliteral root /JHD/ whence *jihād*), meaning "warrior for the faith,"

technically a *ghazi* is not bound by the same legal constraints as a *mujahid*, in that the military jihad cannot be undertaken to acquire spoils, whereas *ghazw* (originally "raiding") can. For discussion of the rules for waging jihad, see Majid Khadduri, *War and Peace in the Law of Islam* (Baltimore: The John Hopkins University Press, 1955), 55–73.

7 It is important to note the difference between the Arabic noun *jihād* (from the verb *jāhada*, "to struggle"), the basic meaning of which is "a striving; struggle; endeavor," and the term *jihād* as it refers specifically to the Islamic doctrine of jihad—i.e., the duty to spread Islam and make God's word supreme in this world, which includes using military means when necessary: Khadduri, *War and Peace in the Law of Islam*, 55–6.

8 The epigraph to this section: Ibn 'Arabi, *al-Wasaya* (Beirut: Mu'assasat al-'A'lami, 1993), 36.

9 For a discussion of the greater jihad in contemporary Western discourse, see David Cook, *Understanding Jihad* (Berkeley and Los Angeles: University of California Press, 2005), 165–6; and Harry S. Neale, *Jihad in Premodern Sufi Writings* (New York: Palgrave Macmillan, 2016), 20–7.

10 The Iranian scholar Sayyid Ja'far Sajjadi discusses the difference between *mujahada* and *jihad*, describing the former as the spiritual struggle against the self, which involves subduing the passions through physical exercises, and the latter as war against the unbelievers for the purpose of either defense or to spread the "light of Islam" among them (though he also discusses *jihad-i akbar* in a following paragraph): Sayyid Ja'far Sajjadi, *Farhang-i istilahat va ta'birat-i 'irfani* (Tehran: Kitabkhana-yi Tahuri, 2004), 295, 697. For further discussion of how Sufi writings distinguish *mujahada* and *jihad*, see Neale, *Jihad in Premodern Sufi Writings*, 47–73.

11 The early mystical treatise *Riyadat al-nafs*, by Muhammad b. Abu 'Abdullah 'Ali (al-Hakim) al-Tirmidhi (d. early fourth/tenth century), uses the terms *mujahada* and *riyada* to describe the spiritual struggle and self-mortification necessary to subdue the lower self; however, it does not refer to this struggle as the "greater jihad": *Riyadat al-nafs*, ed. Ahmad 'Abd al-Rahman al-Sayih and Ahmad 'Abduh 'Awad (Cairo: Maktabat al-Thaqafa al-Diniyya, 2001), 18. Likewise, in his *Sirat al-awliya'*, al-Tirmidhi refers to the spiritual struggle as *mujahada*: *Sirat al-awliya'*, in Bernd Radtke, ed., *Thalath musannafat li'l-Hakim al-Tirmidhi* (Stuttgart: F. Steiner, 1992), 16. In a sermon dealing with how one ought to prepare for the military jihad, the preacher 'Abd al-Rahim b. Muhammad Ibn Nubata (d. 374/ 984) also presages the greater jihad, though like al-Tirmidhi he does not refer to it as such. "Jihad without exertion (*ijtihad*) is of no benefit, just as travel without provisions is not practical; therefore, you must undertake to struggle [*mujahada*] with your heart before seeing battle and overcome your passions before you fight the enemy": *Diwan khutab Ibn Nubata*, ed. Yasir Muhammad Khayr al-Miqdad (Kuwait: al-Wa'i al-Islami, 2012), 300.

12 For extensive treatment of Sufi jihad, including the textual history of the greater jihad and Sufi jihad terminology, see Neale, *Jihad in Premodern Sufi Writings*; and idem, "Books of Zuhd and Jihād" in the *Handbook of Sufi Studies: Prose* (Leiden: E. J. Brill, forthcoming).

13 For discussion of the term "Sufism" in Western scholarship, see Michael Sells, *Early Islamic Mysticism: Sufi, Qur'an, Miraj, Poetic and Theological Writings* (Mahwah, NJ: Paulist Press, 1995), 1; and Carl Ernst, *Sufism: An Introduction to the Mystical Tradition of Islam* (Boston: Shambhala, 2011), 9.

14 *Tasawwuf* is a form-V verbal noun (i.e., the *tafa"ul* pattern). Form-V verbs are created by adding a prefix (/ta-/) to the form-II verbal pattern *fa"ala*, hence *tafa"ala*. Form-II verbs are often causative in meaning, though they can also be intensive or denominative. Form V is the reflexive of form II and, with regard to creeds or religious practices, denotes the adoption of a set of beliefs or self-identification with a particular faith (e.g., *tahawwada*, "to become a Jew"; *tashayya'a*, "to become a Shi'ite"). For an exhaustive discussion of Arabic verb forms, see W. Wright, *A Grammar of the Arabic Language*, I (Cambridge: Cambridge University Press, 1962), 29–49. For discussion of the term *tasawwuf*, see Ernst, *Sufism*, 21–3.

15 This recalls the Sufi dictum "The Sufi owns nothing, and nothing owns him": Abu'l-Hasan 'Ali Hujviri, *Kashf al-mahjub*, ed. Mahmud 'Abidi (Tehran: Soroush Press, 2012), 52.

16 It is, however, generally Sufi hagiography and manuals, rather than non-Sufi sources, that describe the early Sufis as having an affinity for the collection and narration of *hadith*: Jawid Mojaddedi, *The Biographical Tradition in Sufism: The Tabaqat Genre from al-Sulamī to Jāmī* (Richmond, Surrey: Curzon Press, 2001), 187 n. 73.

17 Ignaz Goldziher, *Introduction to Islamic Theology and Law*, trans. A. Hamori and R. Hamori (Princeton: Princeton University Press, 1981), 37–9.

18 For discussion of the role of *hadith* in Sufism, see Hamid Algar, "Hadith in Sufism," *Encyclopædia Iranica*, online edition, http://www.iranicaonline.org/articles/hadith-iv (XI, fasc. 5, 451–3).

19 For discussion of the earliest extant written sources for Sufism in Khurasan, see Jacqueline Chabbi, "Remarques sur le développement historique des mouvements ascétiques et mystiques au Khurasan: IIIe/IXe siècle–IVe/Xe siècle," *Studia Islamica* 46 (1977): 5–72.

20 Hujviri, *Kashf al-mahjub*, 54–5.

21 For example, in the introduction to his hagiography concerning the early Sufi shaykh Abu Sa'id Abu'l-Khayr (d. 440/1049), Muhammad b. Munavvar says that God's friends are second only to prophets and messengers with regard to their sacred function: Muhammad b. Munavvar, *Asrar al-tawhid fi maqamat shaykh Abi Sa'id*, ed. R. Shafi'i Kadkani, I (Tehran: Mu'assasa-yi Intishirat-i Agah, 1997), 2.

22 E.g., 'Attar, *Tadhkirat al-awliya'*, 132: "Association with God's friends is association with God." This dictum is attributed to the early Egyptian ascetic Dhu al-Nun al-Misri (d. 245/859). "Sitting with God's friends is like sitting with God, for a friend of God has died with respect to his own existence and is, thus, like an instrument in the power of God's hand, just as a pen in the hand of a scribe is—whatever comes from the pen is attributed to the scribe and not to the pen": Sultan Valad, *Valad Nama*, ed. Jalal al-Din Huma'i (Tehran: Mu'assasa-yi Nashr-i Huma, 1997), 146.

23 Daphna Ephrat notes that "Sufi shaykhs disseminated the tradition that provided the Muslim believer with the unique combination of spiritual-emotional religious experience, intellectual teaching, and moral guidance [and] established their position as charismatic figures (channels to God)": *Spiritual Wayfarers, Leaders in Piety: Sufis and the Dissemination of Islam in Medieval Palestine* (Cambridge, MA: Harvard Center for Middle Eastern Studies, 2008), 3.

24 'Abd al-Rahman al-Sulami, *Tabaqat al-sufiyya*, ed. Mustafa 'Abd al-Qadir 'Ata (Beirut: Dar al-Kutub al-'Ilmiyya, 2003), 365. The *Sunna* is the proper mode of conduct for Muslims, based on the Prophet's sayings, deeds, and customary behavior as related primarily in the *hadith*.

25 For an excellent overview of early Sufism and the elaboration of Sufi doctrine and practice, see Jamil M. Abun-Nasr, *Muslim Communities of Grace: The Sufi Brotherhoods in Islamic Religious Life* (New York: Columbia University Press, 2007), 26–55.
26 R. G. Jenkins identifies four stages in the development of Sufism and locates the entrance of mysticism into Sufism in the second stage, the first stage being *zuhd* (asceticism; renunciation). He further observes that the second stage was not necessarily a "fusion of asceticism and mysticism" and that some orders "emphasized asceticism rather than mysticism and vice versa": "The Evolution of Religious Brotherhoods in North and Northwest Africa, 1523–1900," in J. R. Willis, ed., *Studies in West African Islamic History*, I, *The Cultivators of Islam* (London: Frank Cass, 1979), 40–77. Whereas Christopher Melchert argues that mysticism (i.e., Sufism) subsumed *zuhd* sometime during the mid-ninth century: Christopher Melchert, "The Transition from Asceticism to Mysticism at the Middle of the 9th Century C.E.," *Studia Islamica* 83 (1966): 51–70, esp. 58. Megan H. Reid, however, contends that *zuhd* continued to exist as a significant aspect of non-Sufi piety among legal scholars and that similarities between their asceticism and austerity with those of Sufis do not suggest these legal scholars had any connection with Sufism: Megan H. Reid, *Law and Piety in Medieval Islam* (Cambridge: Cambridge University Press, 2013), 5–7. Alexander Knysh argues, however, that mysticism and asceticism are generally intertwined and that separating the two "fails to account for the messiness and originality of the thought and practice of real-life 'spiritual athletes'": Alexander Knysh, *Sufism: A New History of Islamic Mysticism* (Princeton: Princeton University Press, 2017), 11.
27 How Western scholarship in European languages and Muslim scholarship in Islamic languages portray and conceptualize Sufism are shaped as much by contemporary cultural, aesthetic, and historical assumptions as they are by Sufi writings and the observation of Sufi practices. To reject one view in favor of another is to diminish our understanding of how the various Sufi "discourses" are intertwined and influence one another. For an extensive and wide-ranging discussion of these matters, see Knysh, *Sufism: A New History of Islamic Mysticism*.
28 William C. Chittick, *Sufism: A Short Introduction* (Oxford: Oneworld, 2000), 18.
29 For discussion of the difficulty of reducing Sufism to a simple definition, see Alexander Knysh, "Sufism as an Explanatory Paradigm: The Issue of the Motivations of Sufi Resistance Movements in Western and Russian Scholarship," *Die Welt des Islams* 42.2 (2002): 139–73; and idem, *Sufism: A New History of Islamic Mysticism*, 58–61.
30 Hamid Algar, "Bektāšīya," *Encyclopædia Iranica,* online edition, http://www.iranicaonline.org/articles/bektasiya (IV, fasc. 2, 118–22).
31 Jamal Malik and John Hinnells, eds., *Sufism in the West* (New York: Routledge, 2006), 3.
32 J. Spencer Trimingham, *The Sufi Orders in Islam* (Oxford: Oxford University Press, 1971), 202–3.
33 J. During and R. Sellheim, "Samā'," *Encyclopædia of Islam, Second Edition* (2012), online edition, http://dx.doi.org/10.1163/1573-3912_islam_COM_0992.
34 Wilfred Madelung, *Religious Trends in Early Islamic Iran* (Albany: Bibliotheca Persica, 1988), 48. Madelung describes the eponym of the order, Abu Ishaq al-Kazaruni, as representing "an activist asceticism." The Iranian scholar 'Abd al-Husayn Zarrinkub has described Abu Ishaq as spending the majority of his career in "preaching, guiding,

warfare, and jihad," and he goes on to say that the shaykhs of the Kazaruni order followed the example of Abu Ishaq in placing particular emphasis on expanding the Abode of Islam by means of jihad. ʿAbd al-Husayn Zarrinkub, *Justuju dar tasavvuf-i Iran* (Tehran: Amir Kabir, 1990), 218.

35 As Chittick points out (*Sufism*, 1), while such labels as "Islamic mysticism" can help orient readers regarding the nature of Sufism, they often end up being "more of a hindrance than a help" in that they may lead to a narrow categorization of the Sufi tradition.

36 "The Qurʾan is a two-sided brocade: some people profit from one side, and some from the other; both are right": Jalal al-Din Rumi, *Kitab-i Fihi ma fihi*, ed. Badiʾ al-Zaman Furuzanfar (Tehran: Intisharat-i Danishgah-i Tihran, 1951), 165. Suhrawardi relates the following *hadith* in this regard—"No verse of the Qurʾan is revealed save that it has an outer aspect and an inner aspect": Shihab al-Din ʿUmar al-Suhrawardi, *ʿAwarif al-maʿarif* (Beirut: Dar Sader, 2010), 30.

37 The early Sufi and author of several treatises Abu Saʾid al-Kharraz (d. 277/890) of Baghdad expressed the complementary nature of Sufism succinctly: "Should any inner [interpretation] contradict an outer [aspect of Islamic practice], then it has no basis" (al-Sulami, *Tabaqat*, 185).

38 Chittick, *Sufism*, 27–8. Chittick makes the significant points that Western scholars and enthusiasts of Sufism often prefer the "drunken" poetry of Sufism to its "sober" prose and that this preference has led to the misconception that Sufis are not overly concerned with matters of outward Islamic practice.

39 Franklin D. Lewis, *Rumi—Past and Present, East and West: The Life, Teachings, and Poetry of Jalâl al-Din Rumi* (London: Oneworld, 2016), 41–128. Lewis's exhaustive analysis, which is both scholarly and accessible, is the definitive study of Rumi available in a European language. Rumi expressed the centrality of the Qurʾan in the quatrain "As long as I have life, I am the bondsman of the Qurʾan": Jalal al-Din Rumi, *rubaʿi* 358, in *Divan-i kamil-i Shams-i Tabrizi*, ed. Badiʾ al-Zaman Furuzanfar and ʿAli Dashti, III (Tehran: Sazman-i Intisharat-i Javidan, 1980), 98.

40 Lewis, *Rumi*, 407–8.

41 Muhammad b. Munavvar, *Asrar al-tawhid*, 275.

42 *Hazar hikayat-i sufiyan*, ed. H. Khatamipur, I (Tehran: Intisharat-i Sukhan, 2000), 457.

43 E.g., the anecdote of Junayd and the *murids* in *Tadhkirat al-awliya*ʾ (Chapter 2) and the anecdote of Shah Jalal and the Sufi *ghazis* in *Gulzar-i abrar* (Chapter 5).

44 For discussion of historical militant Sufism, see David Cook, "Sufism, the Army, and Holy War," in Alexandre Papas, ed., *Handbook of Sufi Studies*, vol. I, *Sufi Institutions* (Leiden: E. J. Brill, 2020), 315–21.

45 Erik S. Ohlander, *Sufism in an Age of Transition: ʿUmar al-Suhrawardi and the Rise of the Islamic Mystical Brotherhoods* (Leiden: E. J. Brill, 2008), 195.

46 For discussion of idealized historiographical and hagiographical Sufi warrior narratives in the subcontinent, see Richard M. Eaton, *The Rise of Islam and the Bengal Frontier, 1204–1760* (Berkeley and Los Angeles: University of California Press, 1993), 71–7; for discussion of the *ghazi* question in relation to early Ottoman history, see Linda Darling, "Contested Territory: Ottoman Holy War in Comparative Context," *Studia Islamica* 91 (2000): 133–63; and Rudi Paul Lindner, "Stimulus and Justification in Early Ottoman History," *Greek Orthodox Theological Review* 27 (1982): 207–24.

47 For a comprehensive study of the life of Muhammad al-Jazuli, see Cornell, *Realm of the Saint*.

48 Saiyid Athar Abbas Rizvi, *A History of Sufism in India*, I (Delhi: Munshiram Manoharlal, 1978), 110.
49 Ira M. Lapidus, *A History of Islamic Societies* (Cambridge: Cambridge University Press, 2002), 364.
50 For discussion of the Sufi role in spreading Islam in India, see Richard M. Eaton, *The Sufis of Bijapur, 1300–1700: Social Roles of Sufis in Medieval India* (Princeton: Princeton University Press, 1978), and idem, *The Rise of Islam and the Bengal Frontier*.
51 As'ad Khatib, *al-Butula wa'l-fida' 'inda al-sufiyya* (Damascus: Dar al-Taqwa, 1997), 149.
52 Michel Balivet, "Miracles chrétiens et islamisation en chrétienté seldjoukide et ottoman entre le XIe et le XVe siècle," in Denise Aigle, ed., *Miracle et karāma: Hagiographies médiévales comparées* (Turnhout: Brepols, 2000), 409.
53 For discussion of the military jihad in Sufi writings, see Neale, *Jihad in Premodern Sufi Writings*, 57–73.
54 For convincing examples of Sufi history that combine a variety of historical and hagiographical sources, see Denise Aigle, "Un fondateur d'ordre en milieu rural: Cheikh Abū Isḥāq de Kāzarūn," in eadem, ed., *Saints orientaux* (Paris: De Boccard, 1995), 181–209, and Richard Eaton's aforementioned (above, nn. 46, 50) monographs regarding Sufis in India. For an analysis of the hagiographical and historical accounts of the Javanese Hindu king Brawijaya, who, after embracing Islam at the hand of one of the Wali Songo (Nine Friends of God), became the Sufi saint Pandan Arang (d. sixteenth century) and converted the inhabitants of central Java to Islam, see Claude Guillot, "The Tembayat Hill: Clergy and Royal Power in Central Java from the 15th to the 17th Century," in Henri Chambert-Loir and Anthony Reid, eds., *The Potent Dead: Ancestors, Saints and Heroes in Contemporary Indonesia* (Honolulu: University of Hawaii Press, 2002), 141–7. For an excellent study of the Sufi role in propagating Islam in the Levant, see Ephrat, *Spiritual Wayfarers, Leaders in Piety*.
55 Aigle, *Miracle et karāma*, 30.
56 The epigraph to this section is from Muhammad Jalal Sharaf's study of Sufism, *Dirasat fi'l-tasawwuf al-islami: shakhsiyat wa-madhahib* (Beirut: Dar al-Nahda al-'Arabiyya, 1980), 9.
57 Regarding the Moroccan hagiographical tradition (though relevant to Sufi hagiography in general), Vincent Cornell underscores the necessity of understanding that although many Muslim friends of God were not Sufis, hagiographers assumed that they were: *Realm of the Saint*, xxxv.
58 For discussion of battle and conquest narratives in early Islamic historiography, see Fred M. Donner, *Narratives of Islamic Origins: The Beginnings of Islamic Historical Writing* (Princeton: Darwin Press, 1998), 174–82. For discussion of how the narratives of early Muslim conquests and the *mujahid*s who participated in them served as models for later Muslims, see Thomas Sizgorich, *Violence and Belief in Late Antiquity: Militant Devotion in Christianity and Islam* (Philadelphia: University of Pennsylvania Press, 2009), 144–67.
59 Ghada Osman, "Oral vs. Written Transmission: The Case of Ṭabarī and Ibn Sa'd," *Arabica* 48 (2001): 67.
60 Muslims wishing to imitate the Prophet saw in *sira* literature the military ideal that he represented in fighting against the unbelievers, which undoubtedly influenced the zeal for carrying out the military jihad during the early centuries of Islam: Michael Bonner, *Aristocratic Violence and Holy War: Studies in the Jihad and the Arab-Byzantine Frontier* (New Haven: American Oriental Society, 1996), 119.

61 For discussion of *thaghr/thughur*, which indicated the border between the eastern region of the Byzantine Empire and the Abode of Islam, see Michael Bonner, "The Naming of the Frontier: 'Awāsim, Thughūr and the Arab Geographers," *Bulletin of the School of Oriental and African Studies* 57 (1994): 17–24. The concepts of *Dar al-Islam* (the Abode of Islam) and *Dar al-harb* (the Abode of War), as well as *Dar al-sulh* (the Abode of Truce), have existed in Islamic jurisprudence since the ninth century. The Abode of Islam is the territory under Muslim rule inhabited by Muslims, as well as non-Muslims who have accepted Muslim rule. The Abode of War is any territory not under Muslim rule. Theoretically, it was the duty of Muslim rulers to bring the Abode of War under Muslim rule if they had the strength and means to do so. The Shafi'i legal school recognized a third category, the Abode of Truce, which is territory ruled by non-Muslims with whom a temporary truce has been made. Not all schools of Sunni Muslim jurisprudence have accepted this category: Majid Khadduri, *The Islamic Law of Nations: Shaybānī's Siyar* (Baltimore: The John Hopkins University Press, 1966), 11–14. (E.g., the Hanafi school has not done.)

62 Edward Lane, *An Arabic-English Lexicon*, III, *Dāl–Zāy* (Beirut: Librairie du Liban, 1968), 1013.

63 Baladhuri gives the following description of the Muslims' border outposts and garrisons: "They are called places of defense (*'awasim*), because the Muslims defend themselves by means of them, and the *'awasim* protect and preserve the Muslims when they have ceased waging war and have left the border (*thaghr*)": Baladhuri, *Futuh al-buldan* (Beirut: Dar al-Kutub al-'Ilmiyya, 2000), 84.

64 'Abd al-Hakim Hissan, *al-Tasawwuf fi al-shi'r al-'arabi: nash'atuh wa-tatawwuruh hatta akhir al-qarn al-thalith al-hijri* (Cairo: Maktabat al-Anjalu al-Misriyya, 1954), 43; for discussion of *ribat* in the Sufi context, see Gerhard Böwering and Matthew Melvin-Koushki, "Ḵānaqāh," *Encyclopædia Iranica*, (edition, http://www.iranicaonline.org/articles/kanaqah (XV, fasc.5, 456–66).

65 Lane, *An Arabic-English Lexicon*, III, *Dāl–Zāy*, 1013–14. In his lexicon of the Qur'an, *Mufradat alfaz al-Qur'an*, 338, al-Raghib al-Isfahani (d. 502/1108) offers a further interpretation of the verbal noun *ribāt/murābata*, which he defines as "defending" or "preserving" (*muhāfaza*).

66 With regard to the allegorical use of military terminology to describe the spiritual struggle of God's friends, it may prove useful to consider a similar use of such terminology to describe the early ascetics of Syrian Christianity in Mesopotamia as found in the extant literature in Syriac, Greek, and Armenian. For example, Saint Ephrem the Syrian (d. 373), a prolific and profoundly influential author of sermons, hymns, poetry, and exegesis in Syriac, described the Christian anchorites as those who went out from the world to make war with the Enemy and his spirits and demons, the Holy Spirit having anointed them as "athletes for combat" (Syriac *atlētē lagōnā*; from Greek ἀθλητής "combatant," "champion," and ἀγών "contest," "struggle," "battle"): Arthur Vööbus, *History of Asceticism in the Syrian Orient: A Contribution to the History of Culture in the Near East*, I (Louvain: Peeters, 1958), 149. Vööbus likewise notes that the early literature referred to these ascetics as "warriors of God": ibid., 150.

67 Several earlier biographies of Sufis are lost, with only quotations from them having survived, notably those composed by Abu Sa'id b. al-Ar'abi (d. 340/952?) and Ja'far al-Khuldi (d. 348/959). Likewise, al-Sulami's history of the Sufis (*Tarikh al-sufiyya*) has not survived: Christopher Melchert, "Origins and Early Sufism," in Lloyd Ridgeon, ed., *The Cambridge Companion to Sufism* (Cambridge: Cambridge University Press, 2015), 19.

68 Mojaddedi, *The Biographical Tradition in Sufism*, 18.
69 Ibid., 24.
70 Abun-Nasr notes that these two hagiographies also differed somewhat in their intent; al-Sulami's hagiography emphasized Sufism as a form of *'ilm* (science) that the preceding generations of religious authorities had passed down, whereas Abu Nu'aym al-Isfahani sought to demonstrate that the fundamental Sufi beliefs and practices were the essence of godliness and Muslim piety: Abun-Nasr, *Muslim Communities of Grace*, 41–2.
71 Jürgen Paul, "Hagiographic Literature," *Encyclopædia Iranica*, online edition, http://www.iranicaonline.org/articles/hagiographic-literature (XI, fasc. 5, 536–9).
72 E.g., two of the earliest extant examples of New Persian prose were composed in the early tenth century and are translations of al-Tabari's history and *tafsir*. Neither of these translations includes the chains of transmission of the originals. The introduction to the *tafsir* contains a fascinating explanation for this, saying that at the behest of the Samanid Amir, they translated al-Tabari's *tafsir* into Persian for the benefit of Muslims who did not know Arabic and while doing so they decided to leave out all the "long chains of transmission": Muhammad b. Jarir Tabari, *Tarjuma-yi Tafsir-i Tabari*, ed. Habib Yaghma'i, I (Tehran: Intisharat-i Tus, 1977), 5.
73 Badi' al-Zaman Furuzanfar, *Sharh-i ahval va naqd va tahlil-i athar-i shaykh Farid al-Din Muhammad 'Attar-i Nishaburi* (Tehran: University of Tehran Press, 1961), 52.
74 For discussion of hagiography and the crystallization of Sufi orders in Central Asia during the thirteenth and fourteenth centuries, see Devin Deweese, *Islamization and Native Religion in the Golden Horde: Baba Tükles and Conversion to Islam in Historical and Epic Tradition* (University Park: Pennsylvania State University Press, 1994), 138–40.
75 For a comprehensive analysis of hagiography as literature, see John Renard, *Friends of God: Islamic Images of Piety, Commitment, and Servanthood* (Berkeley and Los Angeles: University of California Press, 2008), 237–57.
76 Cornell, *Realm of the Saint*, 98.
77 Ibid. Although monographic hagiographical works do exist, they were not as influential in the development of Maghribi Sufism.
78 The epigraph to this section is quoted from 'Unsur al-Ma'ali Kaykavus b. Iskandar b. Qabus, *Qabus Nama*, ed. Ghulamhusayn Yusufi (Tehran: Shirkat-i Intisharat-i 'Ilmi va Farhangi, 2003), 252–3.
79 For comparison of miracles and hagiography in the medieval Christian and Islamic tradition, see Aigle, *Miracle et karāma*. For an example of a particular hagiographical motif shared by Muslim, Hindu, and Sikh hagiography, see Simon Digby, "To Ride a Tiger or a Wall? Strategies of Prestige in Indian Sufi Legend," in Winand M. Callewaert and Rupert Snell, eds., *According to Tradition: Hagiographical Writing in India* (Wiesbaden: Harrassowitz Verlag, 1994), 99–129.
80 Hamid Algar, "The Naqshbandi Order: A Preliminary Study of Its History and Significance," *Studia Islamica* 63 (1976): 134. Vincent Cornell (*Realm of the Saint*, 276) argues that hagiography presents a "typology" of God's friends as embodying correct Islamic practice and that their actions "reflect the collective recollection of social experience."
81 I owe this insight to Jeffrey M. Hurwit's discussion of the role of formulaic language in the Homeric epics in *The Art and Culture of Early Greece, 1100–480 B.C.* (Ithaca: Cornell University Press, 1985), 97. For discussion of the function of repeated hagiographical motifs and miracles see, Aigle, *Miracle et karāma*, 32.

82 For a comprehensive typological compendium of Sufi miracles, see Richard Gramlich, *Die Wunder der Freunde Gottes: Theologien und Erscheinungsformen des islamischen Heiligenwunders* (Wiesbaden: Franz Steiner Verlag, 1987).
83 Renard, *Friends of God*, 25.
84 Khizr (from the Arabic root meaning "green") is a prophet in the Islamic tradition, although he is not named in scripture. It is traditionally believed that the unnamed companion of Moses in Qur'an 18:65–80 is Khizr. In Sufism, Khizr often serves as a guide and preceptor to God's friends; examples may be found herein in the lives of Rumi, Abu Muhammad Chishti, and Baba Palang Pūsh.
85 In the Persian cultural context, hunting is associated with kings, which renders the hunt an ideal locus for the humbling and subsequent conversion of a royal figure such as Ibrahim, who at the time of these wondrous encounters is the king of Balkh. Sizgorich, *Violence and Belief in Late Antiquity*, 173.
86 The motif of repentance, as it developed in Sufi hagiography, emphasized an "unfathomable act of God" whereby He chose His *awliya'* by calling them to Him through wondrous events, rather than it being an individual choice to repent, and this rendered them "divinely inspired" exemplars of Muslim piety: Abun-Nasr, *Muslim Communities of Grace*, 33. For extensive treatment of the topic of *tawba* in early Sufism, see Atif Khalil, *Repentance and the Return to God: Tawba in Early Sufism* (Albany: State University of New York Press, 2019).
87 Renard, *Friends of God*, 43.
88 'Attar, *Tadhkirat al-awliya'*, 300.
89 Muhammad b. Munavvar, *Asrar al-tawhid*, 42.
90 Hamid ibn Fazl Allah Jamali, *Siyar al-'arifin* (Delhi: Matba'-i Rizavi, 1893), 11–12.
91 This *hadith* is found in the compendia of al-Tirmidhi, Abu Dawud, and Ibn Maja.
92 An earlier version of this anecdote is found in *Muruj al-dhahab* of al-Mas'udi (d. 345/956). In *Muruj al-dhahab*, the caliph Harun al-Rashid summons Fudayl and Sufyan b. 'Uyayna to speak with him. Upon entering the court, Fudayl asks Sufyan which one is the Commander of the Faithful, so Sufyan points to Harun al-Rashid. Fudayl then begins to admonish the caliph, saying: "O handsome-faced one, in whose hands is placed the well-being of this religious community! You have assumed a weighty task indeed!" Upon hearing the ascetic's words, Harun begins to weep. He then tries to offer Fudayl a great sum of money; however, Fudayl refuses to take it: al-Mas'udi, *Muruj al-dhahab wa-ma'adin al-jawahir*, III (Beirut: Dar al-Andalus, 1996), 354–5.
93 Abu Nu'aym al-Isfahani, *Hilyat al-awliya' wa-tabaqat al-asfiya'*, VIII (Beirut: Dar al-Fikr, 1996), 105. Other examples of this motif may be found in 'Attar's *Tadhkirat al-awliya'* (e.g., in the life of Shaqiq-i Balkhi, p. 204; and in the life of Dawud-i Ta'i, pp. 231–2).
94 Sizgorich suggests that early Muslims saw the Christian monk as "a model of militant piety." This anecdote may reflect this view, especially when considered alongside *hadith* related by Ibn al-Mubarak concerning jihad as the "monasticism" of Islam. Sizgorich, *Violence and Belief in Late Antiquity*, 161.
95 Attar, *Tadhkirat al-awliya'*, 143, 413, 46, 72; *Pand-i piran*, 13–14.
96 This recalls the colloquial Persian saying *ham khodā-ro mikhād, ham khormā-ro* (He wants both God and the date), which is the equivalent of the English expression "to have one's cake and eat it too."
97 Muhammad b. Ahmad al-Hudaygi, *Tabaqat al-Hudaygi*, ed. Ahmad Bu Mazgu, I (Casablanca: Matba'at al-Najah al-Jadida, 2006), 285.

98   'Attar, *Tadhkirat al-awliya'*, 304–5.
99   Muhammad b. Munavvar, *Asrar al-tawhid*, 31–2.
100 'Attar, *Tadhkirat al-awliya'*, 148–9.
101 'Abd al-Rahman Jami, *Nafahat al-uns*, ed. Mahmud 'Abidi (Tehran: Intisharat-i Ittila'at, 1996), 423.
102 'Attar, *Tadhkirat al-awliya'*, 77–8.
103 'Abdullah ibn As'ad al-Yafi'i, *Nashr al-mahasin al-'aliyya fi fadl al-mashayikh al-sufiyya*, ed. Khalil al-Mansur (Beirut: Dar al-Kutub al-'Ilmiyya, 2000), 39.
104 Abu Nu'aym al-Isfahani, *Hilyat al-awliya'*, VIII, 64.
105 Mirza La'al Bayg La'ali Badakhshi, *Thamarat al-quds min shajarat al-uns*, ed. Sayyid Kamal Hajj Sayyid Jawadi (Tehran: Pizhuhishgah-i 'Ulum-i Insani va Mutala'at-i Farhangi, 1997), 112–13. A slightly different version of this anecdote is related in Chapter 5. A similar motif is found in *Fawa'id al-fu'ad*, where Nizam al-Din Awliya' (d. 725/1325) relates an anecdote in which an official who is devoted to God's friends is journeying in Gujarat when he encounters a Hindu with an unsheathed sword in his hand. The Hindu advances toward him, so he cries out, "O Shaykh, be here!" Forthwith the Hindu lets fall the sword from his hand and beseeches the official to show him mercy. The official is astonished but tells the Hindu he is safe and gives him back his sword. The two men then continue on their separate ways: Khwaja Hasan Dihlavi, *Fawa'id al-fu'ad: Malfuzat-i Khwaja Nizam al-Din Awliya'*, ed. Muhsin Kiyani (Tehran: Intisharat-i Ruzana, 1998), 95–6.
106 E.g., in the tale of King 'Umar Nu'man and his two sons, two young women relate anecdotes about Bishr al-Hafi, Hatim al-Asamm, Ibrahim ibn Adham, and Shaqiq al-Balkhi, including the well-known anecdote in which Ibrahim upbraids Shaqiq for his description of *tawakkul*: "Ibrahim asked Shaqiq, 'How goes it with you in Balkh?' 'If we receive our daily bread, we eat, and if we go hungry, we forbear,' replied Shaqiq. 'Thus do the dogs of Balkh behave! For when *we* receive *our* daily bread, we are delighted, and if we go hungry, we give thanks!' replied Ibrahim. Shaqiq then sat down before Ibrahim and said, 'You are my teacher!'": *Alf layla wa-layla*, I (Beirut: Dar Sader, 1999), 222–3.
107 In English, the heading to this section may be rendered as, "And these things never happened, but they exist forever": Sallustius, *Concerning the Gods and the Universe*, ed. and trans. Arthur Darby Nock (Cambridge: Cambridge University Press, 1926), 8.
108 Ananda Coomaraswamy, *Buddha and the Gospel of Buddhism* (New Hyde Park, NY: University Books, 1969), 11.
109 Peter Chelkowksi and Hamid Dabashi, *Staging a Revolution: The Art of Persuasion in the Islamic Republic of Iran* (New York: New York University Press, 1999), 70–4.
110 Ibid., 89, fig. 5.2.
111 Muhammad Hamidullah, *The Muslim Conduct of State*, 7th ed. (Lahore: SH. Muhammad Ashraf, 1996), 191. For the rules regarding declaring and waging jihad, see Khadduri, *War and Peace in the Law of Islam*, 55–73.
112 Ibn Rushd, *al-Muqaddimat al-mumahhidat*, ed. Muhammad Hajji, I (Beirut: Dar al-Gharb al-Islami, 1988), 341. Ibn Rushd describes the jihad of the heart as "the jihad against Satan by means of *mujahada*." The jihad of the tongue and the hand are concerned with the Qur'anic injunction of enjoining the right and forbidding the wrong (Qur'an 3:104, 110; 9:71, 112; 31:17). It is worth noting that the rest of the chapter in *al-Muqaddimat* that treats the topic of jihad discusses the various aspects of the military jihad.
113 Al-Raghib al-Isfahani, *Mufradat alfaz al-Qur'an*, 208.

114 For a discussion of the contemporary promotion of Sufism for political aims, see Fait Muedini, *Sponsoring Sufism: How Governments Promote "Mystical Islam" in Their Domestic and Foreign Policies* (New York: Palgrave MacMillan, 2015).

Chapter 1

1   In Greater Syria, the Muslims took Damascus in 636, Jerusalem in 638, and Edessa in 641; all Egypt was conquered by 643; the cities of western Iran (i.e., Nihavand, Rayy, Hamadan, Isfahan) were in Arab hands by 644; the Muslim armies completed the conquest of Khurasan by 654: Ira M. Lapidus, *A History of Islamic Societies* (Cambridge: Cambridge University Press, 2002), 32–3.
2   Ignaz Goldziher, *Introduction to IslamicTheology and Law*, trans. A. Hamori and R. Hamori (Princeton: Princeton University Press, 1981), 39.
3   Lapidus, *A History of Islamic Societies*, 33.
4   Muhammad 'Abd al-Hamid Muhammad, *Ibrahim ibn Adham: shaykh al-zahidin wa-imam al-mutasawwifin* (al-Minya: Dar al-Huda li'l-Nashr wa'l-Tawzi', 2007), 151.
5   Ibn 'Asakir, *Tarikh madinat Dimashq*, ed. Muhibb al-Din Abi Sa'id and 'Umar ibn Gharama al-'Amrawi, VI (Beirut: Dar al-Fikr, 1995), 277–350.
6   Ibid.
7   Abu Hatim Muhammad ibn Hibban, *Mashahir 'ulama' al-amsar*, ed. Majdi b. Mansur b. Sayyid al-Shuri (Beirut: Dar al-Kutub al-'Ilmiyya, 1995), 214–15.
8   Ibn al-'Adim, *Bughyat al-talab fi tarikh Halab*, ed. Suhayl Zakkar, X (Beirut: Dar al-Fikr, 1988), 432.
9   Farid al-Din 'Attar, *Tadhkirat al-awliya'*, ed. Muhammad Isti'lami (Tehran: Intisharat-i Zuvvar, 2004), 87–9.
10 *Qaddasa Allah sirrahu*, also sometimes translated as "May God hallow his tomb," is a common honorific phrase appended to the names of God's friends in hagiography.
11 'Attar, *Tadhkirat al-awliya'*, 90.
12 Ibid., 91.
13 *Pand-i piran*, ed. Jalal Matini (Mashhad: Bunyad-i Farhang-i Iran, 1978), 13–14.
14 Abu'l-Qasim al-Qushayri, *al-Risala al-Qushayriyya* (Beirut: Dar Sader, 2011), 97.
15 Allahdia b. Shaykh 'Abd al-Rahim Chishti, *Khwajagan-i Chisht: Siyar al-aqtab*, ed. M. S. Mawla'i (Tehran: Nashr-i 'Ilm, 2007), 43.
16 Literally "supports," "tent pegs." This traditionally refers to four Sufi friends of God who form the third category of the *Rijal al-ghayb* (Men of the Unseen), each of whom surveys one of the four cardinal points.
17 A mountain near Mecca.
18 Safi al-Din 'Abdullah Balkhi (Va'iz-i Balkhi), *Fazayil-i Balkh*, Persian trans. 'Abdullah b. Muhammad Husayni Balkhi, ed. 'Abd al-Hayy Habibi (Tehran: Intisharat-i Bunyad-i Farhang-i Iran, 1971), 95. Similar anecdotes regarding the motif of a friend of God causing something to move or quake simply by mentioning that it can be done are common to Sufi hagiography. Digby notes that "The narrative merely emphasizes that the Master is superior and supernatural powers should not be displayed": Simon Digby, "To Ride a Tiger or a Wall? Strategies of Prestige in Indian Sufi Legend," in Winand M. Callewaert and Rupert Snell, eds., *According to Tradition: Hagiographical Writing in India* (Wiesbaden: Harrassowitz Verlag, 1994), 123.
19 Ibn 'Asakir, *Tarikh madinat Dimashq*, VI: 318.
20 Ibid., 328.

21 'Abd al-Wahhab al-Sha'rani, *al-Tabaqat al-kubra*, ed. Ahmad 'Abd al-Rahim al-Sayih and Tawfiq 'Ali Wahba (Cairo: Maktabat al-Thaqafa al-Diniyya, 2005), 129.
22 Abu Nu'aym al-Isfahani, *Hilyat al-awliya' wa-tabaqat al-asfiya'*, VII (Beirut: Dar al-Fikr, 1996), 373; Also in Ibn 'Asakir, *Tarikh madinat Dimashq*, VI: 295.
23 Ibid., 301.
24 Abu Nu'aym al-Isfahani, *Hilyat al-awliya'*, VIII: 18.
25 Va'iz-i Balkhi, *Fazayil-i Balkh*, 110.
26 Abu Nu'aym al-Isfahani, *Hilyat al-awliya'*, VII: 387.
27 Ibid., 388.
28 It is likely that the 'Abbasid military commander Humayd ibn Ma'yuf al-Hamadani (d. early third/ninth century) is meant, though this would be anachronistic as he was appointed commander of the Levant coastlands in 806, and Ibrahim ibn Adham had died several decades before this date.
29 Abu Nu'aym al-Isfahani, *Hilyat al-awliya'*, VIII: 5–6. Fighting in the path of God at sea is especially meritorious in consideration of the great risk it involves. There are several *hadith* that confirm this: e.g., "The martyr at sea is like two martyrs on land," Ibn Maja, *Sunan*, ed. Muhammad Fu'ad 'Abd al-Baqi, II (Cairo: Dar 'Ihya' al-Kutub al-'Arabiyya, 2009), 928, *hadith* 2778.
30 Ibn 'Asakir, *Tarikh madinat Dimashq*, VI: 325.
31 Va'iz-i Balkhi, *Fazayil-i Balkh*, 112.
32 Ibn Kathir, *al-Bidaya wa'l-nihaya*, X (Beirut: Maktabat al-Ma'arif, 1966), 144–5. Regarding Ibrahim's death, 'Attar relates: "When his life came to an end he vanished, such that his grave was not found. Some say: 'It is in Baghdad,' and others say: 'It is in Syria.' Others say: 'It is in the city of the prophet Lot—upon whom be peace—that sank into the earth.' He fled thither from the people and there he died." 'Attar, *Tadhkirat al-awliya'*, 109.
33 Ibn Hibban gives the year of his death as A.H. 127 (744/45 C.E.): *Mashahir 'ulama' al-amsar*, 180. 'Abdullah ibn As'ad al-Yafi'i, *Mir'at al-janan wa-'ibrat al-yaqzan*, ed. Khalil al-Mansur, I (Beirut: Dar al-Kutub al-'Ilmiyya, 1997), 204; and Ibn al-'Imad, *Shadharat al-dhahab fi akhbar man dhahab*, ed. 'Abd al-Qadir al-Arna'ut, II (Beirut: Dar Ibn Kathir, 1991), 97, say he died four years earlier, in A.H. 123.
34 Ibn Hibban, *Mashahir 'ulama' al-amsar*, 180.
35 'Attar, *Tadhkirat al-awliya'*, 49.
36 Al-Yafi'i, *Mir'at al-janan*, I: 204.
37 Abu Hamid al-Ghazali, *Kimiya-yi sa'adat*, ed. Husayn Khadivjam, II (Tehran: Shirkat-i Intisharat-i 'Ilmi va Farhangi, 2001), 161.
38 Ibid., 496.
39 Abu Bakr Kalabadhi, *al-Ta'arruf li-madhhab ahl al-tasawwuf*, ed. Ahmad Shams al-Din (Beirut: Dar al-Kutub al-'Ilmiyya, 2001), 70.
40 Abu Nu'aym al-Isfahani, *Hilyat al-awliya'*, II: 345.
41 'Attar, *Tadhkirat al-awliya'*, 49.
42 Shams al-Din Muhammad al-Dhahabi, *Siyar a'lam al-nubala'*, ed. Bashshar 'Awwad Ma'ruf, VI (Beirut: Mu'assasat al-Risala, 1996), 120.
43 'Attar, *Tadhkirat al-awliya'*, 49.
44 'Abd al-Malik al-Nisaburi al-Kharkushi, *Tahdhib al-asrar fi adab al-tasawwuf*, ed. Muhammad Ahmad 'Abd al-Halim (Cairo: Maktabat al-Thaqafa al-Diniyya, 2010), 51.
45 Abu Nu'aym al-Isfahani, *Hilyat al-awliya'*, II: 354.
46 'Attar, *Tadhkirat al-awliya'*, 50.
47 Ibid.

48 Yazid b. al-Mulahhab (d. 102/720) was the Umayyad governor of Khurasan.
49 Abu Nu'aym al-Isfahani, *Hilyat al-awliya'*, II: 352. The response of Ibn Wasi' emphasizes his own independence and the governor's lack thereof, in that the latter depends entirely on the army for his power: Richard Gramlich, *Alte Vorbilder des Sufitums*, I (Wiesbaden: Harrassowitz Verlag, 1995), 22.
50 'Abdullah ibn As'ad al-Yafi'i, *Rawd al-rayahin fi hikayat al-salihin*, ed. 'Abd al-Jalil 'Abd al-Salam (Beirut: Dar al-Kutub al-'Ilmiyya, 2017), 301. The early Sufi writer Abu Talib al-Makki (d. 386/996) relates a similar anecdote about an unnamed Sufi *mujahid* who seeks to profit from the sale of a feedbag that he acquires during the military jihad. In a dream he sees two angels recording the true intentions of the various *mujahid*s; when they get to him, they record him as having gone on jihad as a merchant. The Sufi pleads with the angels not to list him as a merchant. The angels amend the Sufi's record to say that he went forth as a warrior but on the way, he bought a feedbag, hoping to make a profit therefrom, and then tell him that God will judge him as He sees fit: Abu Talib al-Makki, *Qut al-qulub fi mu'amalat al-mahbub*, ed. Mahmud Ibrahim Muhammad al-Ridwani (Cairo: Dar al-Turath, 2001), 1364–5.
51 Al-Qushayri, *al-Risala*, 181.
52 Ibn Hibban, *Mashahir 'ulama' al-amsar*, 227.
53 Abu'l-Hasan 'Ali Hujviri, *Kashf al-mahjub*, ed. Mahmud 'Abidi (Tehran: Soroush Press, 2012), 52.
54 'Attar, *Tadhkirat al-awliya'*, 183.
55 Abu Nu'aym al-Isfahani, *Hilyat al-awliya'*, VIII: 162.
56 'Abd al-Ra'uf al-Munawi, *al-Kawakib al-durriyya fi tarajim al-sada al-sufiyya: al-tabaqat al-kubra wa'l-tabaqat al-sughra*, ed. Muhammad Adib al-Jadir, I (Beirut: Dar Sader, 1999), 306.
57 Ibn Kathir, *al-Bidaya wa'l-nihaya*, X: 177.
58 For discussion of the traditional attribution of *Kitab al-jihad* to 'Abdullah ibn al-Mubarak, see Nazih Hamad's introduction to 'Abdullah ibn al-Mubarak, *Kitab al-jihad*, ed. Nazih Hamad (Cairo: Majma' al-Buhuth al-Islamiyya, 1979), 18–21. Although *Kitab al-jihad* is primarily concerned with the military jihad, it does contain references to extramilitary forms of striving (e.g., against the lower self): Christopher Melchert, "Ibn al-Mubārak's *Kitāb al-Jihād* and Early Renunciant Literature," in Robert Gleave and István T. Kristó-Nagy, eds., *Violence in Islamic Thought: From the Qurʾān to the Mongols* (Edinburgh: Edinburgh University Press, 2016), 49–69.
59 Al-Khatib al-Baghdadi, *Tarikh madinat al-salam*, ed. Bashshar 'Awwad Ma'ruf, XI (Beirut: Dar al-Gharb al-Islami, 2001), 389. (This work is typically cited as *Tarikh Baghdad*.)
60 'Attar, *Tadhkirat al-awliya'*, 183, has "One night during winter …. The difference between the two sources for this anecdote is no doubt due to a scribal error: Hujviri, *Kashf al-mahjub*, 147, has *az miyan-i mastan* where the text of *Tadhkirat al-awliya'* has *dar zimistan*.
61 Hujviri, *Kashf al-mahjub*, 147–8. A similar version is related in 'Attar, *Tadhkirat al-awliya'*, 183–4.
62 For discussion of *ahl al-hadith*, those who based legal authority on *hadith*, and *ahl al-ra'y*, those who accepted the application of informed judgment in legal matters, see Lapidus, *A History of Islamic Societies*, 85–7.
63 Hujviri, *Kashf al-mahjub*, 148.
64 Al-Baghdadi, *Tarikh Baghdad*, XI: 393.
65 Hujviri, *Kashf al-mahjub*, 148.

66 'Attar, *Tadhkirat al-awliya*', 184.
67 Hujviri, *Kashf al-mahjub*, 444.
68 Al-Baghdadi, *Tarikh Baghdad*, XI: 393.
69 *al-habib ya'rif al-habib*.
70 Khalil Allah, i.e., the prophet Ibrahim (Abraham).
71 Habib Allah, i.e., the prophet 'Isa (Jesus).
72 *Hazar hikayat-i sufiyan*, 89–90.
73 'Attar, *Tadhkirat al-awliya*', 184–5.
74 Al-Qushayri, *al-Risala*, 68.
75 Abu Nu'aym al-Isfahani, *Hilyat al-awliya*', VIII: 167.
76 Ibid., 168.
77 'Attar, *Tadhkirat al-awliya*', 191.
78 Ibid. Ibn al-Mubarak's statement is an explanation of the *hadith* of Jibril in which the angel Gabriel asks the Prophet to define *Iman, Islam,* and *Ihsan*. In response to Gabriel's question "What is *Ihsan?*" the Prophet says, "That you worship God as though you saw Him; and if you see Him not, verily, He sees you": Muhammad b. Isma'il al-Bukhari, *Sahih al-Bukhari* (Beirut: Dar Ibn Kathir, 2002), "Kitab al-Iman," 23, *hadith* 50.
79 'Attar, *Tadhkirat al-awliya*', 189.
80 From a well-known *hadith* related by Abu Dawud, *Sunan Abi Dawud*, ed. Shu'ayb Arna'ut and Muhammad Kamil Qarah Balili, V (Beirut: Dar al-Islam al-'Alamiyya, 2009), 485.
81 *Hazar hikayat-i sufiyan*, I: 322.
82 'Abdullah ibn al-Mubarak, *Diwan 'Abdullah ibn al-Mubarak*, ed. M. Bahjat (El-Mansoura: Dar al-Wifa', 1987), 44. The traditional commentary says that Ibn al-Mubarak composed these lines of poetry upon seeing the renunciant poet Abu'l-'Atahiya (d. 213/826) clad in a woolen robe. My thanks to Raymond Farrin for his help rendering this poem into English.
83 *Qari'*, "reciter," was another term for renunciant/ascetic (*zahid*), as the early renunciants devoted themselves to reciting the Qur'an: Christopher Melchert, "Origins and Early Sufism," in Lloyd Ridgeon, ed., *The Cambridge Companion to Sufism* (Cambridge: Cambridge University Press, 2015), 3–23.
84 Qur'an 9:12: And if they break their faith after their covenant and speak ill of your religion, then fight the leaders of unbelief, for indeed there is no [binding] oath to them; [fight them] so that they will desist.
85 Qur'an 16:91.
86 *Hazar hikayat-i sufiyan*, I: 665–6. The best-known version of this story is found in 'Attar, *Tadhkirat al-awliya*', 188–9. A shorter version is also related in al-Qushayri, *al-Risala*, 80.
87 Al-Masisa (Mopsuestia; Ancient Greek Μοψυεστία; Turkish Misis) is an ancient city located in the region of Cilicia, in what is now southern Turkey. Al-Masisa was an important Muslim garrison on the *thughur*. Al-Baladhuri (*Futuh al-buldan* [Beirut: Dar al-Kutub al-'Ilmiyya, 2000], 103) relates that the Umayyad prince 'Abdullah b. 'Abd al-Malik conquered Mopsuestia in 703, built a fortress on its ancient foundations, and populated it with Muslim soldiers.
88 Al-Baghdadi, *Tarikh Baghdad*, XI: 394.
89 *Hazar hikayat-i sufiyan*, I: 458–9. A shorter version is also related in al-Baghdadi, *Tarikh Baghdad*, XI: 406.
90 Ibid., XI: 407.

91 Al-Qushayri, *al-Risala*, 201. The *tafsir* of al-Tabari explains *For the like of this* (Qur'an 37:61) as "what God has bestowed in His munificence on the believers in the hereafter": Muhammad b. Jarir al-Tabari, *Jami' al-bayyan 'an ta'wil 'ayy al-Qur'an*, ed. Bashshar 'Awwad Ma'ruf and 'Isam Faris Hurristani, VI (Beirut: Mu'assasat al-Risala, 1994), 307.
92 Al-Baghdadi, *Tarikh Baghdad*, XI: 408.
93 'Attar, *Tadhkirat al-awliya'*, 201.
94 Though brief, *Adab al-'ibadat* is important (assuming it is indeed the work of Shaqiq), as it is the earliest extant description of the mystical path, in that it identifies love of God (*mahabba*) as the highest stage, following *zuhd* (renunciation), *khawf* (fear of God), and *shawq ila al-janna* (yearning for paradise): Shaqiq al-Balkhi, *Adab al-'ibadat*, in Paul Nwyia, ed., *Trois œuvres inédites de mystiques musulmans* (Beirut: Dar al-Mashriq, 1973), 17–22.
95 Hujviri, *Kashf al-mahjub*, 170.
96 Ibn al-'Imad, *Shadharat al-dhahab*, II: 442.
97 Va'iz-i Balkhi, *Fazayil-i Balkh*, 129.
98 The sources differ as to the location and year of Shaqiq's martyrdom; Ibn al-'Imad, *Shadharat al-dhahab*, II: 442; and Ibn al-Mulaqqin, *Tabaqat al-awliya'*, ed. Mustafa 'Abd al-Qadir 'Ata (Beirut: Dar al-Kutub al-'Ilmiyya, 1998), 44, give the year A.H. 194 but no location; Yafi'i gives the same date, but no circumstances, in *Mir'at al-janan*, I: 341. 'Abd al-Rahman Jami gives Khuttalan (modern Khatlan) as the location of Shaqiq's martyrdom in the year A.H. 174, *Nafahat al-uns*, 47; Shams al-Din al-Dhahabi gives Kulan, a region between the land of the Turks and Transoxiana: *Siyar a'lam al-nubala'*, IX: 316.
99 The idol worshiper (Persian *butparast*) in this anecdote may recall the presence of Buddhism in eastern Iranian lands in the pre-Islamic period. Important centers of Buddhism existed in Balkh and Bamiyan, in present-day Afghanistan; Adjina Tepe, in present-day Tajikistan; Termez, near the Amu Darya, in present-day Uzbekistan; and Merv, in present-day Turkmenistan. Indeed, the Persian word *but*—meaning "idol"—was borrowed from the Sogdian *pwt* and was ultimately derived from the Indic *Buddha*. The toponym *Nawbahar*, which occurs in several places in Iran, especially along the old road to Balkh that traverses Khurasan, is most likely a Persianized survival of the Sanskrit *navavihara*, designating the location of a Buddhist monastery, and suggests that Buddhism may have extended farther west than has traditionally been believed: Richard Bulliet, "Naw Bahar and the Survival of Iranian Buddhism," *Iran: Journal of the British Institute of Persian Studies* 14 (1976): 140–5; and A. S. Melikian-Chirvani, "Baztabha-yi adab-i ayin-i Buda dar Iran-i Islami," *Iran Nama* 8 (1990): 277. It has been noted elsewhere (e.g., A. J. Arberry, *Muslim Saints and Mystics: Episodes from the Tadhkirat al-Auliya' of Farid al-Din 'Attar* [London: Routledge, 2008], 62) that Ibrahim ibn Adham's life resembles the Buddha's in significant ways. Likewise, Shaqiq's life contains this anecdote involving a Buddhist temple. It is, thus, possible that the hagiographical lives of these two friends of God preserve a faint memory of Buddhism from Balkh's past.
100 'Attar, *Tadhkirat al-awliya'*, 201–2.
101 *Hazar hikayat-i sufiyan*, I: 106–7. Final quotation from Qur'an 65:3.
102 'Attar, *Tadhkirat al-awliya'*, 201.
103 *Hazar hikayat-i sufiyan*, I: 493.
104 Al-Sulami, *Tabaqat al-sufiyya*, 66.

105 Ibn al-Jawzi, *Sifat al-safwa*, ed. Khalid Mustafa al-Tartusi (Beirut: Dar al-Kitab al-'Arabi, 2012), 782.
106 Abu Nu'aym al-Isfahani, *Hilyat al-awliya'*, VIII: 61.
107 I.e., the Possessor of the Lights Twain, as both his wives were daughters of the Prophet Muhammad.
108 Abu Bakr (d. 13/634), 'Umar (d. 23/644), 'Uthman (d. 36/656), and 'Ali (d. 40/661) are traditionally considered by Sunni Muslims to be the four Rightly Guided Caliphs, who led the Muslims following the death of the Prophet Muhammad in 632.
109 Al-Ghazali, *Kimiya-yi sa'adat*, I: 534–5.
110 Al-Dhahabi, *Siyar a'lam al-nubala'*, IX: 314.
111 'Attar, *Tadhkirat al-awliya'*, 202–3. This well-known anecdote is also found in Abu Nu'aym al-Isfahani, *Hilyat al-awliya'*, VIII: 64; and al-Qushayri, *al-Risala*, 265.
112 'Attar, *Tadhkirat al-awliya'*, 203.
113 Ibn al-'Imad, *Shadharat al-dhahab*, II: 442.

Chapter 2

1 Junayd al-Baghdadi was traditionally said to exemplify sober Sufism; and Bayazid, drunken Sufism. According to those Sufis who preferred drunkenness (*sukr*), this state led to destruction of the human attributes that veil man from God. Those Sufis who preferred sobriety (*sahw*), however, said that drunkenness blinds the seeker, who believes himself to be annihilated when, in fact, his human attributes abide: Abu'l-Hasan 'Ali Hujviri, *Kashf al-mahjub*, ed. Mahmud 'Abidi (Tehran: Soroush Press, 2012), 279–81.
2 Abu 'Abdullah Muhammad b. 'Ali (al-Hakim) al-Tirmidhi, *Riyadat al-nafs*, and *Sirat al-awliya'* (in *Thalath musannafat li'l-Hakim al-Tirmidhi*, ed. Bernd Radtke, 1–134 [Stuttgart: F. Steiner, 1992]), respectively.
3 E.g., the Persian quatrains of Abu Sa'id ibn Abi'l-Khayr, *Sukhanan-i manzum-i Abu Sa'id Abu'l-Khayr*, ed. Sa'id Nafisi (Tehran: Intisharat-i Sana'i, 1997).
4 Abu Nasr al-Sarraj, *Kitab al-luma' fi al-tasawwuf*, ed. R. A. Nicholson (Leiden: E. J. Brill, 1914), 390–1.
5 E.g., in the following dictum attributed to him: "If you behold a man vouchsafed wonders (*karamat*)—even should he ascend in the air—do not be dazzled by him until you behold how he commands [the right] and forbids [the wrong], upholds divine ordinances (*al-hudud*), and carries out God's law (*shari'a*)." Abu'l-Qasim al-Qushayri, *al-Risala al-Qushayriyya* (Beirut: Dar Sader, 2011), 264.
6 Farid al-Din 'Attar, *Tadhkirat al-awliya'*, ed. Muhammad Isti'lami (Tehran: Intisharat-i Zuvvar, 2004), 138.
7 Sibt ibn al-Jawzi, *Mir'at al-zaman fi tawarikh al-a'yan*, ed. M. Barakat et al., XV (Damascus: Dar al-Risala al-'Alamiyya, 2013), 430.
8 Abu Fadl Muhammad al-Sahlagi, *Kitab al-nur min kalimat Abi Tayfur*, in 'Abd al-Rahman Badawi, *Shatahat al-sufiyya* (Kuwait: Wikalat al-Matbu'at, 1976), 60–1.
9 'Abd al-Rahman al-Sulami, *Tabaqat al-sufiyya*, ed. Mustafa 'Abd al-Qadir 'Ata (Beirut: Dar al-Kutub al-'Ilmiyya, 2003), 67.
10 'Attar, *Tadhkirat al-awliya'*, 139.
11 Ibid.
12 Ibid. Ja'far al-Sadiq (d. 148/765) is reckoned the sixth Shi'ite Imam by Twelver Shi'ites and is venerated as a pious and learned descendant of the Prophet Muhammad by

Sunni Muslims. Bayazid's association with him is historically impossible, as he was born almost forty years after the death of Ja'far al-Sadiq.

13 Al-Sahlagi, *Kitab al-nur,* 161–2.
14 Ahmad b. Husayn b. al-Shaykh Kharaqani, *Dastur al-jumhur fi manaqib sultan al-'arifin Abu Yazid Tayfur,* ed. Muhammad Taqi Danishpizhuh and Iraj Afshar (Tehran: Mirath-i Maktub, 2009), 46–7.
15 'Attar, *Tadhkirat al-awliya',* 140.
16 'Abd al-Wahhab al-Sha'rani, *al-Tabaqat al-kubra,* 141–2. Abu 'Ali al-Juzjani (d. fourth/tenth century) was a Sufi shaykh of Khurasan known for *mujahada;* see al-Sulami, *Tabaqat al-sufiyya,* 196. "Struggle" translates *jāhada* in this anecdote.
17 'Attar, *Tadhkirat al-awliya',* 142.
18 Al-Qushayri, *al-Risala,* 167.
19 Ibid., 246.
20 Ibid., 169.
21 'Attar, *Tadhkirat al-awliya',* 141.
22 Muhammad b. Munavvar, *Asrar al-tawhid fi maqamat shaykh Abi Sa'id,* ed. R. Shafi'i Kadkani, I (Tehran: Mu'assasa-yi Intishirat-i Agah, 1997), 253. The motif of a saint riding a lion (or tiger) with a snake whip in his hand is found in Sufi hagiography of the Indian subcontinent, as well as in an earlier Buddhist hagiographical anecdote: Simon Digby, "To Ride a Tiger or a Wall? Strategies of Prestige in Indian Sufi Legend," in Winand M. Callewaert and Rupert Snell, eds., *According to Tradition: Hagiographical Writing in India* (Wiesbaden: Harrassowitz Verlag, 1994), 104.
23 'Attar, *Tadhkirat al-awliya',* 148–9.
24 Al-Qushayri, *al-Risala,* 208.
25 Ibid.
26 'Attar, *Tadhkirat al-awliya',* 182.
27 Al-Qushayri, *al-Risala,* 34.
28 Ibid., 263.
29 'Attar, *Tadhkirat al-awliya',* 159. A similar version of this anecdote also appears in the anonymous early Sufi treatise *Adab al-muluk fi bayan haqa'iq al-tasawwuf,* ed. Bernd Radtke (Stuttgart: Franz Steiner, 1991), 21: "Abu Yazid said, 'My *nafs* opposed me regarding something, so I did not drink water for a year.' This is extreme *mujahada,* and the Sufis have *mujahadat* for matters both outward and inward."
30 'Abd al-Rahman Jami describes al-Nibaji (d. mid-third/ninth century) as one of the early Sufi shaykhs and a contemporary of Dhu al-Nun al-Misri: *Nafahat al-uns,* 91.
31 *Hazar hikayat-i sufiyan,* I, 464.
32 'Attar, *Tadhkirat al-awliya',* 157.
33 Ibid., 181.
34 Ibid.
35 Al-Sahlagi, *Kitab al-nur,* 186.
36 'Attar, *Tadhkirat al-awliya',* 363: "His path is the path of sobriety in contrast to the Tayfuriyan who are the companions of Bayazid."
37 Al-Sulami, *Tabaqat al-sufiyya,* 129.
38 Jamil M. Abun-Nasr, *Muslim Communities of Grace: The Sufi Brotherhoods in Islamic Religious Life* (New York: Columbia University Press, 2007), 36.
39 'Attar, *Tadhkirat al-awliya',* 363.
40 Abun-Nasr, *Muslim Communities of Grace,* 37.
41 Jami, *Nafahat al-uns,* 79.
42 'Attar, *Tadhkirat al-awliya',* 363.

43 For a compendium of Junayd's writings in the original Arabic with English translations, see Ali Hassan Abdel-Kader, *The Life, Personality and Writing of al-Junayd: A Study of a Third/Ninth Century Mystic, with an Edition and Translation of His Writings* (n.p.: Islamic Book Trust, 2013).
44 'Attar, *Tadhkirat al-awliya*', 364.
45 *Zakat* is one of the Five Pillars of Islam, the fundamental religious obligations recognized by all Muslims. The other pillars are the profession of faith (*shahada*), prayer (*salat*), fasting (*sawm*), and pilgrimage (*hajj*).
46 Ibid.
47 Ibid., 364–5.
48 Ibid., 365–6.
49 Hujviri, *Kashf al-mahjub*, 77.
50 Shuniziyya was the location of a well-known cemetery in Baghdad where many early Sufis and friends of God were buried.
51 *Pand-i piran*, 85.
52 Al-Qushayri, *al-Risala*, 130.
53 Qur'an 11:120
54 Abu Bakr Kalabadhi, *al-Ta'arruf li-madhhab ahl al-tasawwuf*, ed. Ahmad Shams al-Din (Beirut: Dar al-Kutub al-'Ilmiyya, 2001), 119.
55 Al-Sulami, *Tabaqat al-sufiyya*, 130.
56 Al-Kalabadhi, *al-Ta'arruf li-madhhab ahl al-tasawwuf*, 19–20.
57 Taj al-Din al-Subki, *al-Tabaqat al-shafi'iyya al-kubra*, ed. Mahmud Muhammad al-Tanahi and 'Abd al-Fattah Hulw, II (Cairo: Dar Ihya' al-Kutub al-'Arabiyya, 1990), 271.
58 Abu Nu'aym al-Isfahani, *Hilyat al-awliya' wa-tabaqat al-asfiya*', X (Beirut: Dar al-Fikr, 1996), 255.
59 Words not in italics are Junayd's exegesis of this verse.
60 Ibn Qayyim al-Jawziyya, *al-Fawa'id*, ed. Muhammad 'Aziz Shams (Mecca: Dar 'Alam al-Fawa'id, 2008), 82–3.
61 'Ali ibn Abi Talib (d. 40/661) was the Prophet's cousin and son-in-law and the fourth of the four Rightly Guided Caliphs according to Sunni sacred history. Shi'ite Islam considers 'Ali the first Imam. With the notable exception of the Naqshbandi order, Sufi orders claim 'Ali as the first transmitter of *walaya* from the Prophet in their initiatic chains (*silsila*). The sword in this anecdote refers to *Dhu'l-Fiqar*, 'Ali's sword, with which he would accompany the Prophet into battle.
62 'Attar, *Tadhkirat al-awliya*', 380.
63 Ibid. A similar anecdote is related in *Hazar hikayat-i sufiyan* regarding a Sufi named Abu'l-Hasan al-Tusi who leads his *murid*s into battle. As his *murid*s are martyred, he looks up and sees a dome of white pearl upon which are seated five houris, each one tending to one of the martyred *murid*s. When there is only one houri left who is not tending to a martyr, Abu'l-Hasan assumes it is he who will be martyred next. One of the unbelievers then comes forward and asks that he teach him the *shahada*. Abu'l-Hasan does so, and the man returns to battle and kills several unbelievers until he is finally slain and becomes a martyr: *Hazar hikayat-i sufiyan*, I: 457–8.
64 'Abdullah ibn As'ad al-Yafi'i, *Rawd al-rayahin fi hikayat al-salihin*, ed. 'Abd al-Jalil 'Abd al-Salam (Beirut: Dar al-Kutub al-'Ilmiyya, 2017), 274.
65 I.e., the second *sura* of the Qur'an.
66 Abu Nu'aym al-Isfahani, *Hilyat al-awliya*', X: 264.
67 'Attar, *Tadhkirat al-awliya*', 392–3.
68 Ibid., 393.
69 *Pand-i piran*, 23.

70 Abu Hamid al-Ghazali, *Kimiya-yi sa'adat*, ed. Husayn Khadivjam, II (Tehran: Shirkat-i Intisharat-i 'Ilmi va Farhangi, 2001), 635; This anecdote is also in 'Attar, *Tadhkirat al-awliya*', 393.
71 Outside the main cities of Perso-Islamic culture (e.g., Isfahan, Nishapur, Merv, Herat, Balkh, Samarqand, Bukhara, etc.), mass conversions to Islam in the countryside did not begin until the ninth and tenth centuries: R. N. Frye, *Islamic Iran and Central Asia (7th–12th Centuries)* (London: Variorum Reprints, 1979), 2–3. Regarding the spread of Islam in the countryside and the predominance of Zoroastrians in Fars, see Jamsheed K. Choksy, *Conflict and Cooperation: Zoroastrian Subalterns and Muslim Elites in Medieval Iranian Society* (New York: Columbia University Press, 1997), 86–8. Concerning conversion statistics during this period, see Richard W. Bulliet, *Conversion to Islam in the Medieval Period: An Essay in Quantitative History* (Cambridge, MA: Harvard University Press, 1979).
72 Hujviri, *Kashf al-mahjub*, 261. The nineteenth-century Indian hagiographer Ghulam Sarvar Lahori related that Abu Ishaq had over 100,000 disciples; a number that must be understood as symbolic: *Khazinat al-asfiya*, II (Khanpur: Munshi Nawal Kishore, 1914), 226.
73 E.g., "My soul attained light from the leader (*murshid*) of the faith": Khwaju Kirmani, *Rawdat al-anwar*, ed. M. 'Abidi (Tehran: Mirath-i Maktub, 2008), 118.
74 Ibn Battuta, *Rihla* (Beirut: Dar Sader, 1998), 217–18.
75 For discussion of the textual history of Mahmud b. 'Uthman's *Firdaws al-murshidiyya*, which was originally composed in Arabic, see Iraj Afshar, "Ferdaws al-Moršedīya fī Asrār al-Ṣamadīya," *Encyclopædia Iranica*, online edition, http://www.iranicaonline.org/articles/ferdaws (IX, fasc. 5, 511–12).
76 'Attar, *Tadhkirat al-awliya*', 663. It should be noted that the life of Abu Ishaq in *Tadhkirat al-awliya*' is in the section of additional lives of God's friends added by a later anonymous author.
77 Mahmud b. 'Uthman, *Firdaws al-murshidiyya*, ed. Fritz Meier (Istanbul: Matba'at Ma'arif, 1943), 14.
78 'Attar, *Tadhkirat al-awliya*', 664. Ibn Khafif (d. 371/981/2) is the subject of an early Sufi hagiography by Abu'l-Hasan al-Daylami, *Sirat al-shaykh al-kabir Abu 'Abdullah ibn al-Khafif al-Shirazi*, ed. Annemarie Schimmel (Tehran: Babak, 1984).
79 Dihlavi, *Fawa'id al-fu'ad*, 303–5. The author of the *Shiraz Nama*, Abu'l-'Abbas Zarkub Shirazi (d. 789/1387), quoting an earlier work that has been lost—the *Mashyakha* of Maqaridi—relates yet another version of how Abu Ishaq was initiated into the Sufi path: "Shaykh Abu Ishaq Ibrahim ibn Shahryar donned the *khirqa* of *tasawwuf* from the hand of Shaykh Husayn-i Akkar. [Abu Ishaq's] father, Shahryar, placed him in the service of [Shaykh Husayn-i Akkar] when [the boy] was seven years old, for he saw the sign of friendship with God in his countenance .... It is said that when Shaykh Ibn-i Khafif was on his deathbed, he summoned Husayn-i Akkar and said, 'You must give our *khirqa* to Abu Ishaq-i Kazaruni.' Husayn-i Akkar was, thus, the means [of Kazaruni's receiving the *khirqa*]": Abu'l-'Abbas Zarkub Shirazi, *Shiraz Nama*, ed. Isma'il Va'iz Javadi (Tehran: Intisharat-i Bunyad-i Farhang-i Iran, 1971), 132.
80 'Attar, *Tadhkirat al-awliya*', 664.
81 Mahmud b. 'Uthman, *Firdaws al-murshidiyya*, 106–7.
82 'Attar, *Tadhkirat al-awliya*', 664–5.
83 Mahmud b. 'Uthman, *Firdaws al-murshidiyya*, 153–4.
84 Ibid., 192.
85 The forenoon prayer (*namaz-i chasht*) is not obligatory.
86 Mahmud b. 'Uthman, *Firdaws al-murshidiyya*, 192.

87 Ibid., 165–6.
88 Ibid., 397.
89 Ibid., 103.
90 The pejorative *gabr* is used here.
91 I have rendered *ghazw* as "military campaign" throughout this section.
92 Mahmud b. 'Uthman, *Firdaws al-murshidiyya*, 197–8.
93 Such graphic descriptions of fighting and plundering unbelievers are not unique to *Firdaws al-murshidiyya*; for example, in the hagiographical narrative of the Central Asian warrior saint Satuq Bughra Khan, the Muslims: "trounced the infidels, hacking them to pieces and making their blood flow like a river. Then they plundered the infidels' goods." Jeff Eden, *Warrior Saints of the Silk Road: Legends of the Qarakhanids* (Leiden: E. J. Brill, 2019), 58.
94 *Himmat*.
95 Mahmud b. 'Uthman, *Firdaws al-murshidiyya*, 198.
96 Ibid., 198–200.
97 Qur'an: 2:255.
98 Mahmud b. 'Uthman, *Firdaws al-murshidiyya*, 410–13.
99 This statement probably refers to the *hadith* "Our Lord descends to the lowest heaven every night when the last third of night remains and says, 'Who would supplicate Me that I may respond to him? Who would ask Me so that I may grant him [what he asks]? Who would seek forgiveness that I may forgive him?'": Muhammad b. Isma'il al-Bukhari, *Sahih al-Bukhari*, "Kitab al-tahajjud," hadith 1145, p. 277.
100 Mahmud b. 'Uthman, *Firdaws al-murshidiyya,* 200–3.

Chapter 3

1 For an early Muslim account of the conquest of the Levant and the Holy Land, see al-Baladhuri, *Futuh al-buldan* (Beirut: Dar al-Kutub al-'Ilmiyya, 2000), 78–92.
2 Ibn al-Athir, *al-Kamil fi al-tarikh*, ed. Abu'l-Fida' 'Abdullah al-Qadi, IX (Beirut: Dar al-Kutub al-'Ilmiyya, 1987), 19–20.
3 Ira M. Lapidus, *A History of Islamic Societies* (Cambridge: Cambridge University Press, 2002), 289.
4 Nur al-Din patronized the *muhaddith* and historian Ibn 'Asakir, whose *Forty Hadith for Inciting Jihad* contributed to the religious and martial enthusiasm that led to Muslim success against the Crusaders: Suleiman Mourad and James Lindsay, *Intensification and Reorientation of Sunni Jihad Ideology in the Crusader Period* (Leiden: E. J. Brill, 2013), 47–50.
5 Lapidus, A History of Islamic Societies, 289–90.
6 Ibid., 291.
7 Devin Deweese, *Islamization and Native Religion in the Golden Horde: Baba Tükles and Conversion to Islam in Historical and Epic Tradition* (University Park: Pennsylvania State University Press, 1994), 138–40.
8 Rajab Muhammad 'Abd al-Halim, *Intishar al-Islam bayna al-Mughul* (Cairo: Dar al-Nahda al-'Arabia, 1986), 84–5; Reuven Amitai, "Il-Khanids: Dynastic History," *Encyclopædia Iranica*, online edition, http://www.iranicaonline.org/articles/il-khanids-i-dynastic-history (XII, fasc. 6: 645–54). It is worth mentioning Stephen Kotkin's view of the Mongol Empire as an "empire of exchange," which, he argues, was based not on language or religion but rather on *Realpolitik*. This empire of exchange,

	among many other things, even helped spread Islam: Stephen Kotkin, "Mongol Commonwealth? Exchange and Governance across the Post-Mongol Space," *Kritika: Explorations in Russian and Eurasian History* 8.3 (2007): 503–4.
9	Mujir al-Din al-'Ulaymi, *al-Uns al-jalil bi-tarikh al-Quds wa'l-Khalil*, ed. 'Adnan Yunis 'Abd al-Majid Abu Tabbana and Mahmud 'Awda Ka'abina, II (Amman: Maktabat al-Dandis, 2000), 238–9. Salah al-Din's son 'Uthman later established a *waqf* for Abu Thawr near Jerusalem.
10	Shams al-Din Ahmad Aflaki, *Manaqib al-'arifin*, ed. T. Yazıcı and Tawfiq H. Subhani (Tehran: Intisharat-i Dustan, 2017), 61–3.
11	For a detailed discussion of the monuments of Kunya Urgench, including the mausoleum of Najm al-Din Kubra, see Edgar Knobloch, *Monuments of Central Asia: A Guide to the Archeology, Art and Architecture of Turkestan* (London: I.B. Tauris, 2001), 80–6.
12	Hamid Algar, trans., "Introduction," in Najm al-Din Razi, *The Path of God's Bondsmen from Origin to Return: A Sufi Compendium* (North Haledon, NJ: Islamic Publications International, 2003), 2–4. Fritz Meier's introduction ("Das Leben des Verfassers") in his edition of Najm al-Din Kubra, *Fawa'ih al-jamal wa-fawatih al-jalal* (Wiesbaden: F. Steiner, 1957), 1–64, remains the definitive study of the shaykh's life in any European language.
13	'Abdullah ibn As'ad al-Yafi'i, *Mir'at al-janan wa-'ibrat al-yaqzan*, ed. Khalil al-Mansur, IV (Beirut: Dar al-Kutub al-'Ilmiyya, 1997), 33.
14	Ibid.
15	The only premodern writer who does not connect Najm al-Din Kubra's death with the Mongol Invasion is Qazvini, who places Kubra's death around 1213 or 1214; however, Fritz Meier deems Qazvini's statement unreliable, as it gives "the impression of being an unverified, vague memory or supposition": Meier, "Das Leben des Verfassers," in Najm al-Din Kubra, *Fawa'ih al-jamal wa-fawatih al-jalal,* 53.
16	*Muhiyy al-sunna* is the cognomen of Abu Muhammad Husayn b. Mas'ud Farra' al-Baghawi (d. 516/1122), who was a renowned scholar of *hadith,* jurisprudence, and *tafsir.* This association with Najm al-Din Kubra is impossible, as al-Baghawi died almost twenty years before his birth.
17	'Abd al-Rahman Jami, *Nafahat al-uns*, ed. Mahmud 'Abidi (Tehran: Intisharat-i Ittila'at, 1996), 423–4.
18	From Qur'an 79:34: And when the great calamity shall come…
19	Jami, *Nafahat al-uns,* 422.
20	Ibid.
21	Ibid., 423.
22	Qur'an 18:9–26.
23	Sa'd al-Din al-Hammu'i (d. 650/1253) was a well-known Sufi shaykh of Khurasan.
24	Jami, *Nafahat al-uns,* 423.
25	The original sources (i.e., al-Yafi'i, Jami, et al.) use the term "Tatar" rather than "Mongol."
26	With the destruction of Khwarazm began the devastating Mongol invasion of the thirteenth century. It is said that the Khwarazmshah Sultan 'Ala' al-Din Muhammad (d. 617/1220) had ordered the massacre of a caravan of merchants from the Mongol Empire in 1218. The sultan's action resulted in the Mongol conquest of Khwarazm and the subsequent calamitous invasion of Central and Western Asia, over the course of which the Mongols destroyed the majority of the great cities of Perso-Islamic civilization (i.e., Nishapur, Merv, Herat, Balkh, Bukhara, Samarqand): J. A. Boyle, "Dynastic and Political History of the Il-Khāns," in J.A. Boyle, ed., *The Cambridge History of Iran,* V (Cambridge: Cambridge University Press, 1968), 303–7.
27	Al-Yafi'i, *Mir'at al-janan,* IV: 34.

28 Ibid.
29 Jami, *Nafahat al-uns*, 427.
30 Ibn al-'Imad, *Shadharat al-dhahab fi akhbar man dhahab*, ed. 'Abd al-Qadir al-Arna'ut, VII (Beirut, Dar Ibn Kathir, 1991), 132.
31 Ibn Kathir, *al-Bidaya wa'l-nihaya*, XIII (Beirut: Maktabat al-Ma'arif, 1966), 93.
32 Ibn al-'Imad, *Shadharat al-dhahab*, VII: 132; and 'Abd al-Ra'uf al-Munawi, *al-Kawakib al-durriyya fi tarajim al-sada al-sufiyya: al-tabaqat al-kubra wa'l-tabaqat al-sughra*, ed. Muhammad Adib al-Jadir, IV (Beirut: Dar Sader, 1999), 398.
33 Al-Yafi'i, -*Mir'at al-janan*, IV: 31.
34 Shams al-Din Muhammad al-Dhahabi, *al-'Ibar fi khabar man ghabar*, ed. Abu Hajar Muhammad al-Sa'id b. Basyuni Zaghlul, III (Beirut: Dar al-Kutub al-'Ilmiyya, 1985), 174.
35 Sibt ibn al-Jawzi, *Mir'at al-zaman fi tawarikh al-a'yan*, ed. M. Barakat et al., XXII (Damascus: Dar al-Risala al-'Alamiyya, 2013), 249.
36 Ibn Kathir, *al-Bidaya wa'l-nihaya*, XIII: 93.
37 Sibt ibn al-Jawzi, *Mir'at al-zaman*, XXII: 249.
38 Ibn Kathir, *al-Bidaya wa'l-nihaya*, XIII: 93.
39 Sibt ibn al-Jawzi, *Mir'at al-zaman*, XXII: 251.
40 Ibid., 250.
41 Al-Amjad Bahramshah (d. 627/1230)—a nephew of Salah al-Din—was the Ayyubid ruler of Baalbek.
42 Al-Yafi'i, *Mir'at al-janan*, IV: 31.
43 A traditional unit of measurement in Egypt and the Levant; one rotl is equal to roughly 2.5 to 3.2 kg, depending on the region.
44 Abu Shama Shihab al-Din al-Maqdisi, *al-Dhayl 'ala al-rawdatayn*, ed. Ibrahim Shams al-Din, V (Beirut: Dar al-Kutub al-'Ilmiyya, 2002), 191.
45 The Ayyubid sultan al-'Adil (d. 615/1218).
46 A town in Syria near the Crusader castle the Krak des Chevaliers.
47 Asad al-Din Shirkuh b. Shadhi (d. 637/1240), known as *al-Malik al-Mujahid*, was the uncle of Salah al-Din and a successful general.
48 Sibt ibn al-Jawzi, *Mir'at al-zaman*, XXII: 251–2.
49 February 5, 1221.
50 Ibn al-'Imad, *Shadharat al-dhahab*, VII: 134–5.
51 Abd al-Ra'uf al-Munawi, *al-Kawakib al-durriyya fi tarajim al-sada al-sufiyya: al-tabaqat al-kubra wa'l-tabaqat al-sughra*, ed. Muhammad Adib al-Jadir, II (Beirut: Dar Sader, 1999), II: 435; 'Abdullah Ibn As'ad al-Yafi'i, *Rawd al-rayahin fi hikayat al-salihin*, 365.
52 Murtada al-Zabidi, *Taj al-'arus min jawahir al-qamus*, ed. 'Abd al-Sattar Farraj et al., XIV (Kuwait: Matba'at Hukumat al-Kuwait, 1974), 310.
53 The village of al-Nuwayra is located in the modern-day Beni Suef Governate, south of Cairo.
54 Al-Zabidi, *Taj al-'arus*, 310.
55 Taj al-Din al-Subki, *al-Tabaqat al-shafi'iyya al-kubra*, ed. Mahmud Muhammad al-Tanahi and 'Abd al-Fattah Hulw, VIII (Cairo: Dar Ihya' al-Kutub al-'Arabiyya, 1990), 170.
56 Ibn Battuta, *Rihla* (Beirut: Dar Sader, 1998), 151.
57 Safi al-Din Ibn Abi'l-Mansur Ibn Zafir, *Risala*, ed. Denis Gril (Cairo: Institut Français d'Archéologie Orientale du Caire, 1986), 73.
58 *Misr*, which can designate both Egypt and modern-day Cairo (known as al-Fustat in the early Islamic period), probably indicates the latter here.

59 The town of Safi (formerly Asfi) is located in modern-day Morocco, on the Atlantic coast.
60 Ibn Zafir relates a slightly different version of this anecdote in another section of the *Risala*: "One day, a Maghribi man from Dukkala, seeing him, let out a cry and lost consciousness for an hour. When he came to, [the man] who came to his aid asked, 'What's wrong with you?' 'I have seen this man several times sitting with our shaykh, Abu Muhammad Salih in Asfi!'" Ibn Zafir, *Risala*, 96.
61 A town in central Egypt where the important archeological site of Oxyrhynchus is located.
62 Na'am, idha kana ma'a ahlihi.
63 Ibn Zafir, *Risala*, 41–2.
64 Located on Roda Island, in central Cairo.
65 Qur'an 3:169.
66 Ibn Zafir, *Risala*, 96–7; Shorter versions of al-Nuwayri's martyrdom are found in al-Munawi, *al-Kawakib al-durriyya*, II: 435–6; and al-Yafi'i, *Rawd al-rayahin*, 365.
67 al-Munawi, *al-Kawakib al-durriyya*, II: 435.
68 The Muslims during this period still referred to Anatolia as *Rūm*—"Rome"—as it had been part of the Byzantine Empire before the Seljuk conquest of the region.
69 Lewis, *Rumi—Past and Present, East and West*, 92.
70 Rumi is also known as *Mawlana/Mawlawi* (Persian *Mawlavi*, Turkish *Mevlevi*), Arabic for "our[/my] master[/protector]."
71 I.e., in the following lines of poetry regarding Rumi: Man namiguyam ki an 'ali janab / hast payghambar vali darad kitab / mathnavi'yi ma'navi'yi mawlavi / hast Qur'ani ba lafz-i Pahlavi (I do not say that exalted one is a prophet, though he does have a book. Mawlavi's Mathnavi-yi ma'navi is a Qur'an in the Persian tongue). Many commentaries cite these lines (or a variation thereof) and attribute them either to the prolific Sufi poet and hagiographer of Herat 'Abd al-Rahman Jami or to the equally prolific Arab Shi'i poet and writer Shaykh Baha' al-Din 'Amili (d. 1030/1621), who emigrated to Isfahan during the Safavid period and was a great admirer of Rumi. I have been unable to find these oft-quoted lines in any of the edited works of either Jami or Shaykh Baha'i (on this conundrum, see Lewis, *Rumi—Past and Present, East and West*, xx), which may indicate the relatively common phenomenon in premodern literature of attributing anonymous quotations, deemed significant, to well-known authors, and thereby rendering them authoritative.
72 "It is the expounder of the Qur'an": Jalal al-Din Rumi, *Mathnavi-yi ma'navi*, ed. 'Abd al-Karim Surush, I (Tehran: Intisharat-i 'Ilmi va Farhangi, 1999), 3. This is found in the Arabic prose introduction, which may not have been composed by Rumi himself.
73 E.g., the story of the fainthearted Sufi in Book 5: Rumi, *Mathnavi-yi ma'navi*, II: 880–1.
74 *Manaqib al-'arifin*, which is the most extensive hagiographical source for Rumi's life, is available in its entirety to English-speaking readers in John O'Kane's splendid translation, *The Feats of the Knowers of God (Manāqeb al-'ārefīn)* (Leiden: E. J. Brill, 2002).
75 I.e., the unknown friends of God—from a *hadith qudsi* (i.e., a *hadith* in which it is believed God spoke directly through Muhammad): *Inna awliya'i tahta qubabi la ya'rifuhum ghayri* (My friends are under my vaults; no one knows them save Me).
76 Aflaki, *Manaqib al-'arifin*, 49.
77 Jami, *Nafahat al-uns*, 461.
78 In a sermon attributed to Baha' al-Din Valad, he accused the ruler, 'Ala' al-Din Muhammad Khwarazmshah (see n. 353 above), and the theologian, *mufassir*, and

philosopher Fakhr al-Din Razi (d. 606/1210), whom Muhammad Khwarazmshah patronized, of innovation (bid'a). If true, this would have rendered his position in Balkh precarious: Baha'-i Valad, Ma'arif: majmu'a-yi mava'iz va sukhanan-i sultan al-'ulama' Baha' al-Din Muhammad b. Husayn Khatibi Balkhi mashhur ba Baha'-i Valad, ed. Badi' al-Zaman Furuzanfar, I (Tehran: Kitabkhana-yi Tahuri, 1973), 81. It is likely that he made other enemies in Balkh as well; see H. Algar, "Bahā' al-Din Moḥammad Valad," Encyclopædia Iranica, online edition, http://www.iranicaonline.org/articles/baha-al-din-mohammad-walad-b (III, fasc. 4, 431–3.)

79 Sultan Valad, Valad Nama, ed. Jalal al-Din Huma'i (Tehran: Mu'assasa-yi Nashr-i Huma, 1997), 161.
80 Jami, Nafahat al-uns, 461. The story of 'Attar and Rumi meeting is clearly apocryphal. It does, however, illustrate the relationship between the works of the two poets, as Rumi continued the use of the *mathnavi*, which Sana'i began and 'Attar perfected, as a means to set forth the mystical teachings of Sufism. Moreover, it may be said that this anecdote serves as a form of premodern literary criticism, in that of his four mystical *mathnavi*s the one 'Attar gives Rumi is his *Asrar Nama*, which is the only one of the four that lacks a frame-tale structure. The other three—*Mantiq al-tayr*, *Ilahi Nama*, and *Musibat Nama*—differ from those of 'Attar's immediate predecessor, Sana'i, and that of Rumi in that they are composed around a unifying frame tale.
81 This refers to the story of Joseph in Egypt as related in Surat Yusuf (Qur'an: 12).
82 Aflaki, Manaqib al-'arifin, 15–16.
83 Ibid., 38. Qur'an: 18:65. Regarding inner knowledge, the following dictum is attributed to Burhan al-Din: "This knowledge comes to one and is not learned." Valad, Valad Nama, 163. This refers to 'ilm-i wahbi (knowledge that God bestows on His friends), as opposed to 'ilm-i kasbi (knowledge one acquires through study).
84 Aflaki, Manaqib al-'arifin, 38–9.
85 Sultan Valad, Valad Nama, 166.
86 The hagiographical sources never refer to him as "Rumi;" rather, the Persian title *khudavandgar-i ma* (our king/lord) is used.
87 Faridun Sipahsalar, Zindagi nama-yi Mawlana Jalal al-Din Mawlavi, ed. Sa'id Nafisi (Tehran: Iqbal, 1999), 23–4.
88 Ibid., 24.
89 Ibid., 83.
90 Ibid.
91 Jami, Nafahat al-uns, 462.
92 Qur'an 6:45.
93 Hulagu (d. 1265), a grandson of Genghis Khan, conquered most of Western Asia, destroying Baghdad in 1258. He founded the dynasty of the Ilkhanate, which would rule much of modern-day Iran and Western Asia until the mid-fourteenth century. Kitbuqa, Hulagu's Nestorian Christian general, was killed at the battle of Ain Jalut, in 1260.
94 Aflaki, Manaqib al-'arifin, 61–3.
95 Sipahsalar, Zindagi nama-yi Mawlana, 115.

Chapter 4

1 The Arabic language arrived in North Africa in two waves: the first occurred in the late seventh century and resulted in the establishment of Qayrawan in present-day

Tunisia, which served as the first center of Arabic language and culture in the Maghrib; the second wave occurred when the Bedouin tribes of the Bani Hilal and Bani Sulaym invaded the region in the eleventh century, coinciding with the arrival of Sufism in North Africa. Though Arabic became the common language of the cities, until this second wave of Arabization, Berber continued to be the language of the majority of the rural population of North Africa: Kees Versteegh, *The Arabic Language*, 2nd ed. (Edinburgh: Edinburgh University Press, 2014), 129.
2   Anwar G. Chejne, *Muslim Spain: Its History and Culture* (Minneapolis: University of Minnesota Press, 1974), 7–9.
3   Charles-André Julien, *Histoire de l'Afrique du Nord: Tunisie, Algérie, Maroc de la conquête arabe à 1830* (Paris: Payot, 1931), 342–3.
4   Georges Drague, *Esquisse d'histoire religieuse du Maroc: Confréries et zaouïas* (Paris: J. Peyronnet, 1951), 279.
5   Vincent J. Cornell, *Realm of the Saint: Power and Authority in Moroccan Sufism* (Austin: University of Texas Press, 1998), 131–8.
6   Ibid., 138.
7   Paul Nwyia, *Ibn 'Abbād de Ronda (1332–1390): Un mystique prédicateur à la Qarawīyīn de Fès* (Beirut: Imprimerie Catholique, 1961), 53–4.
8   Muhammad Jabrun, "al-Haraka al-Sufiyya wa-dawrha fi muwajahat al-ghazw al-salibi li'l-Maghrib," in *al-Tahawwulat al-fikriyya fi'l-'alam al-Islami: a'lam wa-kutub wa-harakat wa-afkar min al-qarn al-'ashir ila al-qarn al-thani 'ashar al-hijri*, ed. A. Jaludi (Herndon, VA: International Institute of Islamic Thought, 2014), 448; Jamil M. Abun-Nasr, *A History of the Maghrib in the Islamic Period* (Cambridge: Cambridge University Press, 1987), 23.
9   Joseph F. O'Callaghan, *Reconquest and Crusade in Medieval Spain* (Philadelphia: University of Pennsylvania Press, 2004), 18–19.
10 Abun-Nasr, *A History of the Maghrib in the Islamic Period*, 147. See also Vincent J. Cornell, "Socioeconomic dimensions of Reconquista and jihad in Morocco: Portuguese Dukkala and the Sadid Sus, 1450–1557," *International Journal of Middle Eastern Studies* 22 (1990): 379–418.
11 Abun-Nasr, *A History of the Maghrib in the Islamic Period*, 134; Mukhtar Habbar, "al-Hudur al-Sufi fi'l-Jaza'ir 'ala al-'ahd al-'Uthmani," *al-Turath al-'Arabi* 57 (1994): 51.
12 Al-Hasan Benabbou, "al-Jam' bayna al-suluk wa'l-fiqh 'inda mutasawwifat al-maghrib," in *Ahmad b. Sulayman al-Simlali al-Jazuli: Ra'id al-tajdid al-sufi fi maghrib al-qarn al-tasi' al-hijri*, ed. Ahmad Bulqadi (Agadir: Kulliyat al-Adab w'al-'Ulum al-Insaniyya, Jami'at Ibn Zahr, 2013), 347. Vincent J. Cornell, "The Logic of Analogy and the Role of the Sufi Shaykh," *International Journal of Middle Eastern Studies* 15 (1983): 75–7.
13 For discussion of *rijal* hagiographical anthologies (i.e., those containing generally brief accounts of God's friends and pious exemplars) and their importance in the development of Sufism in the Maghrib, see Cornell, *Realm of the Saint*, 98.
14 Cornell, *Realm of the Saint*, offers the best sociohistorical analysis of sainthood in Morocco during this period and includes extensive discussions regarding all three of these historical friends of God.
15 For discussion of 'Abd al-Rahman al-Tha'alabi's role in the jihad against the Portuguese in Algeria during the Ottoman period, see Habbar, "al-Hudur al-Sufi fi'l-Jaza'ir 'ala al-'ahd al-'Uthmani."
16 Cornell, *Realm of the Saint*, 285.
17 Cornell, "The Logic of Analogy and the Role of the Sufi Shaykh," 88.
18 Cornell, *Realm of the Saint*, 67.

19   Abun-Nasr, *A History of the Maghrib in the Islamic Period*, 134.
20   Cornell, "The Logic of Analogy and the Role of the Sufi Shaykh," 89.
21   Cornell, *Realm of the Saint*, 239.
22   The Taifa kingdoms, from *Muluk al-tawa'if* (party kings), were essentially feudal city-states ruled by families belonging to various Berber tribes. The Taifa kingdoms came into being in the early eleventh century during the fragmentation of al-Andalus, which preceded the fall of the Umayyads in Cordova in 1031. This chaotic state of affairs ended with the rise of the Almoravids as sole rulers of what remained of al-Andalus at the end of the eleventh century: Chejne, *Muslim Spain*, 50–68.
23   Tahir al-Sadafi, *al-Sirr al-masun fi ma ukrima bihi al-mukhlisun*, ed. Halima Ferhat (Beirut: Dar al-Gharb al-Islami, 1998), 87.
24   Qur'an 37:106. This verse relates God's words regarding the outcome of Abraham's faithfulness.
25   Al-Sadafi, *al-Sirr al-masun*, 87–8.
26   *Mughāwir* denotes one who devotes himself energetically to carrying out surprise attacks (*ghāra*) on an enemy; a raider: Ibn Manzur, *Lisan al-'Arab*, V (Beirut: Dar Sader, 1994), 36.
27   'Abd al-Ra'uf al-Munawi, *al-Kawakib al-durriya fi tarajim al-sada al-sufiyya: al-tabaqat al-kubra wa'l-tabaqat al-sughra*, ed. Muhammad Adib al-Jadir, IV (Beirut: Dar Sader, 1999), 636. Ibn 'Arabi reckoned Yusuf al-Mughawir among the greatest of those wayfarers who undertake jihad in lands where other than God's word is exalted: Ibn 'Arabi, *al-Futuhat al-makkiyya*, ed. Ahmad Shams al-Din, III (Beirut: Dar al-Kutub al-'Ilmiyya, 1999), 51.
28   Ibn al-Mulaqqin, *Tabaqat al-awliya'*, ed. Mustafa 'Abd al-Qadir 'Ata (Beirut: Dar al-Kutub al-'Ilmiyya, 1998), 316.
29   Al-Munawi, *al-Kawakib al-durriya*, has two entries regarding him, one under Abu'l-Hajjaj and the other under Yusuf; Safi al-Din ibn Abi'l-Mansur ibn Zafir, *Risala*, refers to him as Abu'l-Hajjaj Yusuf al-Mughawir. In Ibn al-Mulaqqin's *Tabaqat al-awliya'*, he is Yusuf b. Muhammad b. 'Ali b. Ahmad b. Sulayman al-Hashimi Abu'l-Hajjaj al-Mughawir; al-Sadafi, *al-Sirr al-masun*, names him only *al-Mughawir*. For discussion of the likelihood of their all being the same friend of God, see Halima Ferhat's note in the introduction to *al-Sirr al-masun*, 40.
30   Ibn Zafir, *Risala*, 45.
31   Ibn al-Mulaqqin. *Tabaqat al-awliya'*, 316.
32   Abu 'Abdullah Muhammad b. Ahmad al-Ansari al-Ghazzal (d. sixth/twelfth century?) was a *murid* of Ibn al-'Arif in Almeria.
33   According to many Sufi writers, there is a hierarchy of saints through whom God preserves the earth. These include the Substitutes (*abdal*) and Pillars (*awtad*), as well as several other groups, the chief among whom is the *ghawth* or *qutb* (i.e., the Axis Mundi). Abu'l-Hasan 'Ali Hujviri discusses these categories in *Kashf al-mahjub*, 321. See also Sayyid Ja'far Sajjadi, *Farhang-i istilahat va ta'birat-i 'irfani*, 47–9, 155–6. The *awtad* are usually said to number four; Gril suggests the seven here may refer to the four *awtad*, the *qutb*, and the two Imam assessors. Ibn Zafir, *Risala*, 136 (French translation).
34   Ibid., 45.
35   I.e., the Land of Alfonso king of Castille, in Spain.
36   *Wajd* is derived from the Arabic root /WJD/ (to find) and is described as a visitation from God that one cannot will and that overwhelms the inner heart—through either sadness or happiness—and separates one's outward being therefrom: Sajjadi, *Farhang-i istilahat va ta'birat-i 'irfani*, 780.

37 Ibn Zafir, *Risala*, 45–9.
38 Al-Sadafi, *al-Sirr al-masun*, 93–4. This anecdote is related under the heading *Rajul yuqal lahu al-mughawir* (A man called al-Mughawir).
39 Ibn ʿArabi, *al-Futuhat al-makkiyya*, III: 281. For discussion of this anecdote, see William C. Chittick, *In Search of the Lost Heart: Explorations in Islamic Thought*, ed. Mohammed Rustom, Atif Khalil, and Kazuyo Murata (Albany: State University of New York Press, 2012), 32.
40 ʿAbd al-Haqq al-Badisi, *al-Maqsad al-sharif wa'l-manzaʿ al-latif fi al-taʿrif bi-sulahaʾ al-rif*, ed. Saʿid Iʿrab (Rabat: al-Matbaʿa al-Malakiyya, 1982), 134.
41 Ibid.
42 Muhammad b. Ahmad al-Hudaygi, *Tabaqat al-Hudaygi*, ed. Ahmad Bu Mazgu, I (Casablanca: Matbaʿat al-Najah al-Jadida, 2006), 561; Muhammad al-Hasani al-Shafshawani Ibn ʿAskar, *Dawhat al-nashir li-man kana bi-al-Maghrib min mashayikh al-qarn al-ʿashir*, ed. Muhammad Hajji (Rabat: Dar al-Maghrib, 1977), 34–5; Muhammad al-Mahdi b. Ahmad al-Fasi, *Mumtiʿ al-asmaʿ fi al-Jazuli wa'l-tabbaʿ wa-ma lahuma min al-atbaʿ*, ed. ʿAbd al-Hayy al-ʿAmrawi and ʿAbd al-Karim Murad (Fez: Matbaʿat Muhammad al-Khamis, 1989), 80–1.
43 Abuʾl-ʿAbbas Ahmad b. Khalid al-Nasiri al-Salawi, *Kitab al-istiqsa li-akhbar duwal al-Maghrib al-aqsa*, IV (Casablanca: Dar al-Kitab, 1997), 152.
44 The *Burda* or Mantle of the Prophet. The Sufi al-Busiri (d. 696/1295), of the Shadhili order, composed what is probably the most celebrated extended poem in praise of the Prophet of Islam. The eighth section concerns the Prophet's jihad and begins with the lines "Tidings of his mission struck fear in the hearts of the enemies / as a lion's roar frightens heedless sheep. / [Muhammad] did not cease meeting them in battle / until by means of [the Muslims'] spears [the enemies] resembled meat on a butcher's block": Sharaf al-Din Abi ʿAbdullah Muhammad al-Busiri, *Burdat al-madih: al-qasida al-burda* (Lahore: Hizb al-Qadiriyya, 1997), 27.
45 Ibn ʿAskar, *Dawhat al-nashir*, 34–5; al-Fasi, *Mumtiʿ al-asmaʿ*, 80–1.
46 Al-Hudaygi, *Tabaqat al-Hudaygi*, 561.
47 ʿAbd al-Hadi al-Tazi, *Jamiʿ al-Qarawiyyin, al-masjid wa'l-jamiʿa bi-madinat Fas: mawsuʿa li-tarikhha al-miʿmari wa'l-fikri*, II (Rabat: Dar Nashr al-Maʿrifa, 2000), 508.
48 *Al-Burtughali* means "The Portuguese." He received this nickname on account of his having been held prisoner by the Portuguese for seven years: ʿAbd al-Fattah Miqlad al-Ghunaymi, *Mawsuʿat tarikh al-Maghrib al-ʿArabi*, V (Cairo: Maktabat Madbuli, 1994), 29.
49 *Bilad al-sus* is located in northern Morocco, near Tangier.
50 Bilad al-habt.
51 *Dhimmi* denotes People of the Book who have accepted Muslim rule and must pay the *jizya* in return for being allowed to practice their faiths.
52 The version of the lines of poetry quoted here are from al-Tazi, *Jamiʿ al-Qarawiyyin*, II: 509, as it includes two additional hemistiches that are not quoted in *Dawhat al-nashir*.
53 Ibn ʿAskar, *Dawhat al-nashir*, 59–61. The life of al-Bahluli is also related in al-Hudaygi, *Tabaqat al-Hudaygi*, I: 271–2.
54 Shawqi ʿAta Allah al-Jamal, "Muhammad al-ʿAyyashi wa-jihaduh did al-Isban wa'l-Burtuqal," *al-Manahil* 9 (1977): 105.
55 Al-Hudaygi, *Tabaqat al-Hudaygi*, I: 347.
56 *Murabit* is the active participle of the verb *rābata*, discussed in the introduction: i.e., one who dwells in a *ribat* on the border in order to fight the enemies of the faith.

In this sense, *murabit* is similar to *mujahid* or *ghazi*. The term came into French as *marabout*, for which see this chapter's introductory pages, above.
57   Muhammad ibn al-Tayyib al-Qadiri, *Nashr al-mathani li-ahl al-qarn al-hadi 'ashar wa'l-thani*, ed. Muhammad Hajji and Ahmad Tawfiq, II (Rabat: Maktabat al-Talib, 1982), 7.
58   Julien, *Histoire de l'Afrique du Nord*, 484. The historical Muhammad al-'Ayyashi was drawn into the struggles and upheaval (involving various Berber movements, the Sa'dian dynasty, the Andalusian Muslims, and the Spaniards) that plagued Morocco during the seventeenth century. For an overview of Muhammad al-'Ayyashi's historical biography, see Abun-Nasr, *A History of the Maghrib in the Islamic Period*, 221–5.
59   Al-Hudaygi, *Tabaqat al-Hudaygi*, I: 347.
60   Ibid.
61   Zaydan ibn al-Mansur (d. 1037/1627).
62   Muhammad al-Saghir ibn 'Abdullah al-Ifrani, *Nuzhat al-hadi bi-akhbar muluk al-qarn al-hadi*, ed. 'Abd al-Latif al-Shadhili (Casablanca: Matba'at al-Najah al-Jadida, 1998), 381.
63   Al-Hudaygi, *Tabaqat al-Hudaygi*, I: 347.
64   Ibid., 347–8.
65   Ibid., 348. Another version of this anecdote, which relates that they beheaded him, is narrated in Muhammad al-Saghir ibn 'Abdullah al-Ifrani, *Safwat man intashara min akhbar sulaha' al-qarn al-hadi 'ashar*, ed. 'Abd al-Majid Khayali (Casablanca: Markaz al-Turath al-Thaqafi al-Maghribi, 2004), 168.
66   A town located near the Oum Er-Rbia River, between modern-day Casablanca and Marrakesh.
67   Al-Hudaygi, *Tabaqat al-Hudaygi*, I: 348.
68   Abu Salim 'Abdullah b. Muhammad al-'Ayyashi, *al-Rihla al-'Ayyashiyya*, ed. Sa'id al-Fadili and Sulayman al-Qarshi, II (Abu Dhabi: Dar al-Suwaydi li'l-Nashr wa'l-Tawzi', 2006), 63–4.

Chapter 5

1   S. M. Ikram, *Muslim Civilization in India*, ed. A. Embree (New York: Columbia University Press, 1965), 7.
2   I.e., "Resembling People of the Book."
3   Ikram, *Muslim Civilization in India*, 11–12. According to al-Baladhuri, Muhammad b. Qasim made a truce with the folk of several towns (Sawarandī and al-Rōr—modern-day Rohri), vowing neither to fight them nor to interfere with their worship so long as they paid the tax on non-Muslims. He quotes Muhammad b. Qasim as saying that the temples (*budd*) were "like the churches of the Christians and Jews and the fire temples of the Magians": al-Baladhuri, *Futuh al-buldan* (Beirut: Dar al-Kutub al-'Ilmiyya, 2000), 261. The author of the *Chach Nama* gives a similar quotation, comparing the Hindus to Christians, Zoroastrians, etc.: 'Ali b. Hamid Kufi, *Fathnama-yi Sind ma'ruf ba Chach Nama*, ed. 'Umar b. Muhammad Davud Putah (Tehran: Intisharat-i Asatir, 2005), 214.
4   Khaliq Ahmad Nizami, *Some Aspects of Religion and Politics in India during the Thirteenth Century* (Bombay: Asia Publishing House, 1961), 315.
5   E.g., Sirhindi's letters contain such pronouncements as "The honor of Islam [depends upon] degrading unbelief and those who profess unbelief [by exacting payment of

the *jizya*]" and "It is to the benefit of Islam whenever a Jew is killed": Shaykh Ahmad Sirhindi, *Maktubat-i rabbani*, I (Istanbul: Maktabat al-Haqiqa, 1977), letters 163 and 193, pp. 272, 307–10.

6   For example, the regions of the Indian subcontinent with the largest Muslim populations—modern-day Pakistan and Bangladesh—are quite far from the historical centers of Muslim rule: e.g., Delhi and Jaunpur, in northern India. Thus, if Islam had been spread by the sword, the state of Uttar Pradesh in modern-day India would be predominantly Muslim; however, the great majority of the population was then, and remains today, Hindu: Richard M. Eaton, *The Rise of Islam and the Bengal Frontier, 1204–1760* (Berkeley and Los Angeles: University of California Press, 1993), 115.

7   Ikram, *Muslim Civilization in India*, 25–6. Contemporary and later Muslim accounts of Mahmud's plundering of the temple of Somnath in 1026 framed the raid as religiously motivated: e.g., in his famous elegy for Sultan Mahmud, the poet Farrukhi (d. 429/1037) lamented, "Alas, now all the Brahmins of India will once again build a place for their idols in the temple!": Hakim Farrukhi-yi Sistani, *Divan*, ed. M. D. Siyaqi (Tehran: Intisharat-i Zuvvar, 1999), 91.

8   Bruce Lawrence, *Notes from a Distant Flute: Sufi Literature in Pre-Mughal India* (Tehran: Imperial Iranian Academy of Philosophy, 1978), 19.

9   Shahid Amin, *Conquest and Community: The Afterlife of Warrior Saint Ghazi Miyan* (Chicago: University of Chicago Press, 2015), 9.

10 Regarding early Sufi Mujahids in Bengal, see, Eaton, *The Rise of Islam and the Bengal Frontier*, 72–3.

11 Aziz Ahmad, *Studies in Islamic Culture in the Indian Environment* (Oxford: Oxford University Press, 1964), 84. Eaton notes, however, that Sufis were not always involved in the conversion of Hindus or the development of syncretic Hindu-Muslim practices and even shunned contact with non-Muslims in some cases: Richard M. Eaton, *The Sufis of Bijapur, 1300–1700: Social Roles of Sufis in Medieval India* (Princeton: Princeton University Press, 1978), 133. It is also worth noting in this regard that Shah Mahmud Awrangabadi's *Malfuzat-i Naqshbandiyya*—the hagiographical source for Baba Palang Pūsh—fails to mention any Sufi conversion of Hindus: Simon Digby, "Introduction" in *Sufis and Soldiers in Awrangzeb's Deccan: Malfūzát-i Naqshbandiyya, Translated from the Persian and with an Introduction by Simon Digby* (New Delhi: Oxford University Press, 2001), 8.

12 Eaton, *The Sufis of Bijapur*, 165–73.

13 Ibid., 124.

14 Significant Sufi orders in Indo-Muslim history include the Chishti, Qadiri, Firdawsi, Shattari, and Naqshbandi orders.

15 Jamil M. Abun-Nasr, *Muslim Communities of Grace: The Sufi Brotherhoods in Islamic Religious Life* (New York: Columbia University Press, 2007), 116.

16 Lawrence, *Notes from a Distant Flute*, 20.

17 Nizami, *Some Aspects of Religion and Politics in India*, 178–9.

18 The first significant Naqshbandi shaykh in the subcontinent was al-Baqi Billah (d. 1012/1603), who established a Sufi hospice in Delhi: Abun-Nasr, *Muslim Communities of Grace*, 117.

19 Arthur F. Buehler, *Sufi Heirs of the Prophets: The Indian Naqshbandiyya and the Rise of the Mediating Sufi Shaykh* (Columbia: University of South Carolina Press, 1998), 61; e.g., Khwaja Nasir al-Din 'Ubayd Allah Ahrar (d. 896/1490) assisted the Timurid prince of Tashkent in both subduing and later organizing the defense of Samarqand: Hamid Algar, "A Brief History of the Naqshbandi Order," in Marc Gaborieau, Alexandre Popovic, and Thierry Zarcone, eds., *Naqshbandis: Cheminements et*

situation actuelle d'un ordre mystique musulman; Actes de la Table Ronde de Sèvres, 2–4 mai 1985/Historical Developments and Present Situation of a Muslim Mystical Order; Proceedings of the Sèvres Round Table, May 2–4, 1985 (Paris: Éditions Isis, 1990), 13.

20 The hagiographies and *malfuzat* named in this paragraph represent only a small part of the voluminous Indo-Persian Sufi literary corpus; only compositions used as sources in *Sufi Warrior Saints* are mentioned. Although many Indo-Persian Sufi writings remain in unedited manuscript form, efforts are now being made, particularly in Iran, to edit and publish Indo-Persian Sufi hagiographies (e.g., *Gulzar-i abrar, Akhbar al-akhyar, Thamarat al-quds, Khwajagan-i Chisht*).
21 Lawrence, *Notes from a Distant Flute*, 27.
22 Eaton, *The Rise of Islam and the Bengal Frontier*, 75.
23 Qur'an 2:255: *Allah, there is no god save Him, the Living, the Eternal. Neither slumber nor sleep overtake Him. To Him belongs what is in the heavens and what is on earth. Who may intercede with Him save by His leave? He knows what is before them and what will follow them, and they know naught of His knowledge save what He wills. His seat comprises the heavens and the earth, and their preservation weighs upon Him not. He is the Most High, the Most Mighty.*
24 Allahdia b. Shaykh 'Abd al-Rahim Chishti, *Khwajagan-i Chisht: Siyar al-aqtab*, ed. M. S. Mawla'i (Tehran: Nashr-i 'Ilm, 2007), 126–7.
25 Ikram, *Muslim Civilization in India*, 185.
26 Mahmud of Ghazna plundered the temple of Somnath in 1026: Annemarie Schimmel, *Islam in the Indian Subcontinent* (Lahore: Sang-e Meel Publications, 2003), 7. The fact that this event occurred six years after the death of Abu Muhammad confirms the legendary nature of the anecdote.
27 *Lawh-i mahfuz*, the tablet upon which "the transactions of mankind have been written by God from all eternity." F. Steingass, *A Comprehensive Persian-English Dictionary* (Springfield: Nataraj Books, 2003), 1131.
28 The Tenth of Muharram, which is the first month of the Islamic lunar calendar. This is the date of the martyrdom of the third Imam, Husayn, at Karbala in 680 (A.H. 61).
29 *La ilaha illa Allah wa-Muhammad rasul Allah*.
30 The child's entire response is in Arabic, a further indication of his wondrous precocity.
31 According to Jami, his father also bade Abu Muhammad complete his studies in the outward religious sciences, and Abu Muhammad dutifully fulfilled his father's wish: Jami, *Nafahat al-uns*, 329.
32 *Qawwali* singing has been an important part of Indian Sufism since the thirteenth century. *Qawwāl* is derived from the Arabic root /QWL/, the basic meaning of which is "to speak," "say," "utter." *Qawwali* singing is related to the Sufi practice of *sama'* and incorporates Sufi poetry with various instruments. *Qawwali* singers are still very much active at Sufi shrines in the subcontinent, and the tradition is associated primarily with the Chishti Sufi order: Carl Ernst, *Sufism: An Introduction to the Mystical Tradition of Islam* (Boston: Shambhala, 2011), 186–7.
33 A version of this anecdote is also related in Sayyid Muhammad 'Alavi (Amir Khurd) Kirmani, *Siyar al-awliya' dar ahval va malfuzat-i mashāyikh-i Chisht*, ed. Muhammad Irshad Qurayshi (Islamabad: Markaz-i Tahqiqat-i Farsi-yi Iran va Pakistan, 1978), 50–1.
34 Versions of this anecdote are also related in 'Abd al-Rahman Jami, *Nafahat al-uns*, ed. Mahmud 'Abidi (Tehran: Intisharat-i Ittila'at, 1996), 329; and Mirza La'al Bayg La'ali Badakhshi, *Thamarat al-quds min shajarat al-uns*, ed. Sayyid Kamal Hajj Sayyid Jawadi (Tehran: Pizhuhishgah-i 'Ulum-i Insani va Mutala'at-i Farhangi, 1997), 112–13.
35 Chishti, *Khwajagan-i Chisht*, 67–72.

36 The epigraph to this section is a line of poetry composed in praise of Shah Jalal: Muhammad Ghawthi Shattari Mandavi, *Gulzar-i abrar fi siyar al-akhyar*, ed. Yusuf Bayg Babapur (Tehran: Kitabkhana-yi Muze va Markaz-i Asnad-i Majlis-i Shura-yi Islami, 2012), 148.
37 Eaton, *The Rise of Islam and the Bengal Frontier*, 73. E.g., the main airport near Dhaka, Hazrat Shahjalal International Airport, is named after him.
38 Ibn Battuta, *Rihla* (Beirut: Dar Sader, 1998), 612.
39 Ibid.
40 Mandavi, *Gulzar-i abrar*, 147.
41 Ibid.
42 Ibid.
43 Badakhshi describes Shah Jalal's coming to Bangladesh in somewhat more lurid terms: "He set out for the realm of Bang for the purpose of carrying out war (*ghazā*), and there he eradicated the unbelievers and cleansed that realm of the filth of that unclean folk." Badakhshi, *Thamarat al-quds*, 530.
44 This recalls the number of companions who took part in the battle of Badr with the Prophet Muhammad: Eaton, *The Rise of Islam and the Bengal Frontier*, 75.
45 Qur'an 2:249.
46 Mandavi, *Gulzar-i abrar*, 147–8.
47 Ibid., 148.
48 Badakhshi, *Thamarat al-quds*, 530.
49 One of the meanings of Shah Jalal's epithet al-*Mujarrad* is "the Bachelor."
50 Badakhshi, *Thamarat al-quds*, 530–1. For a comparison of the hagiographical and historical Shah Jalal and Sikandar Ghazi, see Eaton, *The Rise of Islam and the Bengal Frontier*, 73–7.
51 Ibn Battuta consistently uses the term *faqir* (poor, indigent) to refer to Sufis in these anecdotes.
52 Present-day Hangzhou.
53 Present-day Beijing.
54 Ibn Battuta, *Rihla*, 612–14. *'Arafa* is the ninth day of the Month of Pilgrimage, Dhu'l-Hijja; *'Id al-Adha* is the Festival of the Sacrifice, which occurs on the tenth day of Dhu'l-Hijja.
55 Mir 'Ali Sher Qani' Tattawi, *Tuhfat al-kiram*, ed. Nabibakhsh Khan Baluch, trans. Akhtar Razavi (Karachi: Sindhi Adabi Board, 2006), 586 (Urdu translation).
56 Ikram, *Muslim Civilization in India*, 16.
57 The two sources, both composed in the eighteenth century, are Shaykh Muhammad A'zam Tattawi, *Tuhfat al-tahirin*, a short hagiographical work dealing with friends of God in Sindh, and Mir 'Ali Sher Qani' Tattawi, *Tuhfat al-kiram*, a history of Sindh. Neither source gives the date of Sayyid Muluk Shah's death, and I am unaware of any other source regarding this obscure friend of God.
58 Shaykh Muhammad A'zam Tattawi, *Tuhfat al-tahirin*, ed. Badr 'Alam Darani (Karachi: Sindhi Adabi Board, 1956), 168.
59 The great Muslim necropolis located in southern Sindh near the city of Thatta, in present-day Pakistan.
60 Shaykh Muhammad A'zam Tattawi, *Tuhfat al-tahirin*, 167–8.
61 Shah Mahmud Awrangabadi, *Malfuzat-i Naqshbandiyya: Halat-i Hazrat Baba Shah Musafir Sahib* (Hyderabad: Nizamat-i Umur-i Madhhabi-yi Sarkar-i 'Ali, 1939), 2–3.
62 Ibid., 3–4.
63 Ibid., 4–5.
64 Digby, "Introduction," in Sufis and Soldiers in Awrangzeb's Deccan, 11.

65 Ibid., 4. Baba Palang Pūsh arrived in the Deccan during the Mughal annexation of the earlier Bijapur and Golkonda sultanates and the rise of the Hindu Marathas as a serious challenge to Mughal power in the region.
66 Ibid.
67 For discussion of Bilgrami's life of Baba Palang Pūsh and comparison with Awrangabadi's *Malfuzat-i Naqshbandiyya*, see Simon Digby, "Before the Bābās Came to India: A Reconstruction of the Earlier Lives of Bābā Saʿīd Palangpōsh and Bābā Muḥammad Musāfir in 'Wilāyat,'" *Iran* 36 (1998): 139–64.
68 Nile Green, "Stories of Saints and Sultans: Re-membering History at the Sufi Shrines of Aurangabad," *Modern Asian Studies* 38 (2004): 419–46.
69 The Malamati movement arose in Khurasan in the ninth century as a reaction to ostentatious outward manifestations of godliness. Traditionally, the founder of the Malamati movement is said to have been Hamdun Qassar (d. 270/884).
70 I.e., the Prophet Muhammad.
71 Awrangabadi, *Malfuzat-i Naqshbandiyya*, 2–3.
72 This refers to the well-known romance of Majnun and Layla, which originated in Arabia in the seventh century. A young man, Qays, falls in love with Layla, but her father forbids her to have any contact with him. Qays becomes obsessed with Layla and begins to see everything in terms of his love for and separation from her—hence the name *Majnun,* which means "possessed" or "mad" in Arabic. Majnun becomes disillusioned with human society and wanders naked in the wilderness like a wild animal. Sufi poets would later use the story of Majnun and Layla as an allegory for the Sufi wayfarer (Majnun), who seeks union with God (Layla, Majnun's beloved). A. A. Seyed-Gohrab, "LEYLI O MAJNUN," *Encyclopædia Iranica*, online edition, 2009, http://www.iranicaonline.org/articles/leyli-o-majnun-narrative-poem.
73 Regarding Baba Palang Pūsh's meeting with Baba Qul Mazid and his subsequent naked wandering, *Ma'athir al-kiram* relates that Baba Palang Pūsh was studying the religious sciences when he was drawn to Baba Qul Mazid: "At that time, he was seven years old, but he did not desist from seeking [to be the *murid* of Baba Qul Mazid]. That great [shaykh] caused [Baba Palang Pūsh] to be naked and bestowed some breeches on him. At the same time, such a powerful inclination overcame him that he set out for the wilderness. He spent roughly eleven years in the wilderness naked." Mir Ghulam ʿAli Azad Bilgrami, *Ma'athir al-kiram* (Agra: Mufid-i ʿAm, 1910), 172.
74 The text has *sher*, which generally denotes a lion, rather than *palang*, which is the usual word for a leopard.
75 Awrangabadi, *Malfuzat-i Naqshbandiyya*, 4.
76 The text refers to them as *rāfidian* (from the Arabic verb *rafada*, "to refuse"), meaning "apostates," "renegades."
77 ʿAli b. Musa al-Rida (d. 202/818) is the eighth Imam of Twelver Shi'ism. Twelver Shi'ites believe he was martyred at the hands of the Abbasid caliph al-Ma'mun, hence the city's name, Mashhad, i.e., "place of martyrdom."
78 Awrangabadi, *Malfuzat-i Naqshbandiyya*, 5.
79 Yalangtush Bahadur (d. 1066/1656) was the Uzbek advisor to Nadhr Muhammad Khan, who defeated the Qalmaqs in 1643. He also sponsored the building of two *madrasa*s in Samarqand.
80 Nadhr Muhammad Khan (d. 1061/1651?) was the ruler of Balkh at the time of the Qalmaq invasion.
81 The *Fatiha* (from the Arabic verb *fataha*, "to open") is the opening *sura* of the Qur'an and begins with the invocation *In the name of God the compassionate, the merciful.* Its importance for Muslims is similar to that of the Lord's Prayer for Christians.

82　Awrangabadi, *Malfuzat-i Naqshbandiyya*, 5–6.
83　I.e., Muhammad.
84　Hamza ibn 'Abd al-Muttalib (d. 3/625), sometimes known as "The First Martyr," was a Companion of the Prophet Muhammad and a brave fighter in many of the Muslims' early campaigns against the pagan Arabs. It is said that at the battle of Badr (624) he fought before the Prophet with two swords and that at the battle of Uhud (625) he slew thirty-one men before he was killed: Ibn Al-athir, *Usud al-ghaba fi ma'rifat al-sahaba* (Beirut: Dar Ibn Hazm, 2012), 299–300.
85　Awrangabadi, *Malfuzat-i Naqshbandiyya*, 25–6.
86　I.e., "Soldier of the Faith, valiant and victorious in battle."
87　Awrangabadi, *Malfuzat-i Naqshbandiyya*, 26.
88　The text has *qalandar*, a wandering dervish sometimes known for antinomian behavior.
89　Awrangabadi, *Malfuzat-i Naqshbandiyya*, 18.
90　Ibid., 28–9.
91　Ibid, 8.

Conclusion

1　For discussion of the universality of Sufi hagiographical images and motifs, see Jeff Eden, *Warrior Saints of the Silk Road: Legends of the Qarakhanids* (Leiden: E. J. Brill, 2019), 11–12.
2　Reuven Firestone, *Jihad: The Origins of Holy War in Islam* (New York: Oxford University Press, 1999), 23.
3　John Renard, *Friends of God: Islamic Images of Piety, Commitment, and Servanthood* (Berkeley and Los Angeles: University of California Press, 2008), 3–9.
4　See Neale, *Jihad in Premodern Sufi Writings* (New York: Palgrave Macmillan, 2016), 27–31.
5　Thomas Sizgorich, for example, discusses the existence of a "shared semiotic vocabulary" in relation to the forms of "militant piety" common to both late antique Christianity and early Islam: *Violence and Belief in Late Antiquity: Militant Devotion in Christianity and Islam* (Philadelphia: University of Pennsylvania Press, 2009), 145–6.

Glossary

1　Although Jews and Christians who submitted to Muslim rule were to be tolerated, many premodern Muslim writers expressed frustration with their tenacious adherence to the religions of their forebears: e.g., Najm al-Din Razi stated that Jews and Christians were "stubborn" in their refusal to accept the prophethood of Muhammad, whereas they accepted the prophethood of Jesus and Moses on the basis of their miracles: Najm al-Din Razi, *Mirsad al-'ibad min al'mabda' ila al'ma'ad*, ed. Muhammad Amin Riyahi (Tehran: Bungah-i Tarjuma va Nashr-i Kitab, 1973), 140.
2　Sayyid Ja'Far Sajjadi, *Farhang-i istilahat va ta'birat-i 'irfani* (Tehran: Kitbkhana-yi Tahuri, 2004), 565.
3　See Sajjadi, *Farhang-i istilahat va ta'birat-i 'irfani*, 60–1.

4   Ibid., 89–90. The quotation attributed to Abu Sa'id is *al-Islam an yamut 'anaka nafsuka.*
5   The traditional *sira* literature relates that the Prophet Muhammad took part in as many as twenty-seven campaigns: Suleiman Mourad and James Lindsay, *The Intensification and Reorientation of Sunni Jihad Ideology in the Crusader Period* (Leiden: E. J. Brill, 2013), 18.
6   For example, Qur'an 112: *Say, He is God the One, God the everlasting. He begat not, nor was he begotten, and there is no equal to Him.*

Appendix

1   For complete titles and edition-specific bibliographical information, see Bibliography, below. Not all primary sources cited are included in this appendix. Italicized English titles in parentheses are those of readily available translations.

BIBLIOGRAPHY

Primary Sources

Abu Dawud. *Sunan Abi Dawud*. 7 vols. Ed. Shu'ayb Arna'ut and Muhammad Kamil Qarah Balili. Beirut: Dar al-Islam al-'Alamiyya, 2009.
Abu Sa'id ibn Abi'l-Khayr. *Sukhanan-i manzum-i Abu Sa'id Abu'l-Khayr*. Ed. Sa'id Nafisi. Tehran: Intisharat-i Sana'i, 1997.
Adab al-muluk fi bayan haqa'iq al-tasawwuf: Ein Handbuch zur islamischen Mystik aus dem 4./10. Jahrhundert. Ed. Bernd Radtke. Stuttgart: F. Steiner, 1991. [The treatise *Adab al-muluk* is of anonymous authorship.]
Aflaki, Shams al-Din Ahmad. *The Feats of the Knowers of God (Manāqeb al-'ārefīn)*. Trans. John O'Kane. Leiden and Boston: Brill, 2002.
Aflaki, Shams al-Din Ahmad. *Manaqib al-'arifin*. Ed. T. Yazıcı and Tawfiq H. Suhbani. Tehran: Intisharat-i Dustan, 2017.
Alf layla wa-layla. 2 vols. Beirut: Dar Sader, 1999.
'Attar, Farid al-Din. *Mantiq al-tayr*. Ed. M. R. Shafi'i Kadkani. Tehran: Intisharat-i Sukhan, 2010.
'Attar, Farid al-Din. *Tadhkirat al-awliya'*. Ed. Muhammad Isti'lami. Tehran: Intisharat-i Zuvvar, 2004.
Awrangabadi, Shah Mahmud. *Malfuzat-i Naqshbandiyya: Halat-i Hazrat Baba Shah Musafir Sahib*. Hyderabad: Nizamat-i Umur-i Madhhabi-yi Sarkar-i 'Ali, 1939.
al-'Ayyashi, Abu Salim 'Abdullah b. Muhammad. *al-Rihla al-'Ayyashiyya*. 2 vols. Ed. Sa'id al-Fadılı and Sulayman al-Qarshi. Abu Dhabi: Dar al-Suwaydi li'l-Nashr wa'l-Tawzi', 2006.
Badakhshi, Mirza La'al Bayg La'ali. *Thamarat al-quds min shajarat al-uns*. Ed. Sayyid Kamal Hajj Sayyid Jawadi. Tehran: Pizhuhishgah-i 'Ulum-i Insani va Mutala'at-i Farhangi, 1997.
al-Badisi, 'Abd al-Haqq. *al-Maqsad al-sharif wa'l-manza' al-latif fi al-ta'rif bi-sulaha' al-rif*. Ed. Sa'id I'rab. Rabat: al-Matba'a al-Malakiyya, 1982.
al-Baghdadi, al-Khatib. *Tarikh madinat al-salam*. 17 vols. Ed. Bashshar 'Awwad Ma'ruf. Beirut: Dar al-Gharb al-Islami, 2001. [Typically cited as *Tarikh Baghdad*.]
Baha'-i Valad. *Ma'arif: majmu'a-yi mava'iz va sukhanan-i sultan al-'ulama' Baha' al-Din Muhammad b. Husayn Khatibi Balkhi mashhur ba Baha'-i Valad*. 2 vols. Ed. Badi' al-zaman Furuzanfar. Tehran: Kitabkhana-yi Tahuri, 1973.
al-Baladhuri. *Futuh al-buldan*. Beirut: Dar al-Kutub al-'Ilmiyya, 2000.
Balkhi, Safi al-Din 'Abdullah. [Va'iz-i Balkhi.] *Fazayil-i Balkh*. Ed. 'Abd al-Hayy Habibi. Tehran: Intisharat-i Bunyad-i Farhang-i Iran, 1971. [Persian translation by 'Abdullah b. Muhammad Husayn-i Balkhi.]
al-Balkhi, Shaqiq. *Adab al-'ibadat*. In Paul Nwyia, ed., *Trois œuvres inédites de mystiques musulmans*, 17–22. Beirut: Dar al-Mashriq, 1973.
Bilgrami, Mir Ghulam 'Ali Azad. *Ma'athir al-kiram*. Agra: Mufid-i 'Am, 1910.
al-Bukhari, Muhammad b. Isma'il. *Sahih al-Bukhari*. Beirut: Dar Ibn Kathir, 2002.

al-Busiri, Sharaf al-Din Abi 'Abdullah Muhammad. *Burdat al-madih: al qasida al-burda.* Lahore: Hizb al-Qadiriyya, 1997.

Chishti, Allahdia b. Shaykh 'Abd al-Rahim. *Khwajagan-i Chisht: Siyar al-aqtab.* Ed. M. S. Mawla'i. Tehran: Nashr-i 'Ilm, 2007.

al-Daylami, Abu'l-Hasan. *Sirat al-shaykh al-kabir Abu 'Abdullah ibn al-Khafif al-Shirazi.* Ed. Annemarie Schimmel. Tehran: Babak, 1984.

al-Dhahabi, Shams al-Din Muhammad. *al-'Ibar fi khabar man ghabar.* 4 vols. Ed. Abu Hajar Muhammad al-Sa'id b. Basyuni Zaghlul. Beirut: Dar al-Kutub al-'Ilmiyya, 1985.

al-Dhahabi, Shams al-Din Muhammad. *Siyar a'lam al-nubala'.* 25 vols. Ed. Bashshar 'Awwad Ma'ruf. Beirut: Mu'assasat al-Risala, 1996.

Dihlavi, Khwaja Hasan. *Fawa'id al-fu'ad: Malfuzat-i Khwaja Nizam al-Din Awliya'.* Ed. Muhsin Kiyani. Tehran: Intisharat-i Ruzana, 1998.

al-Fasi, Muhammad al-Mahdi b. Ahmad, *Mumti' al-asma' fi al-Jazuli wa'l-tabba' wa-ma lahuma min al-atba'.* Ed. 'Abd al-Hayy al-'Amrawi and 'Abd al-Karim Murad. Fez: Matba'at Muhammad al-Khamis, 1989.

al-Ghazali, Abu Hamid. *Kimiya-yi sa'adat.* 2 vols. Ed. Husayn Khadivjam. Tehran: Shirkat-i Intisharat-i 'Ilmi va Farhangi, 2001.

al-Ghunaymi, 'Abd al-Fattah Miqlad. *Mawsu'at tarikh al-Maghrib al-'Arabi.* 6 vols in 3. Cairo: Maktabat Madbuli, 1994.

Hazar hikayat-i sufiyan. 2 vols. Ed. H. Khatamipur. Tehran: Intisharat-i Sukhan, 2000.

al-Hudaygi, Muhammad b. Ahmad. *Tabaqat al-Hudaygi.* 2 vols. Ed. Ahmad Bu Mazgu. Casablanca: Matba'at al-Najah al-Jadida, 2006.

Hujviri, Abu'l-Hasan 'Ali. *Kashf al-mahjub.* Ed. Mahmud 'Abidi. Tehran: Soroush Press, 2012.

Ibn al-'Adim. *Bughyat al-talab fi tarikh Halab.* 12 vols. Ed. Suhayl Zakkar. Beirut: Dar al-Fikr, 1988.

Ibn 'Arabi. *al-Futuhat al-makkiyya.* 9 vols. Ed. Ahmad Shams al-Din. Beirut: Dar al-Kutub al-'Ilmiyya, 1999.

Ibn 'Arabi. *al-Wasaya.* Beirut: Mu'assasat al-'A'lami, 1993.

Ibn 'Asakir. *Tarikh madinat Dimashq.* 80 vols. Ed. Muhibb al-Din Abi Sa'id and 'Umar ibn Gharama al-'Amrawi. Beirut: Dar al-Fikr, 1995.

Ibn 'Askar, Muhammad al-Hasani al-Shafshawani. *Dawhat al-nashir li-man kana bi-al-Maghrib min mashayikh al-qarn al-'ashir.* Ed. Muhammad Hajji. Rabat: Dar al-Maghrib, 1977.

Ibn al-Athir. *al-Kamil fi al-tarikh.* 11 vols. Ed. Abu'l-Fida' 'Abdullah al-Qadi. Beirut: Dar al-Kutub al-'Ilmiyya, 1987.

Ibn al-Athir. *Usud al-ghaba fi ma'rifat al-sahaba.* Beirut: Dar Ibn Hazm, 2012.

Ibn Battuta. *Rihla.* Beirut: Dar Sader, 1998.

Ibn Hawqal. *Kitab surat al-ard.* Beirut: Dar Maktabat al-Hayat, 1992.

Ibn Hibban, Abu Hatim Muhammad. *Mashahir 'ulama' al-amsar.* Ed. Majdi b. Mansur b. Sayyid al-Shuri. Beirut: Dar al-Kutub al-'Ilmiyya, 1995.

Ibn al-'Imad. *Shadharat al-dhahab fi akhbar man dhahab.* 10 vols. Ed. 'Abd al-Qadir al-Arna'ut. Beirut: Dar Ibn Kathir, 1991.

Ibn al-Jawzi. *Sifat al-safwa.* Ed. Khalid Mustafa al-Tartusi. Beirut: Dar al-Kitab al-'Arabi, 2012.

Ibn Kathir. *al-Bidaya wa'l-nihaya.* 14 vols. Beirut: Maktabat al-Ma'arif, 1966.

Ibn Maja. *Sunan.* 2 vols. Ed. Muhammad Fu'ad 'Abd al-Baqi. Cairo: Dar 'Ihya' al-Kutub al-'Arabiyya, 2009.

Ibn Manzur. *Lisan al-'Arab*. 15 vols. Beirut: Dar Sader, 1994.
Ibn al-Mubarak, 'Abdullah. *Diwan 'Abdullah ibn al-Mubarak*. Ed. M. Bahjat. El-Mansoura: Dar al-Wifa', 1987.
Ibn al-Mubarak, 'Abdullah. *Kitab al-jihad*. Ed. Nazih Hamad. Cairo: Majma' al-Buhuth al-Islamiyya, 1979.
Ibn al-Mubarak, 'Abdullah. *Kitab al-zuhd wa-yalih Kitab al-raqa'iq*. Ed. Habib al-Rahman al-A'zami. Beirut: Dar al-Kutub al-'Ilmiyya, 2004.
Ibn al-Mulaqqin. *Tabaqat al-awliya'*. Ed. Mustafa 'Abd al-Qadir 'Ata. Beirut: Dar al-Kutub al-'Ilmiyya, 1998.
Ibn Nubata, 'Abd al-Rahim b. Muhammad. *Diwan khutab Ibn Nubata*. Ed. Yasir Muhammad Khayr al-Miqdad. Kuwait: al-Wa'i al-Islami, 2012.
Ibn Qayyim al-Jawziyya. *al-Fawa'id*. Ed. Muhammad 'Aziz Shams. Mecca: Dar 'Alam al-Fawa'id, 2008.
Ibn Rushd. *al-Muqaddimat al-mumahhidat*. 3 vols. Ed. Muhammad Hajji. Beirut: Dar al-Gharb al-Islami, 1988.
Ibn Zafir, Safi al-Din Ibn Abi'l-Mansur, *Risala*. Ed. Denis Gril. Cairo: Institut Français d'Archéologie Orientale du Caire, 1986.
al-Ifrani, Muhammad al-Saghir ibn 'Abdullah. *Nuzhat al-hadi bi-akhbar muluk al-qarn al-hadi*. Ed. 'Abd al-Latif al-Shadhili. Casablanca: Matba'at al-Najah al-Jadida, 1998.
al-Ifrani, Muhammad al-Saghir ibn 'Abdullah. *Safwat man intashara min akhbar sulaha'al-qarn al-hadi 'ashar*. Ed. 'Abd al-Majid Khayali. Casablanca: Markaz al-Turath al-Thaqafi al-Maghribi, 2004.
al-Isfahani, Abu Nu'aym. *Hilyat al-awliya' wa-tabaqat al-asfiya'*. 10 vols. Beirut: Dar al-Fikr, 1996.
al-Isfahani, al-Raghib. *Mufradat alfaz al-Qur'an*. Ed. Safwan 'Adnan Dawudi. Damascus: Dar al-Qalam, 1992.
Jamali, Hamid ibn Fazl Allah. *Siyar al-'arifin*. Delhi: Matba'-i Rizavi, 1893.
Jami, 'Abd al-Rahman. *Nafahat al-uns*. Ed. Mahmud 'Abidi. Tehran: Intisharat-i Ittila'at, 1996.
al-Kalabadhi, Abu Bakr. *al-Ta'arruf li-madhhab ahl al-tasawwuf*. Ed. Ahmad Shams al-Din. Beirut: Dar al-Kutub al-'Ilmiyya, 2001.
Kaykavus b. Iskandar b. Qabus, 'Unsur al-Ma'ali. *Qabus Nama*. Ed. Gulamhusayn Yusufi. Tehran: Shirkat-i Intisharat-i 'Ilmi va Faranghi, 2003.
Kharaqani, Ahmad b. Husayn b. al-Shaykh. *Dastur al-jumhur fi manaqib sultan al-'arifin Abu Yazid Tayfur*. Ed. Muhammad Taqi Danishpizhuh and Iraj Afshar. Tehran: Mirath-i Maktub, 2009.
al-Kharkushi, 'Abd al-Malik al-Nisaburi. *Tahdhib al-asrar fi adab al-tasawwuf*. Ed. Muhammad Ahmad 'Abd al-Halim. Cairo: Maktabat al-Thaqafa al-Diniyya, 2010.
Kirmani, Khwaju. *Rawdat al-anwar*. Ed. M. 'Abidi. Tehran: Mirath-i Maktub, 2008.
Kirmani, Sayyid Muhammad 'Alavi. [Amir Khurd.] *Siyar al-awliya' dar ahval va malfuzat-i mashayikh-i Chisht*. Ed. Muhammad Irshad Qurayshi. Islamabad: Markaz-i Tahqiqat-i Farsi-yi Iran va Pakistan, 1978.
Kubra, Najm al-Din. *Fawa'ih al-jamal wa-fawatih al-jalal*. Ed. Fritz Meier. Wiesbaden: F. Steiner, 1957.
Kufi, 'Ali b. Hamid. *Fathnama-yi Sind ma'ruf ba Chach Nama*. Ed. 'Umar b. Muhammad Davud Putah. Tehran: Intisharat-i Asatir, 2005.
Lahori, Ghulam Sarvar. *Khazinat al-asfiya*. 2 vols. Khanpur: Munshi Nawal Kishore, 1914.

Mahmud b. 'Uthman. *Firdaws al-murshidiyya*. Ed. Fritz Meier. Istanbul: Matba'at Ma'arif, 1943.
al-Makki, Abu Talib. *Qut al-qulub fi mu'amalat al-mahbub*. Ed. Mahmud Ibrahim Muhammad al-Ridwani. Cairo: Dar al-Turath, 2001.
Mandavi, Muhammad Ghawthi Shattari. *Gulzar-i abrar fi siyar al-akhyar*. Ed. Yusuf Bayg Babapur. Tehran: Kitabkhana-yi Muze va Markaz-i Asnad-i Majlis-i Shura-yi Islami, 2012.
al-Maqdisi, Abu Shama Shihab al-Din. *al-Dhayl 'ala al-rawdatayn*. 5 vols. Ed. Ibrahim Shams al-Din. Beirut: Dar al-Kutub al-'Ilmiyya, 2002.
al-Mas'udi. *Muruj al-dhahab wa-ma'adin al-jawahir*. 4 vols. in 2. Beirut: Dar al-Andalus, 1996.
Muhammad b. Munavvar. *Asrar al-tawhid fi maqamat shaykh Abi Sa'id*. 2 vols. Ed. R. Shafi'i Kadkani. Tehran: Mu'assasa-yi Intishirat-i Agah, 1997.
al-Munawi, 'Abd al-Ra'uf. *al-Kawakib al-durriyya fi tarajim al-sada al-sufiyya: al-tabaqat al-kubra wa'l-tabaqat al-sughra*. 5 vols. in 6. Ed. Muhammad Adib al-Jadir. Beirut: Dar Sader, 1999.
Pand-i piran. Ed. Jalal Matini. Mashhad: Bunyad-i Farhang-i Iran, 1978.
al-Qadiri, Muhammad ibn al-Tayyib. *Nashr al-mathani li-ahl al-qarn al-hadi 'ashar wa'l-thani*. 4 vols. Ed. Muhammad Hajji and Ahmad Tawfiq. Rabat: Maktabat al-Talib, 1977–86.
al-Qushayri, Abu'l-Qasim. *al-Risala al-Qushayriyya*. Beirut: Dar Sader, 2011.
Razi, Najm al-Din. *Mirsad al-'ibad min al-mabda' ila al'ma'ad*. Ed. Muhammad Amin Riyahi. Tehran: Bungah-i Tarjuma va Nashr-i Kitab, 1973.
Rumi, Jalal al-Din. *Divan-i kamil-i Shams-i Tabrizi*. 3 vols. in 1. Ed. Badi' al-Zaman Furuzanfar and 'Ali Dashti. Tehran: Sazman-i Intisharat-i Javidan, 1980.
Rumi, Jalal al-Din. *Kitab-i Fihi ma fihi*. Ed. Badi' al-Zaman Furuzanfar. Tehran: Intisharat-i Danishgah-i Tihran, 1951.
Rumi, Jalal al-Din. *Mathnavi-yi ma'navi*. 2 vols. Ed. 'Abd al-Karim Surush. Tehran: Intisharat-i 'Ilmi va Farhangi, 1999.
al-Sadafi, Tahir. *al-Sirr al-masun fi ma ukrima bihi al-mukhlisun*. Ed. Halima Ferhat. Beirut: Dar al-Gharb al-Islami, 1998.
al-Sahlagi, Abu Fadl Muhammad. *Kitab al-nur min kalimat Abi Tayfur*. In 'Abd al-Rahman Badawi, *Shatahat al-sufiyya*, 58–187. Kuwait: Wikalat al-Matbu'at, 1976.
al-Sarraj, Abu Nasr. *Kitab al-luma' fi al-tasawwuf*. Ed. R. A. Nicholson. Leiden: E. J. Brill, 1914.
al-Sha'rani, 'Abd al-Wahhab. *al-Tabaqat al-kubra*. 2 vols. Ed. Ahmad 'Abd al-Rahim al-Sayih and Tawfiq 'Ali Wahba. Cairo: Maktabat al-Thaqafa al-Diniyya, 2005.
Shirazi, Abu'l-'Abbas Zarkub. *Shiraz Nama*. Ed. Isma'il Va'iz Javadi. Tehran: Intisharat-i Bunyad-i Farhang-i Iran, 1971.
Sibt ibn al-Jawzi. *Mir'at al-zaman fi tawarikh al-a'yan*. 23 vols. Ed. M. Barakat et al. Damascus: Dar al-Risala al-'Alamiyya, 2013.
Simnani, Sayyid Ashraf Jahangir. *Lata'if-i Ashrafi fi bayan-i tava'if-i sufi*. 2 vols. Karachi: Maktaba Simnani, 1999.
Sipahsalar, Faridun. *Zindagi nama-yi Mawlana Jalal al-Din Mawlavi*. Ed. Sa'id Nafisi. Tehran: Iqbal, 1999.
Sirhindi, Shaykh Ahmad. *Maktubat-i imam rabbani*. Volume I. Istanbul: Maktabat al-Haqiqa, 1977.
Sistani, Hakim Farrukhi. *Divan*. Ed. M. D. Siyaqi. Tehran: Intisharat-i Zuvvar, 1999.

al-Subki, Taj al-Din. *al-Tabaqat al-shafi'iyya al-kubra*. 10 vols. Ed. Mahmud Muhammad al-Tanahi and 'Abd al-Fattah Hulw. Cairo: Dar Ihya' al-Kutub al-'Arabiyya, 1990.
al-Suhrawardi, Shihab al-Din 'Umar. *'Awarif al-ma'arif*. Beirut: Dar Sader, 2010.
al-Sulami, 'Abd al-Rahman. *Tabaqat al-sufiyya*. Ed. Mustafa 'Abd al-Qadir 'Ata. Beirut: Dar al-Kutub al-'Ilmiyya, 2003.
Sultan Valad. *Valad Nama*. Ed. Jalal al-Din Huma'i. Tehran: Mu'assasa-yi Nashr-i Huma, 1997.
al-Tabari, Muhammad b. Jarir. *Jami' al-bayyan 'an ta'wil 'ayy al-Qur'an*. 7 vols. Ed. Bashshar 'Awwad Ma'ruf and 'Isam Faris Hurristani. Beirut: Mu'assasat al-Risala, 1994.
al-Tabari, Muhammad b. Jarir. *Tarjuma-yi Tafsir-i Tabari*. 7 vols. Ed. Habib Yaghma'i. Tehran: Intistharat-i Tus, 1977.
Tattawi, Mir 'Ali Sher Qani'. *Tuhfat al-kiram*. Ed. Nabibakhsh Khan Baluch. Trans. Akhtar Razavi. Karachi: Sindhi Adabi Board, 2006. [Urdu translation.]
Tattawi, Shaykh Muhammad A'zam. *Tuhfat al-tahirin*. Ed. Badr 'Alam Darani. Karachi: Sindhi Adabi Board, 1956.
al-Tirmidhi, Muhammad b. 'Ali. [al-Hakim.] *Riyadat al-nafs*. Ed. Ahmad 'Abd al-Rahman al-Sayih and Ahmad 'Abduh 'Awad. Cairo: Maktabat al-Thaqafa al-Diniyya, 2001.
al-Tirmidhi, Muhammad b. 'Ali. *Sirat al-awliya'*. In Bernd Radtke, ed., *Thalath musannafat li'l-Hakim al-Tirmidhi*, 1–134. Stuttgart: F. Steiner, 1992.
al-'Ulaymi, Mujir al-Din. *al-Uns al-jalil bi-tarikh al-Quds wa'l-Khalil*. 2 vols. Ed. 'Adnan Yunis 'Abd al-Majid Abu Tabbana and Mahmud 'Awda Ka'abina. Amman: Maktabat al-Dandis, 1999–2000.
al-Yafi'i, 'Abdullah ibn As'ad. *Mir'at al-janan wa-'ibrat al-yaqzan*. 4 vols. Ed. Khalil al-Mansur. Beirut: Dar al-Kutub al-'Ilmiyya, 1997.
al-Yafi'i, 'Abdullah ibn As'ad. *Nashr al-mahasin al-'aliyya fi fadl al-mashayikh al-sufiyya*. Ed. Khalil al-Mansur. Beirut: Dar al-Kutub al-'Ilmiyya, 2000.
al-Yafi'i, 'Abdullah ibn As'ad. *Rawd al-rayahin fi hikayat al-salihin*. Ed. 'Abd al-Jalil 'Abd al-Salam. Beirut: Dar al-Kutub al-'Ilmiyya, 2017.
al-Zabidi, Murtada. *Taj al-'arus min jawahir al-qamus*. 40 vols. Ed. 'Abd al-Sattar Farraj et al. Kuwait: Matba'at Hukumat al-Kuwait, 1965–2001.

Secondary Sources

'Abd al-Halim, Rajab Muhammad. *Intishar al-Islam bayna al-Mughul*. Cairo: Dar al-Nahda al-'Arabia, 1986.
Abdel-Kader, Ali Hassan. *The Life, Personality and Writing of al-Junayd: A Study of a Third/Ninth Century Mystic, with an Edition and Translation of His Writings*. N.p.: Islamic Book Trust, 2013.
Abun-Nasr, Jamil M. *A History of the Maghrib in the Islamic Period*. Cambridge: Cambridge University Press, 1987.
Abun-Nasr, Jamil M. *Muslim Communities of Grace: The Sufi Brotherhoods in Islamic Religious Life*. New York: Columbia University Press, 2007.
Afshar, Iraj. "Ferdaws al-Moršedīya fī Asrār al-Ṣamadīya." *Encyclopædia Iranica*, online edition, http://www.iranicaonline.org/pages/articles/ferdaws. [vol. IX, fasc. 5, 511–12.]
Ahmad, Aziz. *Studies in Islamic Culture in the Indian Environment*. Oxford: Oxford University Press, 1964.

Aigle, Denise. "Un fondateur d'ordre en milieu rural: Le cheikh Abū Ishāq de Kāzarūn." In eadem, ed., *Saints orientaux*, 181–209. Paris: De Boccard, 1995.

Aigle, Denise, ed. *Miracle et karāma: Hagiographies médiévales comparées.* Turnhout: Brepols, 2000.

Algar, Hamid. "Bahā' al-Din Moḥammad Valad," *Encyclopædia Iranica*, online edition, http://www.iranicaonline.org/articles/baha-al-din-mohammad-walad-b. [vol. III, fasc. 4, 431–3.]

Algar, Hamid. "Bektāšīya," *Encyclopædia Iranica*, online edition, http://www.iranicaonline.org/articles/bektasiya. [vol. IV, fasc. 2, 118–22.]

Algar, Hamid. "A Brief History of the Naqshbandi Order." In Marc Gaborieau, Alexandre Popovic, and Thierry Zarcone, eds., *Naqshbandis: Cheminements et situation actuelle d'un ordre mystique musulman/Historical Developments and Present Situation of a Muslim Mystical Order; Proceedings of the Sèvres Round Table, 2–4 May 1985*, 3–44. Paris: Éditions Isis, 1990.

Algar, Hamid. "Hadith in Sufism." *Encyclopædia Iranica*, online edition, http://www.iranicaonline.org/articles/hadith-iv. [vol. XI, fasc. 5, 451–53.]

Algar, Hamid. "Introduction." In Najm al-Din Razi, ed., *The Path of God's Bondsmen: From Origin to Return*, 1–22. North Haledon, NJ: Islamic Publications International, 2003.

Algar, Hamid. "The Naqshbandi order: A preliminary study of its history and significance." *Studia Islamica* 63 (1976): 123–52.

Amin, Shahid. *Conquest and Community: The Afterlife of Warrior Saint Ghazi Miyan.* Chicago: University of Chicago Press, 2015.

Amitai, Reuven. "Il-Khanids: Dynastic History." *Encyclopædia Iranica*, online edition, http://www.iranicaonline.org/articles/il-khanids-i-dynastic-history. [vol. XII, fasc. 6, 645–54.]

Arberry, A. J., trans. *Muslim Saints and Mystics: Episodes from the Tadhkirat al-Auliya' of Farid al-Din 'Attar.* London: Routledge, 2008.

Balivet, Michel. "Miracles christiques et islamisation en chrétienté seldjoukide et ottoman entre le XIe et le XVe siècle." In Denise Aigle, ed., *Miracle et karāma: Hagiographies médiévales comparées*, 397–411. Turnhout: Brepols, 2000.

Benabbou, al-Hasan. "al-Jam' bayna al-suluk wa'l-fiqh 'inda mutasawwifat al-maghrib." In Ahmad Bulqadi, ed., *Ahmad b. Sulayman al-Simlali al-Jazuli: Ra'id al-tajdid al-sufi fi maghrib al-qarn al-tasi' al-hijri*, 347–60. Agadir: Kulliyat al-Adab w'al-'Ulum al-Insaniyya, Jami'at Ibn Zahr, 2013.

Bonner, Michael. *Aristocratic Violence and Holy War: Studies in the Jihad and the Arab-Byzantine Frontier.* New Haven: American Oriental Society, 1996.

Bonner, Michael. "The naming of the frontier: 'Awāsim, Thughūr and the Arab geographers." *Bulletin of the School of Oriental and African Studies* 57 (1994): 17–24.

Bosworth, C. Edmund. "The City of Tarsus and the Arab-Byzantine frontiers in early and middle 'Abbāsid Times." *Oriens* 33 (1992): 268–86.

Böwering, Gerhard, and Matthew Melvin-Koushki. "Ḵānaqāh." *Encyclopædia Iranica*, online edition, http://www.iranicaonline.org/articles/kanaqah. [XV, fasc. 5, 456–66.]

Boyle, J. A. "Dynastic and Political History of the Il-Khāns." In J.A. Boyle, ed., *The Cambridge History of Iran* V, 303–421. Cambridge: Cambridge University Press, 1968.

Buehler, Arthur F. *Sufi Heirs of the Prophets: The Indian Naqshbandiyya and the Rise of the Mediating Sufi Shaykh.* Columbia: University of South Carolina Press, 1998.

Bulliet, Richard. *Conversion to Islam in the Medieval Period: An Essay in Quantitative History.* Cambridge, MA: Harvard University Press, 1979.

Bulliet, Richard. "Naw Bahar and the survival of Iranian Buddhism." *Iran: Journal of the British Institute of Persian Studies* 14 (1976): 140–45.
Bulqadi, Ahmad, ed. *Ahmad b. Sulayman al-Simlali al-Jazuli: ra'id al-tajdid al-sufi fi Maghrib al-qarn al-tasi' al-hijri*. Agadir: Kulliyat al-Adab w'al-'Ulum al-Insaniyya, Jami'at Ibn Zahr, 2013.
Chabbi, Jacqueline. "Remarques sur le développement historique des mouvements ascétiques et mystiques au Khurasan: IIIe/IXe siècle–IVe/Xe siècle." *Studia Islamica* 46 (1977): 5–72.
Chejne, Anwar G. *Muslim Spain: Its History and Culture*. Minneapolis: University of Minnesota Press, 1974.
Chelkowksi, Peter, and Hamid Dabashi. *Staging a Revolution: The Art of Persuasion in the Islamic Republic of Iran*. New York: New York University Press, 1999.
Chittick, William C. "Weeping in Islam and the Sufi Tradition." In Mohammed Rustom, Atif Khalil, and Kazuyo Murata ed., *In Search of the Lost Heart: Explorations in Islamic Thought*, 27–38. Albany: State University of New York Press, 2012.
Chittick, William C. *Sufism: A Short Introduction*. Oxford: Oneworld, 2000.
Choksy, Jamsheed K. *Conflict and Cooperation: Zoroastrian Subalterns and Muslim Elites in Medieval Iranian Society*. New York: Columbia University Press, 1997.
Cook, David. "Sufism, the Army, and Holy War." In Alexandre Papas, ed., *Handbook of Sufi Studies*, vol. I, *Sufi Institutions*, 315–21. Leiden: E. J. Brill, 2020.
Cook, David. *Understanding Jihad*. Berkeley and Los Angeles: University of California Press, 2005.
Coomaraswamy, Ananda. *Buddha and the Gospel of Buddhism*. New Hyde Park, NY: University Books, 1969.
Cornell, Vincent J. "The logic of analogy and the role of the Sufi shaykh." *International Journal of Middle Eastern Studies* 15 (1983): 67–93.
Cornell, Vincent J. *Realm of the Saint: Power and Authority in Moroccan Sufism*. Austin: University of Texas Press, 1998.
Cornell, Vincent J. "Socioeconomic dimensions of reconquista and jihad in Morocco: Portuguese Dukkala and the Sadid Sus, 1450–1557." *International Journal of Middle Eastern Studies* 22 (1990): 379–418.
Darling, Linda. "Contested territory: Ottoman Holy War in comparative context." *Studia Islamica* 91 (2000): 133–63.
Deweese, Devin. *Islamization and Native Religion in the Golden Horde: Baba Tükles and Conversion to Islam in Historical and Epic Tradition*. University Park: Pennsylvania State University Press, 1994.
Digby, Simon. "Before the Bābās came to India: A reconstruction of the earlier lives of Bābā Sa'īd Palangpōsh and Bābā Muḥammad Musāfir in 'Wilāyat,'" *Iran* 36 (1998): 139–64.
Digby, Simon, trans. "Introduction." In *Sufis and Soldiers in Awrangzeb's Deccan: Malfūzāt-i Naqshbandiyya, Translated from the Persian and with an Introduction by Simon Digby*, 1–38. New Delhi: Oxford University Press, 2001.
Digby, Simon. "To Ride a Tiger or a Wall? Strategies of Prestige in Indian Sufi Legend." In Winand M. Callewaert and Rupert Snell, eds., *According to Tradition: Hagiographical Writing in India*, 99–129. Wiesbaden: Harrassowitz Verlag, 1994.
Donner, Fred M. *Narratives of Islamic Origins: The Beginnings of Islamic Historical Writing*. Princeton: Darwin Press, 1998.
Drague, Georges. *Esquisse d'histoire religieuse du Maroc: Confréries et zaouïas*. Paris: J. Peyronnet, 1951.

During, J., and R. Sellheim. "Samā'." *Encyclopædia of Islam, Second Edition*, online edition, http://dx.doi.org/10.1163/1573-3912_islam_COM_0992.

Eaton, Richard M. *The Rise of Islam and the Bengal Frontier, 1204–1760*. Berkeley and Los Angeles: University of California Press, 1993.

Eaton, Richard M. *The Sufis of Bijapur, 1300–1700: Social Roles of Sufis in Medieval India*. Princeton: Princeton University Press, 1978.

Eden, Jeff. *Warrior Saints of the Silk Road: Legends of the Qarakhanids*. Leiden: E. J. Brill, 2019.

Ephrat, Daphna. *Spiritual Wayfarers, Leaders in Piety: Sufis and the Dissemination of Islam in Medieval Palestine*. Cambridge, MA: Harvard Center for Middle Eastern Studies, 2008.

Ernst, Carl. *Sufism: An Introduction to the Mystical Tradition of Islam*. Boston: Shambhala, 2011.

Firestone, Reuven. *Jihad: The Origins of Holy War in Islam*. New York: Oxford University Press, 1999.

Frye, R. N. *Islamic Iran and Central Asia (7th–12th Centuries)*. London: Variorum Reprints, 1979.

Furuzanfar, Badi' al-Zaman. *Sharh-i ahval va naqd va tahlil-i athar-i shaykh Farid al-Din Muhammad 'Attar-i Nishaburi*. Tehran: University of Tehran Press, 1961.

Goldziher, Ignaz. *Introduction to Islamic Theology and Law*. Trans. A. Hamori and R. Hamori. Princeton: Princeton University Press, 1981.

Gramlich, Richard. *Alte Vorbilder des Sufitums*. 2 Volumes. Wiesbaden: Harrassowitz Verlag, 1995.

Gramlich, Richard. *Die Wunder der Freunde Gottes: Theologien und Erscheinungsformen des islamischen Heiligenwunders*. Wiesbaden: Franz Steiner Verlag, 1987.

Green, Nile. "Stories of saints and sultans: Re-membering history at the Sufi shrines of Aurangabad." *Modern Asian Studies* 38 (2004): 419–46.

Guillot, Claude. "The Tembayat Hill: Clergy and Royal Power in Central Java from the 15th to the 17th Century." In Henri Chambert-Loir and Anthony Reid, eds., *The Potent Dead: Ancestors, Saints and Heroes in Contemporary Indonesia*, 141–59. Honolulu: University of Hawaii Press, 2002.

Habbar, Mukhtar. "al-Hudur al-Sufi fi'l-Jaza'ir 'ala al-'ahd al-'Uthmani." *al-Turath al-'Arabi* 57 (1994): 51–66.

Hamidullah, Muhammad. *The Muslim Conduct of State*. 7th ed. Lahore: SH. Muhammad Ashraf, 1996.

Hissan, 'Abd al-Hakim. *al-Tasawwuf fi al-shi'r al-'arabi: nash'atuh wa-tatawwuruh hatta al-qarn al-thalith al-hijri*. Cairo: Maktabat al-Anjalu al-Misriyya, 1954.

Hurwit, Jeffrey M., *The Art and Culture of Early Greece, 1100–480 B.C.* Ithaca: Cornell University Press, 1985.

Ikram, S. M. *Muslim Civilization in India*. Ed. A. Embree. New York: Columbia University Press, 1965.

Jabrun, Muhammad. "al-Haraka al-sufiyya wa-dawrha fi muwajahat al-ghazw al-salibi li'l-Maghrib." In A. Jaludi, ed., *al-Tahawwalat al-fikriyya fi'l-'alam al-Islami: a'lam wa-kutub wa-harakat wa-afkar min al-qarn al-'ashir ila al-qarn al-thani 'ashar al-hijri*, 445–58. Herndon, VA: International Institute of Islamic Thought, 2014.

Jaludi, A., ed. *al-Tahawwalat al-fikriyya fi'l-'alam al-Islami: a'lam wa-kutub wa-harakat wa-afkar min al-qarn al-'ashir ila al-qarn al-thani 'ashar al-hijri*. Herndon, VA: International Institute of Islamic Thought, 2014.

Jamal, Shawqi 'Ata Allah. "Muhammad al-'Ayyashi wa-jihaduh did al-Isban wa'l-Burtuqal." *al-Manahil* 9 (1977): 104–45.

Jenkins, R. G. "The Evolution of Religious Brotherhoods in North and Northwest Africa, 1523-1900." In J. R. Willis, ed., *Studies in West African Islamic History*, vol. I, *The Cultivators of Islam*, 40-77. London: Frank Cass, 1979.
Julien, Charles-André. *Histoire de l'Afrique du Nord: Tunisie, Algérie, Maroc de la conquête arabe à 1830*. Paris: Payot, 1931.
Karamustafa, Ahmet T. *God's Unruly Friends: Dervish Groups in the Islamic Later Middle Period, 1200-1550*. Oxford: Oneworld, 2006.
Khadduri, Majid. *The Islamic Law of Nations: Shaybānī's Siyar*. Baltimore: The John Hopkins University Press, 1966.
Khadduri, Majid. *War and Peace in the Law of Islam*. Baltimore: The John Hopkins University Press, 1955.
Khalil, Atif, *Repentance and the Return to God: Tawba in Early Sufism*. Albany: State University of New York Press, 2019.
Khatib, As'ad. *al-Butula wa'l-fida' 'inda al-sufiyya*. Damascus: Dar al-Taqwa, 1997.
Knobloch, Edgar. *Monuments of Central Asia: A Guide to the Archeology, Art and Architecture of Turkestan*. London: I.B. Tauris, 2001.
Knysh, Alexander. *Sufism: A New History of Islamic Mysticism*. Princeton: Princeton University Press, 2017.
Knysh, Alexander. "Sufism as an explanatory paradigm: The issue of the motivations of Sufi resistance movements in Western and Russian scholarship." *Die Welt des Islams* 42.2 (2002): 139-73.
Kotkin, Stephen. "Mongol Commonwealth? Exchange and governance across the post-Mongol space." *Kritika: Explorations in Russian and Eurasian History* 8.3 (2007): 487-531.
Lane, Edward, ed. *An Arabic-English Lexicon*. 8 vols. Beirut: Librairie du Liban, 1968.
Lapidus, Ira M. *A History of Islamic Societies*. Cambridge: Cambridge University Press, 2002.
Lawrence, Bruce. *Notes from a Distant Flute: Sufi Literature in Pre-Mughal India*. Tehran: Imperial Iranian Academy of Philosophy, 1978.
Lewis, Franklin D. *Rumi—Past and Present, East and West: The Life, Teachings, and Poetry of Jalâl al-Din Rumi*. London: Oneworld, 2016.
Lindner, Rudi Paul. "Stimulus and justification in early Ottoman history." *Greek Orthodox Theological Review* 27 (1982): 207-24.
Losensky, Paul, trans. *Farid ad-Din 'Attar's Memorial of God's Friends: Lives and Sayings of Sufis*. New York: Paulist Press, 2009.
Madelung, Wilferd. *Religious Trends in Early Islamic Iran*. Albany: Bibliotheca Persica, 1988.
Malik, Jamal, and John Hinnells, eds. *Sufism in the West*. New York: Routledge, 2006.
Meier, Fritz, ed. "Das Leben des Verfassers." In Ahmad ibn 'Umar, ed., *Fawa'ih al-jamal wa-fawatih al-jalal*, 1-64. Wiesbaden: F. Steiner, 1957.
Melchert, Christopher. "Ibn al-Mubārak's *Kitāb al-Jihād* and Early Renunciant Literature." In Robert Gleave and István T. Kristó-Nagy, eds., *Violence in Islamic Thought: From the Qur'ān to the Mongols*, 49-69. Edinburgh: Edinburgh University Press, 2016.
Melchert, Christopher. "Origins and Early Sufism." In Lloyd Ridgeon, ed., *The Cambridge Companion to Sufism*, 3-23. Cambridge: Cambridge University Press, 2015.
Melchert, Christopher. "The transition from asceticism to mysticism at the middle of the 9th century C.E." *Studia Islamica* 83 (1966): 51-70.
Melikian-Chirvani, A. S. "Baztabha-yi adab-i ayin-i Buda dar Iran-i Islami." *Iran Nama* 8 (1990): 273-80.

Mojaddedi, Jawid. *The Biographical Tradition in Sufism: The Tabaqat Genre from al-Sulamī to Jāmī*. Richmond, Surrey: Curzon Press, 2001.

Mourad, Suleiman, and James Lindsay. *Intensification and Reorientation of Sunni Jihad Ideology in the Crusader Period*. Leiden: E. J. Brill, 2013.

Muedini, Fait. *Sponsoring Sufism: How Governments Promote "Mystical Islam" in Their Domestic and Foreign Policies*. New York: Palgrave MacMillan, 2015.

Muhammad, Muhammad 'Abd al-Hamid. *Ibrahim ibn Adham: shaykh al-zahidin wa-imam al-mutasawwifin*. Al-Minya: Dar al-Huda li'l-Nashr wa'l-Tawzi', 2007.

Neale, Harry S. "Books of Zuhd and Jihād." In Alexander Knysh and Bilal Orfali, eds., *Handbook of Sufi Studies: Prose*. Leiden: E. J. Brill, forthcoming.

Neale, Harry S. *Jihad in Premodern Sufi Writings*. New York: Palgrave Macmillan, 2016.

Nizami, Khaliq Ahmad. *Some Aspects of Religion and Politics in India during the Thirteenth Century*. Bombay: Asia Publishing House, 1961.

Nwyia, Paul. *Ibn 'Abbād de Ronda (1332-1390): Un mystique prédicateur à la Qarawīyīn de Fès*. Beirut: Imprimerie Catholique, 1961.

Nwyia, Paul, ed. *Trois œuvres inédites de mystiques musulmans*. Beirut: Dar al-Mashriq, 1973.

O'Callaghan, Joseph F. *Reconquest and Crusade in Medieval Spain*. Philadelphia: University of Pennsylvania Press, 2004.

Ohlander, Erik S. *Sufism in an Age of Transition: 'Umar al-Suhrawardi and the Rise of the Islamic Mystical Brotherhoods*. Leiden: E. J. Brill, 2008.

Osman, Ghada. "Oral vs. written transmission: The case of Ṭabarī and Ibn Sa'd." *Arabica* 48 (2001): 66-80.

Paul, Jürgen. "Hagiographic Literature." *Encyclopædia Iranica*, online edition, http://www.iranicaonline.org/articles/hagiographic-literature. [vol. XI, fasc. 5, 536-39.]

Reid, Megan H. *Law and Piety in Medieval Islam*. Cambridge: Cambridge University Press, 2013.

Renard, John. *Friends of God: Islamic Images of Piety, Commitment, and Servanthood*. Berkeley and Los Angeles: University of California Press, 2008.

Renard, John, ed. and trans. *Tales of God's Friends: Islamic Hagiography in Translation*. Berkeley and Los Angeles: University of California Press, 2009.

Rizvi, Saiyid Athar Abbas. *A History of Sufism in India. Early Sufism and Its History in India to AD 1600*. Volume I. Delhi: Munshiram Manoharlal, 1978.

Sajjadi, Sayyid Ja'far. *Farhang-i istilahat va ta'birat-i 'irfani*. Tehran: Kitabkhana-yi Tahuri, 2004.

al-Salawi, Abu'l-'Abbas Ahmad b. Khalid al-Nasiri. *Kitab al-istiqsa li-akhbar duwal al-Maghrib al-aqsa*. Volume IV. Casablanca: Dar al-Kitab, 1997.

Sallustius. *Concerning the Gods and the Universe*. Ed. and trans. Arthur Darby Nock. Cambridge: Cambridge University Press, 1926.

Schimmel, Annemarie. *Islam in the Indian Subcontinent*. Lahore: Sang-e Meel Publications, 2003.

Sells, Michael. *Early Islamic Mysticism: Sufi, Qur'an, Miraj, Poetic and Theological Writings*. Mahwah, NJ: Paulist Press, 1995.

Seyed-Gohrab, A. A. "LEYLI O MAJNUN." *Encyclopædia Iranica*, online edition, http://www.iranicaonline.org/articles/leyli-o-majnun-narrative-poem.

Sharaf, Muhammad Jalal. *Dirasat fi'l-tasawwuf al-islami: shakhsiyat wa-madhahib*. Beirut: Dar al-Nahda al-'Arabiyya, 1980.

Sizgorich, Thomas. *Violence and Belief in Late Antiquity: Militant Devotion in Christianity and Islam*. Philadelphia: University of Pennsylvania Press, 2009.

Steingass, F. *A Comprehensive Persian-English Dictionary*. Springfield: Nataraj Books, 2003.

al-Tazi, 'Abd al-Hadi. *Jami' al-Qarawiyyin, al-masjid wa'l-jami'a bi-madinat Fas: mawsu'a li-tarikhha al-mi'mari wa'l-fikri*. 3 vols. Rabat: Dar Nashr al-Ma'rifa, 2000.

Trimingham, J. Spencer. *The Sufi Orders in Islam*. Oxford: Oxford University Press, 1971.

Versteegh, Kees. *The Arabic Language*. 2nd ed. Edinburgh: Edinburgh University Press, 2014.

Vööbus, Arthur. *History of Asceticism in the Syrian Orient: A Contribution to the History of Culture in the Near East*. Volume I. Louvain: Peeters, 1958.

Wright, W. *A Grammar of the Arabic Language*. 2 vols. Cambridge: Cambridge University Press, 1962.

Zarrinkub, 'Abd al-Husayn. *Justuju dar tasavvuf-i Iran*. Tehran: Amir Kabir, 1990.

INDEX

Abbasid Caliphate 10, 23, 31, 36, 41–2, 47, 101
abdal (Substitutes) 152 n.33
'Abd al-Rahman I 77
'Abd al-Samad 66–8
'Abd al-Wahid b. Talha al-'Arusi 87
'Abduh Chihra Aqasi 109
'Abdullah al-Yunini 18, 62
    death of 68
    exempla and wondrous deeds of 66–7
    and military jihad 67–8
'Abid Khan 108
Abu 'Abdullah-i Khafif. *See* Ibn Khafif
Abu 'Abdullah Muhammad b. Ahmad 55
Abu 'Abdullah Muhammad b. al-Shaykh al-Wattasi. *See* al-Burtughali
Abu 'Abdullah Muhammad b. Judhayn 57
Abu Ahmad 98
Abu 'Ali al-Juzjani 45, 143 n.16
Abu 'Amr ibn 'Ali 54
Abu Bakr al-Siddiq (first Rightly Guided Caliph) 108
Abu Dawud, *Sunan Abi Dawud* 140 n.80
Abu Ishaq al-Kazaruni 16–19, 42, 52–60, 115, 130 n.34
    childhood and introduction to Sufi path 53–4
    death of 58–60
    dicta, exempla, and *mujahada* of 54–6
    in *Firdaws al-murshidiyya fi asrar al-samadiyya* 12, 53
    Mawlana Taj al-Din Bukhari 55
    and military jihad 56–8
Abu'l-'Abbas Ahmad al-Daghuri al-Qasri 88
Abu'l-Khayr, Abu Sa'id 7, 15, 26
    in *Asrar al-tawhid fi maqamat shaykh Abi Sa'id* 12, 17, 43, 129 n.21
    on Bayazid 45–6
Abu'l-Qasim al-Junayd al-Baghdadi. *See* Junayd al-Baghdadi
Abu Madyan al-Andalusi 77, 79
Abu Musa 47
Abu Sa'id al-Kharraz 131 n.37
Abu Sa'id b. al-Ar'abi 133 n.67
Abu Tammam 53
Abu Yazid Tayfur al-Bistami. *See* Bayazid al-Bistami
Abu Zakaria b. Yahya b. Bakkar 88
activist asceticism 130 n.34
Adab al-muluk (Unknown author) 122
al-'Adil 67
Aflaki, Shams al-Din Ahmad 62
    Manaqib al-'arifin 125
ahl al-hadith 139 n.62
Ahl al-Kitab (People of the Book) 93
ahl al-ra'y 139 n.62
Ahmad b. Behruz 54
Ahmad-i Havari 15
Ahmad Khizravayh of Balkh 16–17
Akbar (Mughal emperor) 96
akhdha (rapture) 82
Aleppo 62, 74
Alf layla wa-layla 19
'Ali b. Muhammad 65
'Ali b. Musa al-Rida. *See* Imam Reza
'Ali ibn Abi Talib (Fourth Rightly Guided Caliph; first Shi'ite Imam) 38, 144 n.61
'Ali ibn 'Uthman al-Shawi 79, 86–7, 115
Almohads 77–8
Almoravids 77–8, 80, 152 n.22
Amir Hasan (Indian Sufi poet) 95
al-Amjad Bahramshah 67, 148 n.41
al-Andalus 78–81, 85–6, 152 n.22
animals 14, 17, 71, 80–1
al-Aqqawi, Muhammad ibn al-Mubarak 79
Arab/Arabic 1–3, 11–14, 20, 41, 43, 74, 77, 100, 108, 115–16, 127 n.2, 128 n.7, 135 n.84, 137 n.1, 150–1 n.1, 156 n.30. *See also* non-Arabs
Arabian Peninsula 115

archetypes, Sufi 4, 10, 21, 24, 29, 52, 115.
  See also specific person
al-Arkushi, Abu 'Abdullah Muhammad 8,
  20, 79–81
  in *al-Sirr al-masun* 80–1
Asad al-Din Shirkuh b. Shadhi (*al-Malik al-Mujahid*) 68, 148 n.47
Asad al-Sham (The Lion of Greater Syria).
  See 'Abdullah al-Yunini
ascetics/asceticism. *See zahid/zuhhad*
'Attar, Farid al-Din 1, 71
  Asrar Nama 72, 150 n.80
  on Ibrahim's death 138 n.32
  Ilahi Nama 150 n.80
  Mantiq al-tayr 123, 150 n.80
  Musibat Nama 150 n.80
  Tadhkirat al-awliya' 1, 7–8, 12, 20, 24,
    31, 36, 42–3, 48, 53, 114, 123, 129
    n.22, 142 n.111, 143 n.29, 143 n.36,
    145 n.76
'awasim (places of defense) 133 n.63
Awrangabadi, Shah Mahmud, *Malfuzat-i
  Naqshbandiyya: Halat-i Hazrat Baba
  Shah Musafir Sahib* 105–6, 126, 155
  n.11
Awrangzeb 106, 108
awtad (Pillars) 27, 152 n.33
al-'Ayyashi, Abu Salim 'Abdullah b.
  Muhammad (son of Muhammad
  al-'Ayyashi) 91
  al-Rihla al-'Ayyashiyya 89
al-'Ayyashi, Muhammad 79, 89–91
  death of 91
  introduction to Sufi path and jihad
    89–90
  and military jihad 90–1
Ayyubid dynasty 62

Baba Faraj-i Tabrizi 63–4
Bab al-Taq (Baghdad) 49
Baba Palang Push 15, 18–19, 95–7, 105–11,
  155 n.11, 158 n.65, 158 n.73
  admonishes Sharif Khan 109–10
  death of 111
  and defeat of the Qalmaqs 107–8
  journey to Rūm 110–11
  military jihad of 108–9
  on Sufi path 106
  wayfaring and meeting with Khizr 107

Baba Qul Mazid 105–6, 158 n.73
Baba Shah Musafir 106, 108–9, 126
Badakhshi, Mirza La'al Bayg La'ali,
  Thamarat al-quds 101, 126, 136
  n.105, 156 n.34, 157 n.43, 157 n.50
al-Badisi, 'Abd al-Haqq, *al-Maqsad al-sharif* 86, 124
al-Baghawi, Abu Muhammad Husayn
  b. Mas'ud Farra', *Muhiyy al-sunna*
  147 n.16
Baghdad 23–4, 41, 47, 49, 51–2, 59, 61, 72,
  144 n.50, 150 n.93
al-Baghdadi, al-Khatib, *Tarikh Baghdad*
  13, 31, 123
Baha' al-Din Valad 70–2, 149–50 n.78
Bahadur, Yalangtush 158 n.79
al-Bahluli, Muhammad ibn Yahya 79
  in *Dawhat al-nashir* 87–9, 153 n.53
al-Baladhuri, *Futuh al-buldan* 133 n.63,
  140 n.87, 146 n.1
Balkhi, Jalal al-Din. *See* Rumi
baqa' (abiding in God) 42
al-Baqi Billah (Naqshbandi shaykh)
  155 n.18
Battle of Badr 157 n.44, 159 n.84
Battle of Uhud 159 n.84
Bayazid al-Bistami 6, 14–15, 17, 42–7,
  142 n.1, 143 n.12
  Abu Sa'id Abu'l-Khayr on 45–6
  death of 47
  dicta, exempla, and *mujahada* of 44–6
  and military jihad 46–7
  origins and awakening 43–4
  struggle with *nafs* 46
Bedouin tribes 151 n.1
Bektashi Sufi order 5
bid'a (innovation) 150 n.78
Bilgrami, Mir Ghulam 'Ali Azad 158 n.67
  Ma'athir al-kiram 106, 158 n.73
Bishr al-Hafi 16
Brahmins 18, 155 n.7
King Brawijaya 132 n.54
Bu 'Ali Muhammad b. Ishaq b. Ja'far
  53–4
Buddhism/Buddhists 15–16, 93, 114
  important centers of 141 n.99
al-Bukhari, Muhammad b. Isma'il 12, 23
  Sahih al-Bukhari 146 n.99
Burhan al-Din al-Saghirji 104

Burhan al-Din Muhaqqiq 71–3
al-Burtughali 87, 153 n.48
al-Busiri, Sharaf al-Din Abi 'Abdullah Muhammad, al-Burda (Thirteenth-century ode in praise of the Prophet Muhammad) 87, 153 n.44
butparast (idol worshiper) 141 n.99
Buyid dynasty 41
Byzantines 7, 10, 18, 23, 28–9, 31, 34, 42, 53, 61, 133 n.61, 149 n.68

Central Asia 23, 63, 70, 93–4, 101, 106, 109, 113–15, 134 n.74
China 53, 63, 104
Chishti, Abu Muhammad 14–15, 17–18, 94, 96–101
  in *Khwajagan-i Chisht* 97–101
Chishti, Allahdia b. Shaykh 'Abd al-Rahim, *Khwajagan-i Chisht: Siyar al-aqtab* 95–6
Chishti, Mu'in al-Din 15, 94, 96
Chishti Sufi order 94, 96, 155 n.14, 156 n.32
Chittick, William C. 5
Christian/Christianity 3, 8, 49, 61, 67, 80, 87–8, 90–1, 114–15, 127 n.2, 154 n.3, 159 n.1
  anchorites 133 n.66
  monk 16, 32, 60, 135 n.94
  Muslims of Kazarun's campaign against 18
  Spanish 78
  Syrian 133 n.66
  of Western Europe 61
colonialism, European 116
Commander of the Faithful (*Amir al-mu'minin*) 16, 32, 49, 51, 90, 135 n.92
Companions of the Prophet (*Sahaba*) 4, 10–11, 17–18, 26–8, 30, 32, 34, 37, 44, 46, 51, 55–8, 64–5, 69, 73–5, 88–9, 98, 102–4, 106, 109–11
Constantinople, Ottoman conquest of 9
Coomaraswamy, Ananda 21
Crusades/Crusader 8, 18–19, 61–2, 68, 78
  First Crusade 61

Damascus 8, 24, 61–2, 66, 73–4, 137 n.1
Dar al-harb (Abode of War) 7, 102, 133 n.61

Dar al-Islam (Abode of Islam) 8–9, 11, 19, 22–4, 61–2, 78, 87, 133 n.61
Dar al-sulh (Abode of Truce) 133 n.61
al-Dhahabi, Shams al-Din Muhammad 124
  al-'Ibar fi khabar man ghabar 125
  Siyar a'lam al-nubala' 29, 36, 125, 141 n.98
  Tarikh al-Islam 125
dhikr (remembrance of God) 5, 33, 66, 84, 105–6
dhimmi 88, 153 n.51
Dhu al-Nun al-Misri 46
Dihlavi, Khwaja Hasan, *Fawa'id al-fu'ad* 53, 95, 124, 136 n.105
al-Dimashqi, Arslan 8
dogs 14, 17, 34, 45–6, 65, 71, 73, 136 n.106. *See also* animals
du'a (supplicatory prayer) 107

eastern Islamic world 41, 78, 95, 123
Edessa 61–2, 137 n.1
Egypt 62, 68–9, 77, 81, 84, 115, 137 n.1, 148 n.43, 149 n.61
The Eloquent Martyr (*al-shahid al-natiq*). *See* al-Nuwayri, 'Abd al-Rahman

Fakhr al-Din Razi 150 n.78
fall of Granada (1492) 8, 78
fana' (annihilation in God) 42
faqir (poor) 157 n.51
al-Fasi, 'Abd al-Rahman Muhammad 87
Fatiha 107, 111, 158 n.81
fatwa 91
Fez 77–8, 88–90
fiqh (jurisprudence) 47
Firdawsi Sufi order 155 n.14
The Five Pillars of Islam 94, 113, 144 n.45
Franks 67, 69–70
Friday prayer 14–15, 55, 68, 99
friends of God. *See* God's friends (*awliya'*)
Fudayl Ibn 'Iyad 16–18, 27, 36, 135 n.92

al-Ghazali, Abu Hamid Muhammad, *Kimiya-yi sa'adat* 29, 36, 123
ghazi (warrior) 7–11, 18–20, 23–4, 28–9, 34–5, 51, 57–8, 69, 86, 97, 101–2, 116, 127–8 n.6

Ghazi al-Din Bahadur Firuz Jang. *See* Ghazi al-Din Khan
Ghazi al-Din Khan 106, 109–11
Ghazi b. al-shaykh Abi 'Abdullah Muhammad b. Ghazi 88
Ghazi, Sultan Sikandar 102
Ghaznavids 41, 95
ghazw (raiding) 128 n.6, 146 n.91
al-Ghazwani, Abu Muhammad 'Abdullah 87
Ghurids 41, 95
God 4, 14–15, 17, 24, 26, 33, 36–8, 43, 55–6, 58, 71–2, 89–90, 99, 102–3, 111, 141 n.94
  creation of (His creation) 6, 36
  God's Messenger 35, 50, 56, 71–2, 85, 97–8, 129 n.21
  servants of 27, 30, 33, 99
  God's friends (*awliya'*) 1–9, 11–13, 24, 27, 33, 36, 42, 48, 62, 71, 78, 80, 94, 97–8, 113–17, 127 n.2, 129 n.22, 134 n.80, 135 n.86. *See also specific person*
  and Christian saints 127 n.2
  conduct of 41
  Indo-Muslim 96–7
  miraculous events and dreams 18
  in North Africa 78
  recurrent motifs in lives of 1, 11, 13–19, 114–15, 117, 135 n.86, 136 n.105, 137 n.18, 143 n.22 (*see also specific motifs*)
  greater jihad (inner spiritual struggle) 2–3, 20, 22, 37, 101, 128 n.9, 128 nn.11–12
Greater Syria 62, 123, 137 n.1

hadith 1, 4, 11–12, 16, 23, 31–2, 37, 47, 50, 84, 116, 129 n.16, 129 n.18, 129 n.24, 131 n.36, 135 n.91, 138 n.29, 139 n.62, 146 n.99, 149 n.75
hagiography, Sufi 1–2, 4, 8–13, 16, 19–24, 41, 62, 94–7, 113–17, 129 n.16, 132 n.54, 134 n.74, 143 n.22, 159 n.1
  animals in 17
  common motifs in 14
  Indo-Persian 8, 95, 97
  North African (*rijal*) 13, 78, 86, 89, 151 n.13

Hajj (pilgrimage) 30–2, 45, 48, 51, 54, 77, 80, 85, 91, 104, 107, 110, 144 n.45. *See also* Mecca; Medina
Hajji Muhammad 110
Hamza ibn 'Abd al-Muttalib (The First Martyr) 159 n.84
al-Hanbali, Mujir al-Din al-'Ulaymi, *al-Uns al-Jalil bi-tarikh al-Quds wa'l-Khalil* 125
haqiqa 36, 113
harbiyan (unbeliever warriors) 102
Harith al-Muhasibi 54
Harun al-Rashid 16, 32–3, 135 n.92
  and Shaqiq al-Balkhi 38
Hatim al-Asamm 36–9
Hazar hikayat-i sufiyan (Unknown author) 31, 36, 43, 123, 140 n.86, 144 n.63
Herat 97, 145 n.71, 147 n.26, 149 n.71
Hindu(s) 20, 93–4, 96–7, 105, 114, 136 n.105, 155 n.11. *See also* Ahl al-Kitab; Christian/Christianity; Islam; Islamism
Hispano-Arab Sufis 77
al-Hudaygi, Muhammad b. Ahmad, *Tabaqat al-Hudaygi* 13, 86, 89, 126
  'Ali ibn 'Uthman al-Shawi in 87
al-hudud (divine ordinances) 142 n.5
Hujviri, Abu'l-Hasan 'Ali (Data Ganj Bakhsh) 53, 95
  Kashf al-mahjub 31, 36, 48, 95, 122–3, 145 n.72
Hulagu Khan 74, 150 n.93
Humayd ibn Ma'yuf al-Hamadani 28, 138 n.28
Husayn-i Akkar 54, 145 n.79

Iberian Peninsula 8, 23, 77–8, 80, 114–15
Ibn 'Abbad al-Rundi 77
Ibn al-'Ata of Baghdad 47
Ibn al-'Imad, *Shadharat al-dhahab fi akhbar man dhahab* 13, 36, 126, 141 n.98
Ibn al-Jawzi, *Sifat al-safwa* 123
Ibn al-Mubarak, 'Abdullah 10, 15–18, 24, 31–6, 78, 140 n.78
  Book of Jihad (*Kitab al-jihad*) 31, 139 n.58
  Book of Renunciation (*Kitab al-zuhd*) 31

death of 36
dicta, exempla, and miracles of 32–3
Diwan 'Abdullah ibn al-Mubarak 140 n.82
knowledge of *hadith* 32
and military jihad 34–6
pithy sayings attributed to 33–4
poems attributed to 34
repentance of 31–2
Ibn al-Mulaqqin, *Tabaqat al-awliya'* 125, 152 n.29
Ibn al-Sabbagh, Abu'l-Hasan 82, 84–5
Ibn 'Arabi 77
 al-Futuhat al-makkiyya 152 n.27, 153 n.39
 on al-Mughawir 86, 152 n.27
 al-Wasaya 128 n.8
Ibn 'Asakir
 Forty Hadith for Inciting Jihad 146 n.4
 Tarikh madinat Dimashq 13, 24, 123
Ibn 'Askar, *Dawhat al-nashir li-mahasin man kana bi'l-Maghrib min mashayikh al-qarn al-'ashir* 13, 86
 'Ali ibn 'Uthman al-Shawi in 87
 al-Bahluli in 87–9
Ibn Battuta 53, 68, 157 n.51
 Rihla 13, 101, 157 n.54
 on Shah Jalal 103–4
Ibn Hisham, *al-Sira al-nabawiyya* 10
Ibn Kathir 19, 124
 al-Bidaya wa'l-nihaya 13, 24, 66, 125, 138 n.32
Ibn Khafif 54, 145 n.79
Ibn Nubata, 'Abd al-Rahim b. Muhammad 114, 128 n.11
Ibn Qayyim al-Jawziyya 50
 al-Fawa'id 48
Ibn Rushd 22, 114
 al-Muqaddimat al-mumahhidat 136 n.112
Ibn Wasi', Muhammad 18–19, 24, 29–31
 dicta and exempla of 29–30
 emir of Basra and 30
 and military jihad 30–1
Ibn Zafir, Safi al-Din ibn Abi'l-Mansur, *Risala* 68–9, 124, 149 n.60, 149 n.66, 152 n.29, 152 n.33

Ibrahim ibn Adham 10, 15–17, 19, 24, 36, 78, 138 n.28, 141 n.99
 and Abu Qubays Mountain 27
 anecdotes about 27
 wilaya 28–9
 death of 29
 'Attar on 138 n.32
 exemplar of *tawakkul* 27–8
 and military jihad 28–9
 repentance of 24–7
 rigorous *mujahada* 28
 war against unbelievers 29
'Id al-Adha, feast of sacrifice 157 n.54
idol 37, 141 n.99
Idrisid dynasty 77
al-Ifrani, Muhammad al-Saghir ibn 'Abdullah
 Nuzhat al-hadi bi-akhbar muluk al-qarn al-hadi 89
 Safwat man intashara min akhbar sulaha' al-qarn al-hadi 'ashar 89, 154 n.65
ijtihad (exertion) 128 n.11
Ilbari dynasty 95
'ilm-i hal (inner knowledge) 73, 86, 99, 150 n.83
'ilm-i kasbi (knowledge one acquires through study) 150 n.83
'ilm-i laduni (divine knowledge) 73, 99
'ilm-i qal (outer knowledge) 73
'ilm-i wahbi (knowledge that God bestows on His friends) 150 n.83
Imam Reza 106, 158 n.77
India 9, 18, 53, 63, 93–7, 109, 114–15, 132 n.50, 155 nn.6–7
Indo-Muslim culture 94, 96–7, 155 n.14
inner jihad. *See* greater jihad (inner spiritual struggle)
intoxication. *See sukr* (spiritual intoxication)
Iran 41–2, 52, 114–15, 137 n.1
 Iranian Revolution 21
Iraq 21, 24, 29, 36, 41
al-Isfahani, Abu Nu'aym 4, 24, 31, 133 n.65
 Hilyat al-awliya' 12, 16, 18, 24, 31, 36, 48, 122, 138 n.29, 139 n.49
al-Isfahani, al-Raghib 22, 114
 Mufradat alfaz al-Qur'an 127 n.6

Ishaqiyya/Murshidiyya. *See* Kazaruni Sufi order
Islam 2–4, 19, 50, 58, 70, 77, 90, 93, 101, 109, 113–14, 116. *See also* Christian/Christianity; Hindu(s); Muslim(s)
  calendar 23, 156 n.28
  conversion (of unbelievers) to 14, 17–18, 43, 52, 93–4, 132 n.54, 145 n.71 (*see also* proselytization/proselytizers)
  early 23, 115, 132 n.58
  Indian 9, 93–7, 132 n.50
  Islamic doctrine 1–3, 6, 21–2, 114, 116, 128 n.7
  Islamic literature (premodern) 1–2, 4, 13, 117
  Islamic scripture 1, 6, 23, 113–14
  Islamization 9, 62
  jurisprudence 22, 116, 133 n.61
  militant 2, 22
  mystics/mysticism of (*see* mystics/mysticism of Islam)
  sacred history 4, 10, 20–1, 23, 117
  territorial expansion of 23

Islamism 2, 22
isnad (chain of oral transmission) 4

Ja'far al-Sadiq 44, 143 n.12
Jains 94
Jalal al-Din Muhammad Balkhi. *See* Rumi
Jalal al-Din Qassab 74
Jamal al-Din b. Ya'qub 66–7
Jamali, Hamid ibn Fazl Allah. *Siyar al-'arifin* 95
Jami, 'Abd al-Rahman, *Nafahat al-uns* 12, 63, 71, 125, 141 n.98, 143 n.30, 150 n.80, 156 n.31
al-Jazuli, Muhammad 9, 78–9
Jerusalem 26–7, 61–2, 137 n.1
Jews 18, 154 n.3, 155 n.5, 159 n.1
jihad/*jihād* 2, 14, 19–20, 31, 85, 128 n.10
  against Christian invaders 78
  doctrine of 2–3, 22, 114, 116, 128 n.7
  greater 2–3, 20, 22, 37, 101, 128 n.9, 128 nn.11–12
  military (*see* military jihad)
  Sufi 2–3, 6, 10, 16, 19, 42, 95, 115, 128 n.12
  Western definitions of 21
jizya 88, 93, 153 n.51, 155 n.5
Junayd al-Baghdadi 4, 42, 47–52, 142 n.1, 144 n.43
  childhood of 48
  and complementary nature of jihad 50–1
  death of 52
  dicta, exempla, and *mujahada* of 49–50
  and military jihad 51–2
  on the spiritual knower (*'arif*) 50
  thankfulness to God 14

ka'ba 44, 97
al-Kalabadhi, Abu Bakr Muhammad 10, 38
  al-Ta'arruf li-madhhab ahl al-tasawwuf 41, 48, 122
karama/karamat (wonders vouchesafed God's friends) 66, 69, 142 n.5
Karbala (martyrdom of Imam Husayn) 21
Kazaruni Sufi order 5–6, 52–3
Khalid ibn Walid 61
Khalji dynasty 95
khalvat (seclusion) 33, 99
khanaqah (Sufi lodge) 62
Kharaqani, Ahmad b. Husayn b. al-Shaykh, *Dastur al-jumhur fi manaqib sultan al-'arifin Abu Yazid Tayfur* 43, 124
Khatib Abu'l-Qasim (successor of Abu Ishaq al-Kazaruni) 58–60
khawf (fear of god) 141 n.94
khirqa (Sufi cloak) 17–18, 65, 97, 99–100, 105–6
Khizr 15, 25, 76, 99, 107, 135 n.84
Khomeini, Ayatollah 21
Khurasan 8, 18, 29–30, 33, 41, 47, 65, 129 n.19, 137 n.1
  Malamati movement in 158 n.69
  navavihara 141 n.99
Khwarazm 8, 61, 63, 65, 147 n.26
Khwarazmshah, Muhammad 65, 147 n.26, 149–50 n.78
Kirmani, Khwaju 53

Kirmani, Sayyid Muhammad 'Alavi, *Siyar al-awliya' dar ahval va malfuzat-i mashayikh-i Chisht* 95, 156 n.33
Kubra, Najm al-Din 4, 8, 14, 17–18, 62–6
  anecdotes and exempla of 64–5
  death of 147 n.15
  military jihad and martyrdom of 65–6
  spiritual awakening of 63–4
Kubrawi Sufi order 63, 105
Kunya Urgench, monuments of 147 n.11

Lahori, Ghulam Sarvar 145 n.71

Maghribi Sufis/Sufism 8, 11, 16, 77–9, 103, 134 n.77, 151 n.1
mahabba (love of God) 141 n.94
Mahmud b. 'Uthman, *Firdaws al-murshidiyya* 12, 53, 124, 145 n.75
Mahmud of Ghazna 156 n.26
al-Makki, Abu Talib Muhammad, *Qut al-qulub* 122, 139 n.50
Malamati movement (Path of Blame) 106, 158 n.69
malfuzat genre 95, 156 n.20
Malik ibn Dinar 16, 18, 31
Mamluk 61
al-Ma'mura 89–90
manaqib genre 12–13, 78
Mandavi, Muhammad Ghawthi Shattari, *Gulzar-i abrar* 8, 95, 126, 157 n.36
  Shah Jalal al-Din Mujarrad in 101–2
al-Maqdisi, Abu Shama Shihab al-Din, *al-Dhayl 'ala al-rawdatayn* 66, 124
marabout 78, 89, 153–4 n.56
ma'rifa (knowledge of God) 32
Marinid dynasty 77
al-Masisa 35, 140 n.87
al-Mas'udi, *Muruj al-dhahab wa-ma'adin al-jawahir* 135 n.92
Mawlana Zia al-Din Hakim 15
Mecca 14, 26, 32–3, 48, 68, 72, 74, 77, 82, 84, 104
Medina 44, 68, 77, 91
Mesopotamia 61–2, 133 n.66
Mevlevi Sufi order 5, 13, 62, 71
military jihad 2, 8–9, 16, 19, 22, 24, 31, 42–3, 62, 79, 128 n.6, 132 n.53
  and 'Abdullah al-Yunini 67–8
  and Abu Ishaq al-Kazaruni 56–8

  and Baba Palang Pūsh 108–9
  and Bayazid 46–7
  and Ibn al-Mubarak 34–6
  and Ibn Wasi' 30–1
  and Ibrahim ibn Adham 28
  and Junayd 51–2
  and Muhammad al-'Ayyashi 89–91
  and Najm al-Din Kubra 65–6
  and al-Nuwayri 69–70
  and Rumi 74–5
  and Shaqiq al-Balkhi 38–9
  and 'Umar al-Tanji 86
Mir Shihab al-Din (Shihab al-Din Khan) 108–9
Misr (Egypt/Cairo) 148 n.58
Mongol invasion of Central Asia and Iran 8, 61–2, 70, 147 n.26
Morocco 77, 79, 87–9, 151 n.14
  Bilad al-sus 153 n.49
  Safi (Asfi) 149 n.59
Mosul 61–2
Mughal period 93–4, 96, 158 n.65
mughāwir 152 n.26
al-Mughawir, Abu'l-Hajjaj 17, 79, 81–6
  Ibn 'Arabi on 86, 152 n.27
  in Ibn Zafir's *Risala* 81–5
al-Mughawir, Yusuf 86
muhaddith (hadith scholar) 4, 63, 146 n.4
Muhammad b. Munavvar, *Asrar al-tawhid fi maqamat shaykh Abi Sa'id* 7, 129 n.21, 143 n.22
Muhammad ibn Qasim 93, 154 n.3
Muhammad ibn Wasi' al-Azdi. *See* Ibn Wasi', Muhammad
Muharram ('Ashura) 21, 156 n.28
mujahada (individual spiritual struggle) 3, 10–11, 14–17, 19, 22, 26, 32, 41–3, 46, 56, 66, 73, 79, 97, 100–2, 114–15, 128 nn.10–11. *See also riyada* (self-mortification)
mujahid (one who carries out jihad) 1–3, 5, 7–11, 13–14, 18–20, 22, 24, 36, 38, 42, 44, 62, 68, 78–80, 86–7, 89, 91, 93–4, 96, 115–16, 132 n.58
Muluk al-tawa'if (party kings) 152 n.22
al-Munawi, 'Abd al-Ra'uf 31, 70
  al-Kawakib al-durriyya fi tarajim al-sufiyya 69, 126, 152 n.29

murid (Sufi initiate) 6–8, 17–18, 36, 38–9, 46, 50–1, 54, 56, 64–5, 71, 74, 99, 101, 105–6, 110–11, 144 n.63
Muslim ibn al-Hajjaj 23
Muslims 16, 18–20, 23, 35, 38, 43–4, 52–3, 56, 58–60, 62, 64, 69–70, 79–80, 83, 87, 94, 102–5, 113, 115–17. *See also* Christian/Christianity; Hindu(s); Islam; Islamism; non-Muslims
   conquest of North Africa 77
   of Greater Syria 62
   Iberian 78
   India 9, 93–7, 132 n.50
   Persian-speaking 1
   premodern Muslim culture 1, 7, 22, 79, 113–17
   Turkic 93, 95
   warriors 10–11, 20, 23, 77, 115
   of Western Asia 62
mystics/mysticism of Islam 2–3, 5–7, 21, 42, 113–14, 130 n.26, 131 n.35

Nadhr Muhammad Khan 107, 158 nn.79–80
nafs (lower self) 3, 16–17, 19, 22, 27–8, 34, 42, 44, 50, 115, 128 n.11
   Bayazid's struggle with 46
Najm al-Din Razi 159 n.1
Naqshbandi Sufi order 5, 12, 94–5, 105, 144 n.61, 155 n.14
Nasrabadi, Abu'l-Qasim 5
Near East 23, 115
Ne'matollahi Sufi order 5
Nizam al-Din Awliya' 95, 136 n.105
non-Arabs 103. *See also* Arab/Arabic
non-Muslims 14, 16, 94, 114, 116, 133 n.61, 155 n.11. *See also* Islam; Islamism; Muslim(s)
North Africa 1, 8, 23, 77–8, 87, 89, 113–15, 150–1 n.1
Nur al-Din Zengi 62, 146 n.4
al-Nuri, Abu'l-Husayn 16
al-Nuwayra, Cairo 148 n.53
al-Nuwayri, 'Abd al-Rahman 18, 62, 68–70
   concerning Sufism of 70
   military jihad and martyrdom of 69–70

orthodoxy, religious 6, 41, 94
Ottoman Empire 9

Pand-i piran (Unknown author) 24, 48, 122, 127 n.1
Persian culture/Persian language 95, 116
   hunting 135 n.85
   New Persian 41, 134 n.72
   Perso-Islamic culture 145 n.71, 147 n.26
piety 1, 4, 7, 10, 21–2, 52, 66, 78–9, 94, 96–7, 114, 116, 130 n.26
Pope Urban II 61
Portugal/Portuguese 8–9, 23, 78, 87–8, 151 n.15, 153 n.48
Prophet Muhammad 4, 10, 73, 98, 100, 115, 142 n.12, 153 n.44, 160 n.5
   and Companions (*Sahaba*) 4, 10–11, 108, 115, 159 n.84
proselytization/proselytizers 9, 12, 14, 17–18, 22, 94

Qaddasa Allah sirrahu (May God hallow his secret/tomb) 137 n.10
al-Qadiri, Muhammad ibn al-Tayyib. *Nashr al-mathani li-ahl al-qarn al-hadi 'ashar wa'l-thani* 89
Qadiri Sufi order 5, 155 n.14
qalandar 159 n.88
qari' (reciter) 140 n.83
qawwali 99–100, 156 n.32
qibla (direction of Mecca) 82, 97
Qur'an 1, 5, 16–20, 31, 42–3, 50, 52–3, 55, 70, 73–4, 80, 86–7, 99, 131 n.36, 140 n.84, 150 n.83, 152 n.24, 156 n.23, 158 n.81, 160 n.6
   Ayat al-Kursi 58
   Rumi on 6
   Surat Ali 'Imran verse in 11
   Surat Ya Sin 86
al-Qushayri, Abu'l-Qasim 4
   al-Risala al-Qushayriyya 24, 31, 43, 48, 123, 127 n.1, 141 n.91, 142 n.5
Qutayba ibn Muslim 30

Rabi'a 16
Radi al-Din 'Ali Lala 65
Raja Gour Govinda 102
Rajputs 96
rak'at (bowing in prayer) 29, 33, 44, 49, 52, 54
Reconquista period 8, 78

religious sciences 4, 14–15, 47, 54, 72, 98
religious tradition 3, 14, 20–2
repentance (*tawba*) 14–16, 31, 135 n.86
　of Ibn al-Mubarak 31–2
　of Ibrahim ibn Adham 24–7
　of Shaqiq al-Balkhi 36–7
ribat/ribāt 10–11, 32, 62, 84, 133 n.64, 153 n.56
Rightly Guided Caliphs 106, 142 n.108, 144 n.61
rihla (travel-narrative) 13, 101
Rijal al-ghayb (Men of the Unseen) 137 n.16
riyada (self-mortification) 3, 15–17, 22, 24, 26, 29–30, 42, 44, 46, 66, 73, 99–102, 115, 128 n.11. *See also mujahada* (individual spiritual struggle)
riyadat wa-mujahadat (spiritual struggle) 66, 115
Rūm (Byzantine Anatolia) 7, 13, 18, 51, 57–8, 84, 149 n.68
　Baba Palang Pūsh's journey to 110–11
Rumi 2, 6, 14, 62, 70–5, 115, 149 n.70
　childhood and introduction to Sufism 71–3
　death of 75
　dicta, exempla, and wonders of 73
　and Islam 7
　Kitab-i Fihi ma fihi 71, 131 n.36
　in *Manaqib al-'arifin* 13, 71, 149 n.74
　Mathnavi-yi ma'navi 7, 71, 149 n.71, 150 n.80
　and military jihad 74–5
　poetry of 6, 149 n.71
　on Qur'an 6

Sa'adian dynasty 77
Sabuktigin, Sultan Mahmud 99
sacred history 4, 9–10, 20–1, 23, 41, 117
sacred time 21
al-Sadafi, Tahir 80, 85
　al-Sirr al-masun 153 n.38
Sa'd al-Din Hammu'i 64–5, 147 n.23
al-Sahlagi, Abu Fadl Muhammad, *Kitab al-nur* 42–3, 123
sahw (sobriety) 6–7, 142 n.1

Saint Ephrem the Syrian 133 n.66
Salah al-Din (Saladin) 62, 147 n.9
salat (the prescribed five daily prayers of Islam) 144 n.45
sama' (musical audition) 5, 69, 99–100, 156 n.32
Samanid Empire 41, 95
al-Sanusi, Muhammad 90
Sari al-Saqati 47–8
al-Sarraj, Abu Nasr, *Kitab al-luma'* 41, 48, 122
Satuq Bughra Khan 146 n.93
sawm (fasting) 144 n.45
sayyid (a man descended from the Prophet) 51
Sayyid Hamza 108
Sayyid Muluk Shah 96, 104–5
　in *Tuhfat al-tahirin* 105
Seljuks 41, 61–2
Shadhili order 5, 79
shahada (profession of faith) 5, 50, 58, 70, 144 n.45
Shah Jahan 96, 110
Shah Jalal al-Din Mujarrad 94, 96–7, 101–4, 157 n.43
　death of 103
　in *Gulzar-i abrar* and *Thamarat al-quds* 101–2
　Ibn Battuta on 103–4
Shah Khaki 110
Shaqiq al-Balkhi 15–16, 18, 24, 27, 136 n.106, 141 n.99
　Adab al-'ibadat 36
　death of 39
　dicta and exempla of 37–8
　and Harun al-Rashid 38
　and military jihad 38–9
　repentance of 36–7
al-Sha'rani, 'Abd al-Wahhab, *al-Tabaqat al-kubra* 24, 43
shari'a (Divine Law) 6, 15, 31, 36, 45, 50, 94, 113, 142 n.5
Sharif Khan 109–10
Sharushan (grandfather of Bayazid) 43
Shattari Sufi order 155 n.14
shawq ila al-janna (yearning for paradise) 141 n.94
Shaykh-i Murshid. *See* Abu Ishaq al-Kazaruni

Shaykh Muhammad A'zam Tattawi, *Tuhfat al-tahirin* 126, 157 n.57
Shihab al-Din 'Umar al-Suhrawardi, *'Awarif al-ma'arif* 131 n.36
Shi'ite Islam 3, 21, 107, 144 n.61
Shirazi, Abu'l-'Abbas Zarkub. *Shiraz Nama* 53, 145 n.79
Shuniziyya Mosque, Baghdad 144 n.50
Sibt ibn al-Jawzi, *Mir'at al-zaman* 42, 66
Sidi 'Abd al-Wahid b. 'Ashir 90
Sidi 'Abdullah ibn Hassun 89
Sidi al-'Arabi al-Fasi 90
Sidi Ibrahim al-Hilali 90
silsila (initiatic chain) 144 n.61
Simnani, Sayyid Ashraf Jahangir, *Lata'if-i Ashrafi fi bayan-i tava'if-i sufi* 95
Sindh 93, 104, 157 n.57, 157 n.59
al-Sindi, Baha' al-Din 18
Sipahsalar, Faridun, *Zindagi nama-yi Mawlana Jalal al-Din Mawlavi* 71
sira literature 10, 115, 117, 132 n.60, 160 n.5
Sirhindi, Ahmad 93
  Maktubat-i rabbani 155 n.5
snake motif 17, 27, 32
Southern Asia 113
Spain 8, 23, 77–8, 87
storytelling 22, 50, 114
al Subki, Taj al Din, *Tabaqat al shafi'iyya* 125
Sufis/Sufism 2–5, 8–9, 11–12, 19, 21–2, 31, 35, 62–3, 113, 116, 130 n.27. *See also specific orders*
  anecdotes of 1–2, 6–8, 10, 13–20, 22, 24, 31, 36, 42, 95–6
  development stages of (Jenkins) 130 n.26
  doctrine 7, 41, 116, 130 n.25
  drunken 5–6, 41–2, 131 n.38, 142 n.1
  formative period of 4–5, 7, 41
  in India 93–4
  jihad 2–3, 6, 10, 16, 19, 115, 128 n.12
  Maghribi (*see* Maghribi Sufis/Sufism)
  manifestations of 6, 20, 113
  mysticism of (*see* mystics/mysticism of Islam)
  poetry 1–2, 6–7, 19, 24
  pre-*tariqa* phase of 94
  in Scholarship in Islamic languages 5
  sober 5–6, 41, 47, 131 n.38, 142 n.1
  and *tasawwuf* 3–7
  warriors 93–4
  in Western scholarship 128 n.13
Sufyan b. 'Uyayna 135 n.92
sukr (spiritual intoxication) 6–7
al-Sulami, 'Abd al-Rahman 4, 24, 133 n.67, 134 n.70
  Tabaqat al-sufiyya 1, 5, 11–12, 43, 48, 122, 129 n.24
Sultan 'Ala' al-Din Muhammad 147 n.26
Sultan Mahmud 95–7, 155 n.7
Sultan Valad, *Valad Nama* 71, 129 n.22, 150 n.83
Sunna 5–7, 48, 63, 68, 87, 129 n.24
Sunni Islam 3–4, 6–7, 11–12, 19, 21, 41–2, 94, 113–14, 116, 127 n.2, 133 n.61, 142 n.108, 143 n.12
sura 32, 64, 158 n.81
Syria 61–2, 67, 71, 74
  Syrian Christianity 133 n.66

al-Tabari, Muhammad b. Jarir, *Tarikh al-rusul wa'l-muluk* 10
tadhkira (memorial/memoir) 1
al-Tadili, Abu Ya'qub, *Kitab al-tashawwuf ila rijal al-tasawwuf* 13
tafsir (exegesis) 23, 71, 114, 134 n.72, 141 n.91
Tahirids 41
The Taifa kingdoms 79, 152 n.22
al-Tamazuti, Muhammad ibn Ahmad 16
al-Tamimi, Muhammad 'Qasim, *Kitab al-mustafad fi dhikr al-salihin wa'l-'ubbad* 13
al-Tamma al-kubra (The Great Calamity). *See* Kubra, Najm al-Din
al-Tanji, 'Umar 8, 79, 108
  military jihad in *al-Maqsad al-sharif* 86
Tariq ibn Ziyad 23, 77
Tatar 147 n.25
tavājud (ecstasy) 99
tawakkul (reliance on God) 4, 17, 24, 27, 36–7, 46, 50, 81, 136 n.106
al-Tazi, Muhammad ibn Yajjabsh 78–9
  Jami' al-Qarawiyyin 87, 153 n.52
thaghr/thughur (the border region between the Byzantines and the Muslims) 10, 23, 56, 78, 133 n.61

al-Tha'alabi, 'Abd al-Rahman 79, 151 n.15
al-Tirmidhi, Hakim 41
   Riyadat al-nafs 128 n.11
   Sirat al-awliya' 128 n.11
Transoxiana 8, 29, 41, 107
Tughluq dynasty 95
Turkic dynasties 41
Twelver Shi'ism 5, 142 n.12, 158 n.77
tyrants 16, 19, 42, 55, 67, 85, 114

Umayyad Caliphate 10, 23, 77, 93, 152 n.22
unbelievers (*kafir/kuffar*) 3, 9, 12, 14, 16–18, 22, 28–9, 34–5, 38, 42, 46–7, 51, 56–9, 65–6, 82–3, 88, 90–1, 96, 99, 102–4, 107, 114, 128 n.10, 146 n.93
unknown friends of God 149 n.75. *See also* God's friends (*awliya'*)

Va'iz-i Balkhi, *Fazayil-i Balkh* 24, 124, 137 n.18

Wahhabism 116
wajd (spiritual ecstasy) 64, 84, 152 n.36
walaya (friendship with God) 13, 17, 64, 73, 97, 127 n.2, 144 n.61
wali. *See* God's friends (*awliya'*)
wandering in the wilderness (motif of God's friends) 15–16, 44, 158 n.72

al-Waqidi 10
wara' (scrupulosity) 4, 24, 28, 86
   Bayazid exemplified 43
Wattasid dynasty 77, 87
Western Asia 23, 62, 94, 113
wilaya (wondrous power of God's friends) 16, 18, 20, 28–9, 55, 57, 62, 65, 96–7, 127 n.2

al-Yafi'i, 'Abdullah ibn As'ad
   Mir'at al-janan 13, 29, 63, 66, 125
   Nashr al-mahasin 125
   Rawd al-rayahin 125, 139 n.50
Yalangtush 107–8
Yasavi, Ahmad 101
Yasavi, Sayyed Ahmad 101
Yazid b. al-Mulahhab 30
Yazid I 21

zahid/zuhhad (renunciants/ascetics) 4, 10, 18–19, 28–30, 33–4, 38, 52, 130 n.26, 141 n.94
zakat (prescribed alms) 48, 144 n.45
zawiya (Sufi hospice; chiefly North Africa) 66–7, 78, 84–5
Zoroastrian 15–16, 37, 42–3, 52–3, 55–6, 114, 145 n.71
zuhd (renunciation/asceticism) 18, 28–9, 130 n.26, 141 n.94

www.ingramcontent.com/pod-product-compliance
Lightning Source LLC
Chambersburg PA
CBHW061833300426
44115CB00013B/2355